Also by Sonoko Sakai

The Poetical Pursuit of Food: Japanese Recipes for American Cooks

Rice Craft

Japanese Home Cooking: Simple Meals, Authentic Flavors

Mai and the Missing Melon

WAFU
COOKING

Everyday Recipes
with Japanese Style

WAFU
COOKING

Sonoko Sakai

Photographs by Rick Poon

Illustrations by Juliette Bellocq

ALFRED A. KNOPF
New York
2024

THIS IS A BORZOI BOOK
PUBLISHED BY ALFRED A. KNOPF

Copyright © 2024 by Sonoko Sakai
Photographs copyright © 2024 by Rick Poon
Illustrations copyright © 2024 by Juliette Bellocq

All rights reserved. Published in the United States by Alfred A. Knopf,
a division of Penguin Random House LLC, New York, and distributed
in Canada by Penguin Random House Canada Limited, Toronto.

www.aaknopf.com

Knopf, Borzoi Books, and the colophon are registered
trademarks of Penguin Random House LLC.

Library of Congress Cataloging-in-Publication Data
Names: Sakai, Sonoko, [date] author. | Poon, Rick, photographer. |
Bellocq, Juliette, illustrator.
Title: Wafu cooking : everyday recipes with Japanese style / Sonoko Sakai ;
Photographs by Rick Poon ; Illustrations by Juliette Bellocq.
Description: First edition. | New York : Alfred A. Knopf, 2024. | Includes index. |
Identifiers: LCCN 2023053187 (print) | LCCN 2023053188 (ebook) |
ISBN 9780593535271 (hardcover) | ISBN 9780593535288 (ebook)
Subjects: LCSH: Cooking, Japanese. | LCGFT: Cookbooks.
Classification: LCC TX724.5.J3 S255 2024 (print) | LCC TX724.5.J3 (ebook) |
DDC 641.5952—dc23/eng/20231220
LC record available at https://lccn.loc.gov/2023053187
LC ebook record available at https://lccn.loc.gov/2023053188

Cover illustrations by Juliette Bellocq
Cover design by Kelly Blair

Manufactured in China
First Edition

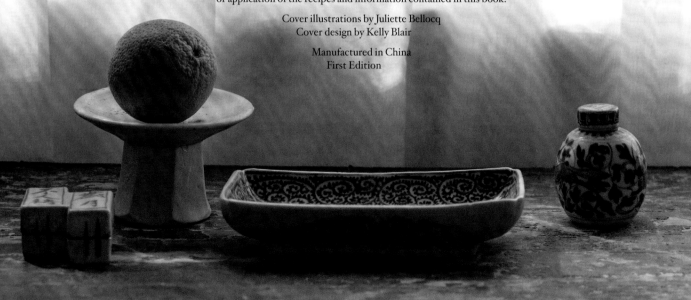

This book is for my son, Sakae,
who makes an excellent tonjiru.
I hope he uses Wafu Cooking
to continue his home cooking journey.

And in memory of my 25-year-old cat,
Kinchan, who loved bonito flakes

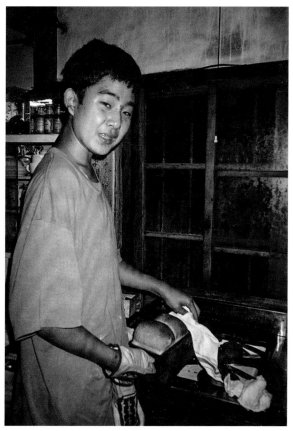

Sakae baking his first milk bread with Hiobachama
(his great-grandmother)

Contents

All-Day Breakfast   43

Soups   69

Plants and Vegetables   91

SALADA (SALAD-ISH DISHES)   93

VEGETABLES AND BEANS   111

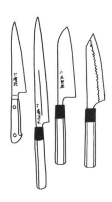

Noodles and Dumplings 231

Sweets and Baked Goods 271

Introduction

There is no goodness superior to the goodness of nature.

—Rosanjin (1883–1959), artist and epicure

It can be easy to think of Japanese cuisine as timeless and unchanging. But in reality, even dishes as distinctly "Japanese" as ramen and tonkatsu (pork cutlet) are the product of cultural intermingling.

Wafu cooking (the words "wa" and "fu" mean "Japanese" and "style") describes anything done in the "Japanese style" and is the name for any dish imbued with Japanese ingredients, seasonings, techniques, presentation, or sensibilities. To me, this is what cooking is all about: tasting foods from all around the world and, when the opportunity arises, combining them in harmony.

"Wafu" is a term that is hard to translate, and can feel somewhat amorphous, so for the purposes of this book, I've limited myself to writing about dishes that capture the cultural exchange between Japan and the rest of the world. Some are foods from elsewhere that have been wafu-ed (yes, I use the word as a verb), sometimes over the course of centuries (things like soy sauce, tofu, and noodles), others are more recent innovations, like Shaki Shaki Salada with Ponzu Dressing (page 102) or Miso Apple

Pie (page 281). Some, like tempura, ramen, and karei raisu (Japanese-style curry), have become so established that many Japanese people even think of them as truly "national dishes" while others are modern-day inventions—many of them my own. And in the process of writing this book, all of these recipes—new and old—have been transformed as they have traveled through my own California kitchen.

The dishes in this book represent who I am. I was born in New York to Japanese parents, the first American-born child and the eldest daughter of five. I have Italian Swiss ancestors on my mother's side and was raised by my maternal grandmother and a mother who took pride and joy in our European roots, but lived in a traditional Japanese culture.

In addition to my multicultural family lineage, I was raised in many places, including San Francisco, Mexico City, Kamakura, Tokyo, and Los Angeles. When I was growing up, my family moved every few years, whenever my father got transferred. My mother adjusted and adapted her cooking with each move, creating her own wafu dishes for me and my four siblings. Her specialty was lasagna, made from scratch. She would set a big stock pot full of Bolognese sauce cooking on the range like an Italian mama and roll out the pasta by hand. I don't know where she got the recipe, but her lasagna was distinctly wafu in two ways: she used miso in her Bolognese sauce as her kakushiaji—her secret ingredient—and she served it with rice. It was hard for me to shake off the rice habit. Even now, when the Cavallos, my Italian Swiss relatives, treat me to lasagna, I still fondly remember that mound of rice that my mother served with hers.

I now live with my husband, Katsuhisa Sakai, in Los Angeles and in Tehachapi (two hours northeast of Los Angeles in the high desert), on a ranch with two old mules (Fuyu and Sono), two cats (Chapi and Kinchan), and a dog (Kinako). Our family has become more diverse through our extended families—Japanese, Chinese,

English, and Finnish. My son, Sakae, lives in Seattle with his wife, Binah; my stepson, Tyler, lives in London with his wife, Emmalina, and their two children, Masa and Mai. I cherish this diversity and amalgamation of many cultures. I wear a Mexican gold medallion of Our Lady of Guadalupe that my father gave me, and need a tortilla fix when I am away from Los Angeles for too long. I swear to everyone that my last meal will be natto—gooey fermented soybeans—on rice.

For me, it is this exchange that's the true joy of cooking. While I love and revere traditional Japanese cooking—it's my culinary foundation, and you'll see that throughout the book—it is the melding of flavors and ingredients from all different cultures that creates the tasty, comforting, and simple dishes that I appreciate and am inspired by. This way of cooking is

representative of the way I, and so many others, like to cook and eat these days—crossing from Japan to the United States or to Mexico or to Italy on the same plate without even blinking.

The evolution taking place in our culinary culture—an exchange of ingredients, seasonings, techniques, presentation, or sensibilities as diverse as you can possibly imagine, working together in pursuit of harmony—is, to me, one of the great pleasures of life.

The cultural mixing of foods is becoming more and more common these days. In part, this is due to how accessible international ingredients are now. It's mind-boggling, actually. I never thought the world would acquire a taste for matcha—a fragrant but subtly bitter beverage I sipped as a girl in my grandmother's formal tearoom. Now I can be at our ranch in Tehachapi and find matcha lattes at the drive-through—not to mention that I can source soy sauce, tamari, miso, sake, and nori in my local grocery store. It means I can make just about anything wafu, and you can too.

In that spirit, most of the recipes in this book are wafu-ed weekday and weeknight dishes. I begin with a chapter on the wafu pantry and recipes for a few traditional Japanese condiments and culinary building blocks, which you can use to integrate Japanese-style cooking into any meal. These are the ingredients you want to have on hand to wafu anything you cook—not only my recipes, but as you start to invent your own. Once you understand the characteristics of the wafu pantry and have made a few of the

fundamental recipes, you will be well set up to explore the others in the book.

The majority of the recipes here will take less than thirty minutes to reach the table. There are a few that take more time in the kitchen, like homemade miso, breads, and ramen; for these, there are no shortcuts. They are particularly hands-on, for those days when you've got time and want to put in an extra effort for an extra reward.

In my previous book, *Japanese Home Cooking*, I shared Japanese dishes and ideas with an intention to help identify and preserve authenticity. In this book, the recipes are more relaxed, exploratory, and accessible, but still respectful of tradition. They are meant to be eaten and enjoyed with family and friends.

This book was created with the love and support of so many people. Arigato to everybody involved and to you, the reader!

What Is Wafu?

Although the use of the word "wafu" is relatively new, the culinary exchange between Japan and other parts of the world is as old as Japan itself. Japanese cuisine is the product of history, tradition, religion, and geography. Many ingredients and culinary practices originally came from China and traveled to Japan via the Korean peninsula and later by way of Europe and other parts of the world. Buddhist practice prohibited the eating of meat for twelve hundred years—land is too scarce in Japan to graze cattle—and Japan's ruling Tokugawa shogunate imposed the Sakoku policy, which closed its ports to the outside world for more than two hundred years in fear of influences from the Western world, namely colonialism and Christianity. Only in Dejima—a man-made island off Nagasaki in Kyushu—were the Europeans (the Dutch exclusively) and the Chinese allowed to trade on a limited basis with the Japanese.

My great-great-grandfather Hakuai Nakamura was one of a handful of young and progressive samurais from the Satsuma and Choshu clans of Kyushu who illegally traveled abroad to study in Europe in the 1860s. They returned to Japan to become active leaders in the Meiji Restoration period that ended the feudalistic closed-door policy. During this time, the new Meiji government's goal was to build a nation capable of standing equal among Western powers. They encouraged Japanese people to modernize and adopt Western customs, including dietary habits so they would become bigger and stronger people, like Westerners. Western dishes like stew, curry, croquettes, steaks, and dairy foods like butter, cheese, and ice cream. This is when they began seriously tinkering in their kitchens and the idea of wafu really blossomed. The Japanese call authentically Japanese dishes "washoku," whereas Western dishes are "yoshoku" and "seiyo ryori." Breaded pork cutlets (côtelette) served with demiglace sauce are "seiyo ryori"—authentic Western cuisine. Those cutlets became wafu when they morphed into tonkatsu, a sliced pork cutlet served with shredded cabbage, tonkatsu sauce, miso soup, rice, and pickles—a meal that can be eaten with chopsticks. Japanese people call dishes like these, that have become theirs over a period of time, "yoshoku." Something Western in style is "yofu." The same has happened with chugoku ryori, authentic Chinese cuisine. Many Chinese dishes, like gyoza (fried dumplings) and ramen, are products of adaptation, and they are referred to as "chuka ryori," Japanese-style Chinese cooking. Something Chinese in style is "chukafu." All of these cuisines are forms of wafu cooking.

I grew up eating yoshoku like Neapolitan spaghetti (pasta seasoned with ketchup) and mentaiko spaghetti (spaghetti with pickled cod roe, nori, and shiso). We didn't call these dishes wafu. They were simply the best Western-style noodles we could eat in family restaurants in the late 1960s, when few Japanese people traveled abroad.

It was around that time that Toichiro Nakashima (1883–1973), a pioneering Japanese businessman and founder of Kewpie Mayonnaise, introduced their French Dressing in 1958, the first bottled dressing in Japan, to meet the growing interest in Western salads. This was followed in 1965 by the first Japanese-style dressing, which was seasoned with soy sauce and sold as Oriental Dressing. In 1978, the company came out with a new salad dressing seasoned with soy sauce called Wafu Dressing, and it is around this period that the term "wafu" appears to have become common with Japanese people, including me, to define food that was Japanese in style.

I like to think of wafu cooking as divided into three periods. The first is traditional wafu, which includes dishes that developed over centuries, like noodles and dumplings, which were introduced from China; or tempura, bread, and confections, which came from Portugal in the sixteenth century. Then there is classic wafu, dishes that developed between the Meiji Restoration (in the late nineteenth century) and the 1960s, like tonkatsu, ramen, and gyoza. Finally, modern wafu consists of the adaptations and creations of the last half century. This book features mostly modern wafu dishes that we can cook at home, but I include examples from across all three periods to show that this cultural exchange is nothing new and is now happening not only with Western and Chinese dishes but also with those from India, Korea, the Middle East, and many other parts of the world, as well.

WAFU FLAVORS

My pantry is filled with all the familiar seasonings and condiments that you probably have in yours: salt, pepper, olive oil, honey, mustard, vinegar, and ketchup. What makes my kitchen distinctive are the jars full of dried seaweeds, shiitake mushrooms, and bonito flakes; the fermented seasonings, like sake, mirin, and miso; and the garnishes—yakumi and furikake—that can transform all kinds of foods, not just those from Japan, into delicious wafu dishes. This is what Japanese cooks have been doing for centuries—adapting, substituting, and melding to create something new and delicious.

In this chapter, I provide you with a few foundational recipes, so you can see how these wafu flavor agents are used in traditional Japanese dishes before you incorporate them into your own cooking. You might prepare a big batch of Kombu and Bonito Dashi (page 20) at the start of the week, to make traditional miso soup for breakfast and then Mushroom Dashi Risotto (page 133) or Grilled Seafood with Shiso Salsa Verde (page 190) later in the week. Miso is just as versatile. Use it to make Miso-Honey Butter (page 50) to spread on

your morning toast, and then as a flavor enhancer in your Pan-Roasted Baby Beets, Carrots, Turnips, and Orange with Lemon-Miso Yogurt (page 122), or in Miso Apple Pie (page 281) for a hint of caramel.

These pantry essentials can crisscross from one plate to another—from Japan to the United States or Peru and back—without flinching. That's the way people want to eat these days. I certainly do. When your friends and family ask why your pasta sauce tastes so good, you can tell them it's because you wafu-ed it!

As I mature as a cook and grow older, I have come to appreciate the wafu way of "less is more" when seasoning foods. This doesn't mean bland or tasteless. It's the absolute opposite. Seasonings are used prudently so you taste and appreciate the natural and seasonal flavors of food. This is the underlying principle of wafu cooking. Any condiment, wafu or otherwise, can enhance or do just the opposite—overwhelm. They should complement an ingredient and be in harmony. Always taste first, before you reach for flavor agents to add. Then, fine-tune to find your own wafu balance.

Yakumi and Furikake

In traditional Japanese cooking, garnishes are used to enhance the presentation of a dish—to add color, aroma, taste, texture, and form but without overwhelming. Some garnishes, like cherry blossoms, bring the season to a dish. There are essentially two forms of garnishes: raw and fresh garnishes called yakumi, that are used on most everything—from sashimi, soups, rice, noodles, salads, and grilled vegetables to meat and fish, pickles, and hot pots—to enhance the dish and clear the palate; and fuikake, which is a dry or wet condiment that's sprinkled on food (not only rice but also salads, vegetables, and meats) to accent the dish before serving.

Think of sashimi. Soy sauce alone will not do. You must also have yakumi, such as a dab of spicy wasabi or grated ginger, or green shiso leaf to clear the palate. Thinly sliced daikon radish is commonly served as a bed for sashimi. It helps to keep the fish fresh by absorbing any excess moisture. Or consider onigiri. Rice alone would be plain. Scatter furikake—the name comes from the Japanese "furi kakeru," meaning "to sprinkle over"—such as gomashio (toasted sesame seeds and salt), for a good crunch and nutty aroma, or bonito flakes for an oceanic flavor.

In some cases, furikake and yakumi perform medicinal functions—wasabai, for instance, is an antiseptic that can kill any harmful bacteria in raw fish, while shichimi pepper can improve blood circulation. In fact, furikake was first invented for medicinal use, by an early-twentieth-century Japanese pharmacist named Suekichi Yoshimaru. Originally a mixture of ground dried sardines, sesame and poppy seeds, and seaweed—all ingredients rich in minerals and nutrients—Japanese rice lovers welcomed it as a health supplement to eat with rice. Your grocery store may carry only one particular brand or blend, but there are tons of commercial furikakes available that come in a variety of flavors and textures that range from sweet to salty, spicy, wet, and crunchy. I prefer furikakes that are made with natural ingredients.

Furikake are easy and fun to make at home. Start with Surigoma (Ground Toasted Sesame Seeds) (page 6), a basic furikake that can be used as a base for more complex versions. My first

lesson as a young cook was making surigoma with a suribachi and surigoki, a mortar and pestle. My grandmother asked me to turn the pestle until the freshly toasted sesame seeds released their fragrant oils as they were crushed. I can still smell the nutty aroma of the ground seeds. She taught me about natural ingredients—how they contribute to freshness, flavors, texture, and colors. I recommend you give it a try.

In addition to wasabi, ginger, daikon, and shiso, other common yakumi include edible flowers and citrus fruits. Yakumi are used whole or cut into small pieces; root vegetables are grated, and fruit peels are cut into slivers or coins, rather than zested.

You might have difficulty finding some wafu garnishes in your local market. That was my experience for a long time, although now farmers grow many of my favorite yakumi, such as daikon radish, yuzu, shiso, chives, scallions, young ginger, wasabi, and myoga. Before they were widely available, I grew them myself. I still do. I have also learned to substitute and adapt the ingredients that I cannot find and often discover an even more exciting ingredient, like Meyer lemons or Mexican limes or oro blanco in place of yuzu, or dill, parsley, and basil instead of mitsuba and shiso.

DAIKON OROSHI

Fresh Daikon Radish Sauce

Makes about ½ cup (114 grams) grated daikon radish

8 ounces (230 grams)
daikon radish, peeled

Daikon oroshi is a fresh, versatile sauce, made with only one ingredient: daikon radish. It is slightly spicy. If you can't find daikon, you can use other varieties of radishes, like purple and red radishes, which are milder in flavor and smaller in size but just as effective as yakumi.

I highly recommend that you invest in a Japanese grater—an oroshiki—which can be found in Japanese markets and online. They are great for grating daikon as well as ginger and wasabi. They have compartments that collect the juices and are much more effective than a microplane or four-sided grater. Use the daikon oroshi as a garnish with fresh, grilled, and deep-fried dishes.

Grate the daikon by moving it against the grater in a circular motion. The grated daikon will be juicy. Drain the juice and lightly press to remove excess moisture. (Don't throw away the juice; it's spicy but high in vitamin C.) Serve the grated daikon with grilled and deep-fried dishes like Cedar Plank Salmon with Shio Koji Marinade (page 201), Crispy Tofu with Dipping Sauce (page 125), or Pork and Cabbage Hot Pot (page 221).

KITCHEN NOTE When grated and left standing, daikon emits a sulfurous smell common to cabbage and mustard families. To minimize this unpleasant smell, grate the daikon just before serving and use it right away.

SURIGOMA

Ground Toasted Sesame Seeds

Makes 1 cup (140 grams)

1 cup (140 grams) white
sesame seeds

This is a basic sesame furikake with many uses. I urge you to use a suribachi and surigoki—a versatile Japanese mortar and pestle. The suribachi has a textured interior that makes grinding easy. You can use a coffee or spice grinder, but the manual mortar and pestle is much gentler on the seeds. Unlike in an electric grinder, they will grind without overheating.

Heat a dry, medium skillet over medium-low heat. Add the sesame seeds, stirring constantly, until they become fragrant and lightly toasted (but not burned). Transfer the seeds to a mortar placed on a nonslip surface. Hold the pestle straight with one hand and the mortar with the other and grind the seeds clockwise.

Light Grind (5 minutes)
The seeds will be slippery and smooth in the beginning but will begin to break and turn coarse within about 5 minutes. This grind is great for salad toppings and using on noodles and rice, and for making gomashio (see Variation).

Medium Grind (10 minutes)
Continue grinding the sesame seeds until they start to get oily and pasty and stick to the grooves of the mortar. This texture is suitable as a mochi topping when combined with sugar.

Heavy Grind (15 minutes)
The sesame seeds will be finer and smoother with time, becoming a thick paste with some sesame seeds still in pieces throughout. You can add a tablespoon of light sesame oil to make the paste creamier and turn it into nerigoma (Japanese-style tahini). This can be used as a base for a sesame dressing.

Variation Mix 1 cup of toasted light-grind sesame seeds with a couple teaspoons of sea salt to turn surigoma into gomashio furikake.

GRAPEFRUIT FURIKAKE

1 cup (140 grams) white
sesame seeds

½ cup (70 grams) black
sesame seeds

¼ cup dehydrated grapefruit
peels (see Kitchen Note)

½ cup dehydrated kale, crumbled
(see Kitchen Note)

¼ cup dried Alaskan kelp
(or nori or wakame seaweed),
crumbled

1½ tablespoons sea salt,
or more to taste

1 tablespoon cane sugar,
or more to taste

1 teaspoon sansho pepper,
or more to taste

Makes 4 cups (250 grams)

Toasted black and white sesame seeds are the primary ingredients here, but it is the grapefruit peel and sansho pepper that brighten the flavors. Kale brings in the greens and eye appeal, kelp the oceanic flavors. You can use other dehydrated fruits like tangerines, lemons, or limes, or vegetables like tomatoes, carrots, beets, or radishes, if you prefer. The flavor profile will change according to what you add to the mix. Add ingredients in small increments and taste as you go.

Below, I give a variation that is made with dehydrated cherry tomatoes. My kitchen assistant Cassie eagerly climbed the tree to pick the fruit and helped me develop the furikake recipes. The cherry tomato one won first place in the Good Food Awards 2023 category, and this grapefruit version was a finalist.

I use this furikake on toast, noodles, salads, grilled vegetables, focaccia, meat, and seafood. If you can't find Alaskan kelp, use nori or wakame seaweed.

In a frying pan, toast the white sesame seeds over medium-low heat, stirring constantly, until they turn slightly brown and fragrant. When a few seeds begin to pop, remove from the heat and transfer to a bowl. The whole process should take less than 4 or 5 minutes. Let the seeds cool while you repeat the process with the black sesame seeds. You won't see any browning, so simply remove from the heat when the seeds turn fragrant, in 3 to 4 minutes. Bring to room temperature.

Grind the dehydrated grapefruit peels in a food processor until they turn into a coarse powder. You want to leave some texture, so don't overprocess. Measure out ¼ cup ground grapefruit peels and transfer it to the bowl of sesame seeds. Repeat with the dried kale and the kelp, measuring out ½ cup of kale and ¼ cup of kelp, and adding it to the bowl.

Add 1 tablespoon of the salt, 2 teaspoons of the sugar, and ½ teaspoon of sansho pepper to the bowl and give the furikake a good stir. Taste. Then add more salt, sugar, and sansho pepper until you reach the desired flavor. Stored in an airtight container, this furikake keeps fresh for 6 months.

KITCHEN NOTE A dehydrator is a great tool to use for dehydrating fruits and vegetables. I got one from my son Sakae for Christmas. If you don't have a dehydrator, an oven will do. To make dehydrated grapefruit peel, preheat the oven to 200°F (95°C). Line a baking sheet with parchment paper. Peel 2 cleaned and dried grapefruits. Scrape away as much of the pith as possible (the size of the peels does not matter). Spread the peels on the lined baking sheet in an even layer and bake in the oven for 3 hours or until they are dried and crumbly. For kale leaves, remove the stems from the leaves and bake them in the oven until they are dry and crumbly, about 40 minutes. For cherry tomatoes, halve them, spread them on a sheet tray, and bake for 5 hours or until they are crispy and completely dry.

Variation Use ¼ cup dehydrated cherry tomatoes instead of grapefruit peels. Begin with 20 cherry tomatoes, halved and dehydrated (see Kitchen Note). Put the dehydrated tomatoes in a blender and coarsely grind. The flakes should be about the size of sesame seeds or finer. Combine with the other furikake ingredients, in place of the grapefruit, and proceed as directed.

YUZU KOSHO

Spicy Yuzu Paste

Makes about ⅔ cup (157 ml)

About ¾ cup (2½ ounces/ 70 grams) peeled and minced yuzu (or other citrus; see headnote), from about 3 dozen yuzu

About ¾ cup (2½ ounces/ 70 grams) finely chopped fresh green chilies (such as Thai, Calabria, jalapeño), stems and seeds removed

1¾ tablespoons sea salt (Adjust salt level to taste. I use 15–20% of the metric weight of the minced yuzu and chilies.)

½ cup (120 ml) yuzu juice (or other citrus juice)

When the yuzu season arrives in late fall to early winter, I start making yuzu kosho, a spicy, salty, aromatic condiment made from yuzu peel, chilies, and salt. It's a pungent flavor enhancer that brightens almost any dish—udon noodles, ramen, sashimi, gyoza, grilled foods, salad dressings, hot pots, and even on fresh pineapple! This year, my son, Sakae, and his wife, Binah, helped me peel the yuzu and mince the chilies. I owe them a lot of yuzu kosho. Because yuzu can be difficult to find in the U.S., other types of citrus, such as lemon, lime, or sudachi, can be substituted. Be careful when handling chilies. Wear rubber gloves and goggles if you have sensitive eyes.

In a medium bowl, combine the peeled and minced yuzu, chilies, and salt. Let stand for 30 minutes. Transfer to a food processor or high-speed blender, add the yuzu juice, and process until pureed with a little texture left. Transfer to a sterilized small jar, cover, and refrigerate for 3 days before using. The yuzu kosho will keep for up to a year in the refrigerator.

Dashi

At the heart of wafu cooking is the broth— dashi—which enhances the flavor deeply and heartily and brings harmony to your dishes by adding umami. Umami, which is now recognized as one of the five tastes, with sweet, sour, salty, and bitter, was discovered by Kikunae Ikeda, a Japanese chemist who, one evening while having dinner with his family, noticed that his soup was tastier than usual thanks to the addition of kombu (kelp). He studied the chemical composition of kombu and discovered that its savory flavor comes from the amino acid glutamate.

Every cook interested in wafu cooking should learn how to make a good dashi. "Dashi" just means "broth" in Japanese, and literally translated means "to extract the essence" of ingredients.

Traditional dashi is made with a variety of ingredients like kombu, bonito flakes, dried anchovies, and dried shiitake mushrooms. Use of these authentic dashis can give a non-Japanese dish a distinctive wafu complexity, whereas dashi made from meat bones and tomatoes, carrots, peas, garlic, onions, cabbage, and potatoes, and herbs and spices like garlic, nutmeg, saffron, thyme, oregano, sage, or basil, can give classic Japanese dishes a yofu—Western—flavor and

dashi made from chicken carcass, bay leaf, scallions, star anise, peppercorns, and ginger can give them a chukafu—Chinese—flavor. I use dashi not only to make miso soups and rice dishes like risotto and paella, but also as kakushiaji, a secret flavor enhancer, in my salads and pickles. When using dashi in this way, you will discover that you don't need to add a drizzle of oil to get a good flavor.

Making dashi is fairly fast, about 15 minutes, but the resulting stock will set you up for a week of meals. You can make a single-ingredient dashi—with kombu, bonito flakes, shiitake mushrooms, or dried anchovies—or blend two or more ingredients together. When you combine one or more specific amino acids—glutamic acid from kombu, inosinic acid from bonito flakes, dried anchovies, meat bones, and shellfish, or guanylyl acid from shiitakes—their synergy creates an even deeper umami-rich dashi.

To make dashi, the ingredients are gently infused into water (preferably filtered water), almost like making tea. When using seaweed or seafood, the goal is to achieve a pleasant oceanic flavor rather than something "fishy" or "slimy," which can happen for a number of reasons: if you cut slits in your kombu (some kombu, such as

rishiri, are naturally more slimy than the others because they contain water soluble dietary fibers); if you leave the kombu soaking for longer than twelve hours; if you boil the ingredients too harshly; or if you press the steeped kombu and bonito flakes when you are straining the dashi. While the neba neba (a term Japanese use when referring to slimy foods) of kombu is loaded with vitamin B and fiber, and considered medicinal

and a distinct texture, it can be unpleasant in a dashi. Always strain the liquid through a sieve lined with a paper towel or cheesecloth. Attention to such details will help you make a fragrant, clean-tasting dashi.

Other styles of dashis, like bone broth, may be made from an array of bones and vegetables. I absolutely love bone-based dashis and always keep homemade meat bone dashi in stock; it can be used interchangeably or in combination with more traditional dashis in Japanese cooking. Many Americans associate ramen with tonkotsu-style dashi because that style landed in the United States first and became hugely popular. Tonkotsu dashi is made of mostly pork bones with tendons, joints, and collagen-rich parts like the femur, trotter, and leg. During the simmering process, which can take hours, the collagen breaks down into gelatin and creates a richer, thicker liquid that makes for a fat-laden, creamy soup. I use a pork bone dashi to make both ramen and Posole Japonesa (page 87). It is hard to find femur bones in grocery stores in the U.S., so look for trotters and leg and neck bones, particularly in Asian and Latino markets. You can also use Chicken Dashi (page 25) or Quick Chintan Dashi (page 26) instead. Or use chicken and pork bones with kombu, bonito flakes, sardines, and shiitakes to make your own blend of wafu dashi.

KOMBU DASHI

Cold Brew Method

Makes 8 cups (about 2 liters)

8 cups (2 liters) water

One 5 x 5 inch (12 x 12 cm) piece
dried kombu (20 grams)

I always have cold brew kombu dashi on standby to use as the base for miso soup in the morning and to season my dishes. It has a subtly briny taste. When soaked in water, kombu reconstitutes itself and will double or triple in size. The spent kombu can be used in several ways. You can make a secondary dashi (see Kitchen Notes) or do as I do and slice it up and enjoy the chew or add to your salads and stir-fry. My husband makes an improvised pickle by placing spent kombu in rice vinegar with a little salt and sugar, and now my son, Sakae, does the same. I also compost spent kombu—my plants love it.

———————

Fill a pitcher with the water. Add the dried kombu and let it steep for at least 1 hour and up to overnight in the fridge but not more than 12 hours to avoid the dashi getting slimy, because the kombu is water soluble. Remove the kombu. The dashi is now ready to use. It can be stored in the fridge for up to 1 week or in the freezer for up to 3 months.

KITCHEN NOTES

If you have a digital scale, weigh the kombu in grams. You will get a more accurate reading because the width and length of kombu can vary. You can make a second round of dashi by adding 2 quarts (2 liters) water to the spent kombu and bring it to a boil over medium heat for 4 to 5 minutes. Drain. Compost the kombu or slice it into strips and add them to your pickle. See the pickles section (beginning on page 137) for more ways to use kombu.

For a stronger dashi, cook over low heat for 10 minutes before removing the kombu. ❯

Kombu and Dried Anchovy Dashi

This dashi is a strong, aromatic broth that works well in miso soup and noodle soups. Katakuchi iwashi (Japanese anchovies) and other silvery-skinned fish that have been cooked and then dried are called niboshi or iriko, and this dashi can be made simply by soaking the fish in water overnight. The number of dried anchovies depends on the size of the fish and how strong you want your dashi to be, so try making a batch or two, and adjust accordingly. Look for dried anchovies that are silvery and shiny rather than yellowish with an oily surface, which is a sign that the fish have oxidized. Once the package is opened, keep it in the refrigerator.

Break off the heads and remove the bitter innards of 30 dried anchovies (2 ounces/50 grams) with your fingers. Place the fish in a bowl with the water at the same time as the kombu. Let stand in the fridge overnight. Strain and use the liquid as a light dashi. You can make a stronger dashi by cooking the liquid in a saucepan over medium heat before you remove the anchovies. Bring to a boil and lower the heat to maintain a simmer for 7 to 8 minutes. Skim off any foam. Strain the liquid through a sieve lined with a paper towel, cheesecloth, or unbleached flannel cotton.

Kombu and Toasted Dried Anchovy Dashi

If you would like a smokier version of the previous dashi, toast the anchovies in a medium frying pan over medium-low heat until lightly browned. Then follow the instructions for Kombu and Dried Anchovy Dashi (above). ➤

Kombu

Kombu is a seaweed cultivated both wild and farmed in Japan, Korea, Australia, South Africa, Canada, and on both the Pacific and Atlantic coasts of the United States. Japanese kombu comes primarily from the coastlines of Hokkaido and the northeastern parts of Honshu Island, where the mineral-rich sea meets the ice that drifts from Siberia to Hokkaido, providing an ideal habitat for seaweed.

Since ancient times, kombu has been a vital part of the diet of the indigenous Ainu people in Hokkaido, who harvested it as a source of salt. The word "kombu" is believed to come from the Ainu word "kompu," which means "plants that grow on underwater rocks." During the seventeenth century, Japanese commercial boats (kitamae-bune) plied the trade route known as the Kombu Route between Hokkaido and Osaka, and farther south to the Ryukyu dynasty (Okinawa) and Qing dynasty (China).

Kombu has long been an important ingredient not only for culinary purposes but also for celebrations and religious ceremonies in Japan. For New Year's gatherings I prepare osechi ryori, a variety of dishes that represent good luck—such as mochi for endurance, beans for diligence, and eggs for fertility—and include kombu because it sounds similar to "yorokobu," the word for happiness.

Just as there are many different types of lettuces, there are many varieties of kombu, of several shapes, textures, and flavors. They can be a lot to take in at first glance when you visit a Japanese market. See below for a description of the most common ones, all of which make good dashi. All Japanese kombu goes through a quality-control process and is graded from standard to premium. As soon as kombu is harvested, it is laid out in the sun to dry on rocks. Then it is brought indoors for further processing. Premium-grade kombu undergoes a further dehydration and maturation process which can last two to three years to remove the distinctive odor and improve the flavor. Kombu is labeled by the place of origin, whether it was grown wild or farmed, and when it was harvested. It has a shelf life of two to three years.

Hidaka: A good, economical kombu for an everyday dashi base, widely used by Japanese home cooks. Tender and slim. Used for wrapping fish and vegetables to infuse them with umami.

Makombu: Thick and wide kombu, considered one of the highest species of kombu. Rich with umami. It possesses a refined sweetness.

Rausu: Regarded as a premium kombu, like makombu. Produces a rich, fragrant, golden-colored dashi with deep umami.

Rishiri: Slightly tougher than makombu or rausu kombu. It produces a clear and briny dashi, favored by chefs in Kyoto.

Vegetable Dashi

Makes 10½ cups (2.5 liters)

5 quarts (5 liters) water

One 3 x 7 inch (7 x 25 cm) piece dried kombu (10 grams)

3 dried shiitake mushrooms

1 yellow onion, quartered

1 carrot, cut into 4 pieces

1 medium tomato, halved

4 garlic cloves, smashed

1 leek, green parts only

¼ cup (60 ml) vegetable oil (grapeseed, olive, rice bran, light sesame)

1 dried bay leaf

1 ounce (28 grams) ginger, sliced

5 whole black peppercorns

1 dried chili pepper, seeded (optional)

Sea salt, to taste

Freshly ground black pepper, to taste

This fragrant vegetable dashi infused with kombu and vegetables is a versatile broth that can serve as the base for many vegan dishes.

———————

Fill a heavy-bottomed stock pot with the water. Add the kombu and dried shiitake mushrooms and leave them to steep on the kitchen counter or in the refrigerator for 6 hours or overnight to make a cold brew dashi.

Preheat your oven to the broil setting. Set a rack about 5 inches (13 cm) from the broiler and line a sheet pan with aluminum foil. Place the onions, carrots, tomatoes, garlic, and leek on the pan and toss them with the oil. Put the sheet pan under the broiler and brown the vegetables until toasted evenly across the tops, about 2 to 3 minutes. Remove from the oven.

Add all the vegetables to the dashi along with the bay leaf, ginger, peppercorns, and chilies, if using. Set the stock pot over medium heat and allow the dashi to come to a boil. Remove the kombu, lower the heat, and continue to simmer for about 2 hours, stirring the pot every 15 minutes to prevent any scorching on the bottom. Simmer until the liquid has reduced to about half of its original volume. Remove the pot from the heat and allow the dashi to rest for 20 minutes undisturbed.

Remove any large vegetable chunks from the broth and then strain the dashi. Skim off any surface fat before using. Your dashi is now ready to be seasoned with salt and pepper, or any seasonings of your choice. Store in the fridge for up to 1 week or in the freezer for up to 3 months.

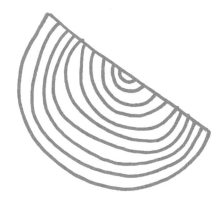

BONITO DASHI

Makes 7 cups (1.6 liters)

8 cups (2 liters) water

5 cups (40 grams) bonito flakes

The beauty of dashi made from bonito (dried tuna flakes; see box about Bonito Flakes, page 23) is its clean oceanic, smoky flavor. Some say it is the king of dashi, others that kombu dashi is. Either way, they are both incredibly powerful agents of umami, and bonito dashi has its own special qualities. It's perfect when I want a hint of smokiness. I love using this dashi for Udon al Yuzu Kosho (page 246), because the smokiness pairs well with the creamy, lemony sauce, creating an even richer umami.

In a large saucepan, over medium-high heat, bring the water to a full boil, about 5 or 6 minutes. Turn off the heat and add the bonito flakes. Gently stir once and let the flakes steep in the liquid for 2 minutes, undisturbed.

To strain the dashi, pour the liquid through a fine-mesh sieve lined with a paper towel or damp cheesecloth. Do not press the bonito flakes while straining, as it will cloud the dashi. Reserve the spent bonito flakes to make another pot of dashi (see Kitchen Note). The dashi can be stored in the fridge for up to 1 week or in the freezer for up to 1 month.

KITCHEN NOTE You can use the bonito flakes to make a second round of dashi, called niban dashi, or "number 2 dashi." Simply add another 8 cups (2 liters) of water to the pot, along with the spent bonito flakes, and bring to a boil over medium heat. Simmer for 20 minutes. Strain the dashi, following the directions above. This method also works for Kombu Dashi and its variations (pages 15–18). ›

Bonito and Kombu Dashi

Makes 7 cups (1.6 liters)

8 cups (2 liters) water

One 5 x 5 inch (13 x 13 cm) piece
dried kombu (20 grams)

5 cups (40 grams) bonito flakes

When used in combination, kombu and bonito flakes create a synergy of two amino acids working together to create a much deeper umami. It is the most widely used classic dashi by Japanese chefs and cooks. I always keep a pitcher on standby. Adjust the amount of bonito flakes or kombu based on the depth of umami you wish to achieve. I add an additional cup of bonito flakes and a couple of dried shiitake mushrooms to this recipe when I'm making a noodle soup, so I get that extra-deep oceanic and earthy flavor.

In a medium saucepan set over medium heat combine the water and kombu and cook until the water begins to simmer and bubbles form around the kombu, about 4 to 5 minutes. Remove the kombu before the water comes to a full boil and set aside. Lower the heat to a simmer and add the bonito flakes. Turn off the heat. Gently stir once and let the flakes steep in the liquid for 2 minutes.

To strain the dashi, pour the liquid through a fine-mesh sieve lined with a paper towel or damp cheesecloth. Do not press the bonito flakes while straining, as it will cloud the dashi. Use the spent kombu and bonito flakes to make another pot of dashi (see Kitchen Note below). The dashi can be stored in the fridge for up to 1 week or in the freezer for up to 1 month.

KITCHEN NOTE You can use the bonito flakes and kombu to make a second round of dashi, called niban dashi, or "number 2 dashi" (page 19). ›

Bonito, Kombu, and Dried Shiitake Mushroom Dashi

This trio of ingredients—bonito flakes, dried shiitake mushrooms, and kombu—is what my soba master Takashi Hosokawa of Hosokawa Soba in Tokyo used every morning to make dashi. The clean fragrance of the dashi filled up the kitchen while he rolled out the dough to make the soba. He would go back into the kitchen, taste, and adjust the flavor as needed. I was a dish washer but he always let me taste the dashi—a fundamental and essential lesson for making a good noodle dish. I was in charge of washing the large flannel cotton cloth after the dashi was strained and hanging it outside to dry in the sun. I loved that morning ritual.

To make the dashi, add two or three pieces of dried shiitake mushrooms and one 5 x 5 inch (13 x 13 cm) kombu to 8 cups of water, and let it stand in the refrigerator for 3 hours to overnight, and proceed with the instructions, following the Kombu and Bonito Dashi recipe.

Bonito Flakes

When I was growing up in Japan, it was common for every household to be equipped with a katsuobushi no kezuriki—a plane for shaving blocks of bonito (dried tuna) to make bonito flakes (katsuobushi). I vividly remember the comforting sound of my grandmother shaving bonito, moving her hands steadily to produce a box full of long curly flakes, which were used for making Bonito Dashi (page 19), for sprinkling on ohitashi (see Baby Bok Choy Ohitashi, page 114), and to munch on as the tastiest snack ever: meaty, like beef jerky, in texture and smoky in flavor. Over the past fifty years, shaving bonito flakes at home has fallen out of practice. The standard katsuobushi you find in the market is arabushi, made from tuna that has been gutted, boiled, deboned, dried, and smoked and then shaved into flakes and conveniently vacuum packed for shelf stability. This process takes about thirty days. There is also namabushi, which undergoes a shorter processing period than arabushi, yielding a block that is softer and easier to shave but has a shorter shelf life (six months in the fridge). The more expensive, higher-grade katsuobushi is hongarebushi, which has an ash-brown color that is the result of inoculating the bonito block with a fungus called *Aspergillus glaucus* four to five times to further reduce the moisture level, deepen the umami, and elevate the aroma. This latter process can take six months or more. I keep a few blocks of dried bonito for cooking with and bring out my katsuobushi no kezuriki when I want to sprinkle fresh shaved bonito flakes on my ohitashi, risotto, or soba noodles, because nothing compares to the smoky flavor of freshly shaved flakes.

When I am in Japan, I always visit Yagicho Honten, a nearly three-hundred-year-old shop in Tokyo now run by my childhood friend Mamiko Nishiyama, and treat myself to freshly shaved bonito flakes to order to bring back in my suitcase.

Use katsuobushi (also called kezuribushi or hanakatsuo) for making dashi. Itokezuri, finely shredded bonito flakes, are used as a finishing garnish, not for making dashi.

To prevent oxidation, be sure to seal the bag of unused bonito flakes and store it in the fridge or freezer. Once you've opened it, use it within a year.

PORK BONE DASHI

Makes about 3 quarts (3 liters)

3 pounds (1.3 kilograms) pork bones (femur bones, trotters, neck, shanks)

2 chicken backs

1 yellow onion, halved

5 garlic cloves, peeled and left whole

1 bay leaf

3 dried shiitake mushrooms

One 2 x 2 inch (5 x 5 cm) piece kombu hydrated in 4 cups (1 liter) water for 1 hour or overnight, soaking liquid reserved

2 leeks, cut lengthwise and in sixths

1 carrot, peeled and cut into chunks

1 ounce (28 grams) ginger, unpeeled and sliced

1 dried red chili pepper (optional)

½ teaspoon whole black peppercorns

This dashi is the product of a rich synergy of ingredients: pig trotters and leg bones, chicken, kombu, shiitake mushrooms, onions, and aromatics. I use it as the base for ramen soup, stews, curries, and my Posole Japonesa (page 87).

———————

Fill a large saucepan with water and bring it to a boil. Place the pork bones and chicken backs in a colander and pour the hot water over them. Rinse briefly under cold running water and set them aside. This blanching method is commonly used in Japan to remove impurities and odors from meats.

In a stock pot, add the onions, garlic, bay leaf, shiitake mushrooms, kombu, leeks, carrots, ginger, chili pepper (if using), peppercorns, and the blanched bones. Fill with water and the reserved kombu soaking liquid to cover the ingredients by 2 inches (5 cm) and bring to a boil. Lower the heat and simmer for 6 hours. Periodically skim off any foam that floats to the surface. Strain through a fine mesh strainer lined with damp cheesecloth and reserve the stock. Discard the solids.

If you wish to remove the fat from the dashi, allow it to chill in the fridge overnight. The fat will rise to the surface and will be easier to remove. The flavor is in the fat, so reserve it for use in ramen soup and other broths. Store in the fridge for up to 4 days or in the freezer for up to 1 month.

Variation Combine the Pork Bone Dashi with Kombu and Bonito Dashi (page 20) or Kombu and Toasted Dried Anchovy Dashi (page 16) for a layer of smoky oceanic umami flavor—a method often used by ramen chefs.

CHICKEN DASHI

Makes 3 quarts (3 liters)

1 whole chicken (4 pounds/ 1.8 kilograms), cut into large pieces, skin on

One 2 x 2 inch (5 x 5 cm) piece kombu

3 dried shiitake mushrooms

1 carrot, unpeeled, cut into 3 parts

3 garlic cloves, mashed

1 ounce (28 grams) ginger, peeled and sliced into ¼ inch (6 mm) coins

1 yellow onion, skin removed, quartered

2 leeks, green parts only

¼ cup (60 ml) sake

½ teaspoon whole black peppercorns

5 quarts (5 liters) water

This dashi is made with a rich combination of umami-heavy ingredients, including a whole chicken, vegetables, and shiitake mushrooms. It is the perfect base for soups, stews, dumplings, rice dishes, ramen, and more. Ginger, which is not an ingredient used in Western broths, is essential in Japanese meat bone dashi to brighten its flavor. Blanching the bones before you start cooking them yields a cleaner-tasting dashi.

———————

Fill a large saucepan with water and bring it to a boil. Place the chicken parts in a colander and pour the hot water over them. Rinse briefly under cold running water.

In the same saucepan, combine the rinsed chicken parts, kombu, shiitake mushrooms, carrots, garlic, ginger, onions, leeks, sake, peppercorns, and water. Bring to a boil over medium heat. Remove the kombu, simmer the dashi for 2 hours, and then take out the chicken pieces; the chicken will be cooked through. Allow the chicken to cool on a cutting board for 10 minutes, then pull out the breast meat, leg meat, and thigh meat. You can use the meat for soups, salads, and other dishes. (You can use the spent kombu in a number of ways; see Kombu Dashi headnote, page 15.)

Return the bones to the pot and continue to cook the dashi at a bare simmer for 5 hours, skimming off any foam that accumulates on the surface. The temperature of the dashi should not exceed 200°F (95°C) while simmering. Remove from the heat and discard the solids. Slowly strain the liquid through a fine mesh sieve lined with cheesecloth or paper towel. You will have about 3 quarts (3 liters) of dashi. Let the dashi cool to room temperature before storing it in the fridge or freezer.

If you wish to remove the fat from the dashi, allow it to chill in the fridge overnight. The fat will rise to the surface and will be easier to remove. The flavor is in the fat, so reserve it for use in ramen soup and Aonori Potato Pancake with Miso-Stewed Apples (page 60). Store in the fridge for up to 4 days or in the freezer for up to 1 month.

KITCHEN NOTE When using onion and garlic in your broth, leaving the skins on or removing them comes down to personal preference. Leaving them will result in a darker broth, with deeper, earthier flavors. Removing them results in a lighter-colored broth. The preference is yours.

QUICK CHINTAN DASHI

Quick Pork and Chicken Broth

Makes 7 cups (1.7 liters)

10 cups (2.25 liters) water

One 3 x 3 inch (7 x 7 cm) piece kombu (10 grams)

1 pound (454 grams) ground pork

1 pound (454 grams) ground chicken (preferably white meat)

1 ounce (28 grams) ginger, peeled and sliced into ¼ inch (6 mm) coins

2 garlic cloves, smashed

1 leek, green parts only, cut into 3 inch (7 cm) pieces crosswise then sliced thinly

Sea salt, to taste

Freshly ground black pepper, to taste

The question I get asked the most in my ramen workshops is "Where can I find bones to make ramen broth?" The marrow and cartilage from pork femur bones contain fats and collagens that produce the exceptionally thick and creamy tonkotsu dashi that many Americans associate with ramen. If you are willing to spend your time getting the right pork bones and cooking them for hours, that's fine, but the ramen broth universe is immense and there are so many other ways to make dashi. My quick all-purpose dashi these days is chintan dashi. It is a simple "clear" broth, Chinese in origin, and wafu-ed with kombu. It is far less complicated to make than Pork Bone Dashi (page 24) and works well for ramen and other dishes when you are in a hurry. From start to finish, it only takes thirty minutes, as the process is accelerated by using ground meat. In this recipe, I use a combination of ground pork and ground chicken. You can also make it with one or the other or another combination, like ground pork and ground beef. You can use the spent meat in stir-fried vegetables and fried rice (see Dry Curry Omuraisu, page 165), so nothing is wasted.

———————

Fill a large pot with the water. Without turning the heat on, add the kombu and ground pork and stir with a pair of long cooking chopsticks or a spatula to distribute it into the water. Add the ground chicken and repeat. Add the ginger, garlic, and leeks. The water will look a bit cloudy.

Turn the heat on medium-high and bring the water to a boil, then lower to a bare simmer (200°F/95°C). Let the dashi simmer for 30 minutes, until it becomes clear. Do not disturb the ingredients or stir.

Pour the dashi through a fine mesh strainer lined with paper towel or damp cheesecloth. The dashi is ready to be used.

If not using immediately, let the dashi come to room temperature and then refrigerate. Fat will rise to the surface; you can skim it off or leave some for a deeper umami. Season with salt and pepper or any seasonings of your choice. Store in the fridge for up to 1 week or in the freezer for up to 3 months.

Variation For another layer of umami, pour the strained dashi back into the pot. Roughly chop 1 yellow onion and 1 carrot, add to dashi, and bring to a boil over medium heat. Lower the heat to a simmer and cook for another 30 minutes. Strain and discard (or compost) the vegetables.

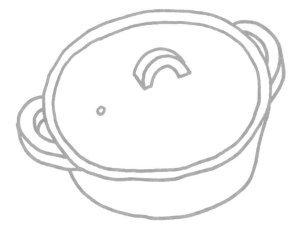

SHIITAKE MUSHROOM DASHI POWDER

Makes ¼ cup (12 grams)

1 ounce (28 grams)
dried shiitake mushrooms

All dashi introduced earlier are in liquid form. This homemade mushroom powder is used for making instant dashi. Just add hot water! No soaking needed. It is a versatile and natural umami booster that I use in soups, curries, stews, pasta sauces, salad dressings, and more. It's like bouillon or MSG without the chemical additives. I use this powder so often that I keep it in an airtight container next to my salt and pepper shakers.

———————

Remove the stems from the mushrooms and discard. Place the mushrooms in a blender. Close the lid and blend to a very fine powder. Do not open the lid while blending, to prevent getting yourself dusty with mushroom powder. Wait for the powder to settle completely before opening. Transfer to an airtight container; it will keep for up to a year.

For a single serving of instant miso soup, add 2 teaspoons of miso to 1 cup of heated mushroom dashi and stir. Don't forget the veggies.

Keep the reconstituted dashi in the refrigerator for 4 to 5 days. You can also combine it with other dashis where dried shiitake mushrooms are called for.

Fermented Condiments

In addition to dashi, my Japanese pantry is defined by fermented seasonings: namely, soy sauce, miso, shio koji (fermented salt), mirin, sake, and rice vinegar, many of which originated in China and were brought to Japan in ancient times.

These fermented condiments are used alone or in combination to impart the five basic tastes—sweet, sour, salty, umami, and bitter.

Differences in base ingredient (the type of grain or legume) as well as brewing method (natural versus industrial fermentation) determine the flavors of these condiments and can add another layer that can be described in Japanese as koku (depth of flavor) and marumi (roundness of flavor). Luckily, most of these condiments, including some artisanal brands, are available online or in specialty grocery stores.

Shoyu (Japanese-Style Soy Sauce)

Soy sauce is the base seasoning for many wafu recipes: soups, simmered dishes, marinades, and salad dressings. There are a variety of Japanese soy sauces—shoyu—on the market, but the most common ones for cooking are koikuchi shoyu (dark-colored); usukuchi shoyu (light-colored); and tamari (also referred to as tamari shoyu, darker in color and thicker than koikuchi shoyu, it is made with more soybeans and is mostly gluten free). In ancient times, tamari was what most Japanese people cooked with. Both tamari and koikuchi shoyu tend to be more pungent and fragrant in flavor and darker in color than usukuchi, which is slightly saltier than the others and often used to preserve the color and fragrance of the dish. I like to use usukuchi shoyu when making noodle soups and salad dressings and koikuchi shoyu and tamari for sashimi, braising, and stir-frying. There are many artisanal varieties of Japanese soy sauce that you can purchase online and at specialty shops. I prefer ones made with organic whole soybeans, organic wheat, and salt without added alcohol, chemical seasoning, and preservatives. Once shoyu is opened, keep it in the refrigerator.

Tare: Sauces Made with Soy Sauce

Soy sauce can be used plain or in combination with other fermented ingredients, like mirin, sake, rice vinegar, miso, and shio koji. Sauces made with soy sauce are called tare. Combine soy sauce with mirin and dashi to make noodle soup, or with mirin and sake to make a teriyaki sauce for basting grilled meats and seafood. With vinegar or citrus juice and grated ginger, it can turn into a versatile sauce for your vegetables; add oil, and it becomes a salad dressing. I'm including some simple recipes that will give a wafu punch to any dish you use them in. The ratios can be altered to suit your palate.

BASIC SHOYU TARE

¼ cup (60 ml) mirin

2 teaspoons cane sugar

1 cup (240 ml) soy sauce
(usukuchi shoyu,
koikuchi shoyu, or tamari)

This is an all-purpose sauce made by combining soy sauce and mirin, both seasonings that add umami, saltiness, and mild sweetness to dishes. The strength can be adjusted according to your preference. When basic shoyu tare is diluted with dashi, it turns into mentsuyu. The word "mentsuyu" is used to refer to a base for soup or a dipping sauce, depending on the amount of dashi (see Basic Soup for Noodles, page 34). Or it can be used to season many dishes in this book. It's slightly sweet without being sugary sweet like a lot of commercial sauces tend to be.

Combine the mirin and sugar in a small pan set over medium heat and stir until the sugar dissolves. Add the soy sauce and cook for an additional 2 minutes over low heat. Remove from the heat and set aside to cool to room temperature. Store in a container in the refrigerator, where it will keep for up to 6 months.

TERIYAKI SAUCE

⅓ cup (80 ml) koikuchi or usukuchi soy sauce, or tamari

⅓ cup (80 ml) sake

⅓ cup (80 ml) mirin

Makes 1 cup (240 ml)

This is an all-purpose tare that works well with stews like Quick Amakarani Beef and Shirataki (page 169) and for basting grilled meat and onigiri for an amakara—salty and sweet—flavor, using equal parts soy sauce, mirin, and sake. If you like a sweeter sauce, you can omit the sake or add 1 tablespoon (12 grams) of sugar.

Combine the soy sauce, sake, and mirin and mix well. The sauce will keep, tightly covered, in the refrigerator for up to 3 months.

Sake and Mirin

Sake and mirin are both made by fermenting rice. You are probably familiar with sake—a delicious alcoholic beverage, light in body, with complex flavors that can range from earthy to floral and delicate. Sake is also a versatile seasoning—it tenderizes, subtly sweetens, acts as an antiseptic, removes odors from meat and seafood, and adds umami without coloring or overwhelming the natural flavor of ingredients. Mirin is a type of sake but made with sweet rice (also called glutinous rice) and has a mildly syrupy texture and sweet flavor. The combination of equal parts mirin and soy sauce or sake and soy sauce makes an instant teriyaki sauce to season any of your dishes. Look for hon mirin—pure mirin that does not have added corn syrup. Since mirin has a lower glycemic index than cane sugar, honey, or maple syrup, it makes a viable substitute for those looking to consume less sugar. Sakes brewed in the United States are the most reasonably priced and are good for everyday cooking. I keep a large bottle in my pantry just for that.

BASIC SOUP
FOR NOODLES

7 cups (1.6 liters) dashi of your
choice (see Kitchen Note)

½ cup (120 ml) Basic Shoyu Tare
(page 32), or more as needed

1 tablespoon mirin or sake
(optional)

Makes about 7 cups (1.6 liters), or 4 servings

This is an essential soup base recipe that is made by combining dashi and basic shoyu tare. I use this recipe for udon, soba, somen, and ramen soups. In this recipe, I used a ratio of about 7 percent tare to 93 percent dashi. Remember, if you start with good dashi, you've basically completed 90 percent or more of the job. This soup goes by many different names. While most ramen chefs call it soup, udon and soba chefs call it "mentsuyu" or "tsuyu." The word "mentsuyu" applies to both a soup base and a dipping sauce, which can be confusing to a foreigner. You just have to remember that the dipping sauce is denser in flavor than the other.

In a medium pot set over medium heat, combine the dashi with the shoyu tare. Bring to a boil, then remove from the heat. Taste and adjust the seasoning with more tare or a splash of sake or mirin for more sweetness, as needed. It keeps for 1 week in the fridge.

KITCHEN NOTE Allow 1½–2 cups (350–473 ml) of soup per serving, depending on the size of the bowl you are serving it in. When making soup for soba and udon noodles, I prefer light-colored soy sauce (usukuchi shoyu), and I use Bonito, Kombu, and Dried Shiitake Mushroom Dashi (page 22). For ramen, I use Chicken Dashi (page 25), Pork Bone Dashi (page 24), Bonito, Kombu, and Dried Shiitake Mushroom Dashi (page 22), and Vegetable Dashi (page 18), or Quick Chintan Dashi (Quick Pork and Chicken Broth) (page 26).

BASIC DIPPING SAUCE

Tsuyu, Tsukejiru, or Mentsuyu

Makes about 4 cups (960 ml)

3 cups (720 ml) Kombu and
Bonito Dashi (page 20)

1 cup (240 ml) Basic
Shoyu Tare (page 32)

This is a basic dipping sauce for noodles and tempura. Like my Basic Soup for Noodles (page 34), it is most often called mentsuyu, but it is made with less dashi and more shoyu tare. In this recipe, I used a ratio of 25 percent shoyu tare to 75 percent dashi for a medium-strength sauce that you can pour over noodles or use as a dip with tempura. For dipping noodles, I make a stronger sauce: 30 percent basic shoyu tare to 70 percent dashi. The ritual of dipping noodles involves dipping the noodle about a third of the way instead of dunking the whole thing so you can taste the noodle.

In a medium pot set over medium heat, combine the dashi and the shoyu tare. Bring to a boil, then remove from the heat. Serve hot or cold as a dipping sauce for noodles or tempura. It will keep for a week in the fridge.

KITCHEN NOTE Allow ⅓–½ cup (80–120 ml) of dipping sauce per serving.

Vinegar

For my wafu cooking, I use mostly rice vinegar, which is brewed and fermented from white and brown rice. Komezu, white rice vinegar, is light and mellow. Genmaizu, brown rice vinegar, is darker and stronger in flavor. I use them interchangeably for making salad dressings, sunomono (vinegared dishes), and sushi rice. I prefer organic seichi-hakko, which is rice vinegar slowly made using a traditional two-step method. First, sake is brewed using rice, water, and *Aspergillus* mold. Then the sake is converted into vinegar, a slow fermentation process that can take six months or longer. Other vinegars in my pantry include umami-rich kurozu, amber-brown rice vinegar, which is produced very, very slowly, over the course of one to three years, allowing seichi-hakko, or slow fermentation. Kurozu is suitable as a finishing vinegar for Chashu Pork (page 215) and Pork, Napa Cabbage, and Garlic Chive Gyoza (page 253). You can find artisan rice vinegars at Japanese markets, specialty stores, and online.

CLASSIC PONZU SAUCE

Makes about ¾ cup (180 ml)

2 tablespoons mirin

1 tablespoon sake

6 tablespoons (90 ml) freshly squeezed tangerine, yuzu, or grapefruit juice, or combination of citrus fruit, strained

1 teaspoon rice vinegar

¼ cup (60 ml) soy sauce

1 x 1 inch (2.2 x 2.2 cm) kombu

¼ cup (4 grams) bonito flakes

This umami-rich ponzu sauce is easy to make but needs two to four weeks of resting to ferment and mature to achieve the synergy of various amino acids in the kombu, bonito flakes, and soy sauce. This is a versatile sauce that can be used for sashimi, salads, pastas, grilled vegetables, seafood, and meat dishes.

————————

Heat the mirin and sake in a small pot over low heat and bring to a boil. Remove from heat. Let cool. Combine with all the remaining ingredients in a sterilized mason jar. Stir to combine. Let stand in the refrigerator for a week and then strain out the bonito and kombu. The flavor will mature slowly but surely. Keeps for 5 months in the fridge.

QUICK PONZU SAUCE

Makes about ¾ cup (180 ml)

6 tablespoons (90 ml) soy sauce

⅛ ounce (3.5 grams) kombu (optional)

¼ cup (60 ml) rice vinegar

1 tablespoon light or toasted sesame oil (optional)

2 tablespoons citrus juice (yuzu, lime, lemon, grapefruit, or orange)

If you are in a hurry and need a quick ponzu sauce, make this version, which requires no resting. It is a citrusy sauce that can serve as an oil-free dressing for vegetables and salads, or as a true salad dressing with the addition of a few tablespoons of extra-virgin olive oil or sesame oil (light or toasted). It also works well with grilled seafood and meats.

————————

Combine the soy sauce, kombu (if using), vinegar, sesame oil (if using), and citrus juice and mix well. Taste and make adjustments. The umami of the kombu will kick in if you allow the sauce to rest for a couple of days, but you can start using it right away if you need it in a hurry. The sauce will keep, tightly covered, in the refrigerator for up to 4 weeks.

SHIO KOJI

Fermented Koji Salt

¾ cup (170 grams) freeze-dried rice koji, at room temperature

4 tablespoons (60 grams) sea salt

1 cup (240 ml) warm water (80–90°F/26–32°C)

Makes 1⅓ cups (300 ml)

Shio koji is a relative newcomer among fermented wafu seasonings. It's a cousin of miso, but creamier, mellower, and easier to use. Like miso, it has many health benefits; it contains a number of enzymes known to be beneficial for well-being, including amylase, which aids in digestion and promotes a healthy gut. You can buy it in Japanese markets or online, but I prefer to make my own. I rub my seafood, meat, and tofu with shio koji and use it like a marinade. My roast chicken (Shio Koji Marinated Roast Chicken, page 209) has never gotten more accolades than when cooked with shio koji. I also add it to pickles, water kimchi, soups, stews, and even ice cream. It's my secret seasoning.

One tablespoon of shio koji contains approximately ¼ teaspoon of salt. When using it to season, marinate, or tenderize, you want to use an amount equivalent to about 7 to 10 percent of the weight of the ingredient you are applying it to. For example, if you want to make a quick cabbage pickle with 1 pound (454 grams) of napa cabbage, you should use about 2 to 3 tablespoons (36 to 45 grams) of shio koji. A digital scale will come in handy to do the math, but once you get used to using shio koji, you can trust your taste buds to do the measuring.

———

In a medium bowl, mix together the rice koji and the salt. Combine thoroughly.

Add the warm water to the rice and salt mixture. Stir together to distribute the water evenly. Put a kitchen towel on top and leave the shio koji on the kitchen counter to ferment at room temperature, out of direct sunlight, for 2 to 3 days. Mix it once a day to allow for proper hydration and fermentation.

The fermentation is complete when the shio koji becomes thicker and creamier and begins to develop a sweet aroma. Transfer to an airtight container and store in the refrigerator for up to 4 months. For an even creamier shio koji, put the fermented shio koji through a blender before storing in the refrigerator.

Miso

For more than a decade, I have made miso every year, and of all the things I have learned to make by hand, it's one of the most rewarding. More than a seasoning, it is a "living food." The second bedroom of our house has been transformed into a nursery where fermentation crocks and big Cambro containers house millions of microorganisms. When you open them, the sweet, earthy aroma hits your nostrils right away. Some people think miso smells funky, but I love it.

Miso has been an essential part of the Japanese diet for generations. Like its close cousin, soy sauce, it was introduced from China more than a thousand years ago. In fact, it is believed that it was during the process of making soy sauce that someone tasted the fermenting paste and found it so delicious that it became a product of its own. Each region in Japan makes its own type of miso, differing in flavor and texture. What makes every miso distinct is the unique confluence of grains, soybeans, koji, and water, as well as salt content, temperature, and the duration of fermentation.

I allow three months to a year for my miso to ferment, but I start using it when it is still young and white, about three months old, if it tastes good. It is simply too irresistible to wait. I make a red miso, using a slightly higher ratio of rice koji to soybeans. We refer to a miso as "white miso" when the koji-soybean ratio is two to one, which allows the miso to ferment faster and makes it taste naturally sweeter. White miso has a shorter shelf life than red miso and should be eaten within a year if stored in the fridge, while red miso will last a few years. There are many miso makers out there making fine miso, and the best way to deepen your appreciation for this staple of Japanese cooking is to taste as many as you can. But use misos that are unpasteurized so you can get the full probiotic benefits.

Throughout this cookbook, you will see me adding miso to a variety of wafu dishes, both sweet and savory. It is truly a magical condiment—but it's salty, so use it wisely.

RED MISO

Special Equipment

Metric digital scale
(recommended)

Cambro container or slow cooker,
sterilized

Pressure cooker
(or large stock pot)

10 pounds (4.5 kilograms)
weights (such as clean rocks)

Food thermometer

Brown paper, to cover
the container

Kitchen twine

Ingredients

1.1 pounds (500 grams) soybeans

2.2 pounds (1 kilogram)
freeze-dried rice koji

10 ounces (300 grams) sea salt,
divided (set aside 3 tablespoons,
or 1½ ounces/42 grams, for
salting the container)

Miso making lends itself to community building. Whenever I teach a miso workshop, I have my students working in teams of three or four, because it's a lot of work. Plus, the beans and koji cultures are happier when there are lots of hands to knead the paste. This recipe uses a high ratio of rice koji to soybeans and takes about six months to ferment and produce a mildly pungent red miso. Start tasting the miso when it's about three months old; if it has a pleasant miso smell and flavor, you can start using it. You can find freeze-dried rice koji in the refrigerated section of most Japanese markets or online. I strongly suggest using a metric digital scale to weigh the ingredients in grams for accuracy. You will need about 1 tablespoon (15 grams) of miso and 1 cup (240 ml) of the dashi of your choice (see dashi section beginning on page 13) to make a cup of miso soup.

Rinse the soybeans and place them in a large bowl with water to cover. Soak for 18 hours. The beans must stay completely submerged in the water. Check the water level and replenish as needed. The beans are completely hydrated when they have tripled in size and turned from round to oblong. Cut open one of the beans. If there is no white core in the center, the hydration is complete. Drain the water.

Transfer the beans to a pressure cooker and cook following the manufacturer's directions for cooking beans. (If you don't have a pressure cooker, use a large stock pot.) Put the cooked beans in a large pot, fill with water to cover the beans by 2 inches (5 cm), and bring to a boil. Then lower the heat and cook for 4 to 5 hours or until the beans are done. Add water to keep the beans submerged while cooking. Remove and discard any white foam from the surface. Test the doneness of the beans by squashing one with your fingers; if it is easily squashed, the beans are cooked. Allow the cooked beans to cool down to 100°F (37°C). Meanwhile, reserve 2 cups of the cooking liquid and allow it to cool to the same temperature.

In a medium bowl, combine 1 cup of the cooled cooking liquid (100 F°/37°C) with the rice koji and mix well to hydrate the koji granules. Let stand for 1 hour, until the grains feel moist. Then add the salt, setting 2 tablespoons aside for sprinkling the bottom of the container and on top later, and massage the koji mixture for a couple of minutes. Reserve the remaining cooking liquid.

When the beans have cooled down, remove them from the water and transfer to a large bowl. Start smashing the beans with the heel and knuckles of your hands or put them through a food processor to make a paste.

Measure the temperature of the soybean paste. Once it has cooled down to 100°F (37°C), add the koji mixture and mix well, turning the mixture over from the bottom. Repeat a few times, until the two mixtures are totally incorporated to form a paste. If the paste feels dry and crumbly, add the remaining cooking broth and mix well.

Form the paste into balls, each about the size of a ping-pong ball. They should be firm, slightly moist but not wet, with no air bubbles trapped inside. Salt the bottom of the Cambro or fermenting crock with 1 tablespoon of salt. Drop one ball in the middle of the container and use your hand to smash it into a disc. Repeat with the remaining balls. Spread the paste evenly throughout the container, packing it well so there are no visible air holes. Sprinkle the remaining 1 tablespoon of salt over the top. Cover the miso with parchment paper and then cover with weights equal to or double the weight of the miso (about 10 pounds/4.5 kilograms) or divide the miso into two containers and apply 5 pounds (2.25 kilograms) of weight on top of each. The weights serve to prevent the miso paste from getting moldy.

Loosely cover the container with brown paper and tie it with string. Let the paste ferment in a cool dark place. The miso will start to transform, turning from light to dark in approximately 3 weeks. Use a clean wooden spoon or spatula to turn the miso after 2 months, bringing what's on the bottom of the container to the top, and pack it down again so there are no air bubbles. This step ensures even fermentation throughout the miso. Clean the side of the container with a paper towel. When you turn and repack the miso, sprinkle a tablespoon of salt on top to prevent mold from building on the surface. Put a fresh piece of parchment paper and the weights back on top of the paste, and cover the container loosely with the brown paper. If the paste tastes like miso after 4 months—and the texture feels smooth, and it smells insanely good—you've got miso. It takes about 10 months to fully mature. If you want a stronger fermentation, leave it out for another month or two. Otherwise, store in the fridge once the desired miso flavor is reached.

Variation For dashi miso, add a 3 x 3 inch (7 x 7 cm) piece of kombu on top of the paste once you've set it to ferment. Once the miso is ready, mix 1 tablespoon miso for every 1 cup (240 ml) of water, and you have instant miso soup! You can eat the pickled kombu, too. Slice it into thin strips and enjoy it with rice or on its own.

ALL-DAY BREAKFAST

Every morning, I make my husband a traditional Japanese breakfast of vegetable miso soup, rice, eggs, natto (fermented soybeans), and a pickled ume plum. That may sound like a lot, but after making this meal for four decades I can almost do it with my eyes closed. For breakfast, I sometimes like to follow the Japanese meal composition of ichiju sansai: one soup and three dishes, plus pickles and rice. It's a nutritionally balanced meal plan with a little bit of everything. I always have dashi in the fridge or use homemade Shiitake Mushroom Dashi Powder (page 29). Just add some veggies or tofu that are begging to be used up in the fridge to the heated dashi with miso, about 1 tablespoon for 1 cup of dashi, and you have miso soup ready in five minutes. (No recipe needed!) It is a classic Japanese breakfast soup. The "three dishes" can be anything you like: a fried egg, Maple Tamagoyaki (page 55), Cedar Plank Salmon with Shio Koji Marinade (page 201), or any leftovers from last night's dinner.

Personally, I prefer a modern wafu breakfast of Yogurt with Sweet Black Soybeans, Fruit, and Toasted Coconut Flakes (page 59) or Dashi Cheese Grits with Miso-Honey Butter (page 45). Or have a spoonful of natto on avocado toast with some nori. You can mix and match wafu and yofu—Western-style—dishes in any way you like. But I always aim for harmony of flavors and nutritional balance, because in my family, and perhaps yours too, breakfast is the most important meal of the day. Not that these recipes need to be limited to the morning only—they can just as easily be eaten as a light snack, lunch, or dinner.

DASHI CHEESE GRITS WITH MISO-HONEY BUTTER

Makes 4 servings

2 cups (480 ml) Chicken Dashi (page 25) or store-bought low-sodium chicken broth

2 cups (480 ml) whole milk

1 cup (250 grams) stone-ground grits

1 garlic clove, minced (optional)

4 ounces (113 grams) shredded sharp cheddar cheese

Sea salt, to taste

Freshly ground black pepper, to taste

3 tablespoons Miso-Honey Butter (page 50)

2 tablespoons chopped fresh parsley or sliced scallions, for garnish (optional)

Fried eggs and bacon, to serve (optional)

Shrimp and Bacon Topping (recipe on following page) (optional)

I learned to make cheese grits while doing a cooking workshop at Sequatchie Cove Farm in Chattanooga, Tennessee. The farm is run by four generations of the Keener Family—Bill and Miriam Keener, their son Kelsey and his wife Ashley (and their children Fletcher, Oliver, and Ella Mae), and Miriam's parents, Jim and Emily. They grow all their produce, and their animals are raised using organic and biodynamic practices.

One morning, Kelsey and Ashley invited me over for breakfast. I stood next to Kelsey and watched him stir a big batch of grits. "Grits are like the rice of Tennessee," says Kelsey. "We cook with them all the time; they're great for a classic southern breakfast like cheese grits, with bacon and eggs, and shrimp, as well as all kinds of other dishes such as beef casserole. The trick is to stir often with a wooden spoon. You don't want them to stick to the bottom of the pot!" It was one of the most delicious breakfasts I've ever had, and I try to find every excuse to be back there. This is my wafu twist on those southern grits. I use chicken dashi as a base to give it another layer of umami, and I top the grits with a dollop of butter infused with miso and honey that gives the dish a salted caramel–like flavor.

Bring the dashi and milk to a boil in a medium saucepan. Add the grits and stir with a whisk to ensure that you don't get lumps. Add the garlic, if using, reduce the heat to medium-low, and cook, stirring frequently, until the grits are tender, about 20 to 30 minutes. The cooking time will depend on the coarseness of the grits. You can always add more dashi or water if the grits are getting too thick.

Remove from the heat and add the cheese, salt, and pepper to taste. Top with miso-honey butter. Sprinkle with chopped fresh parsley or scallions, and serve with fried eggs and bacon, or shrimp and bacon topping, if desired. ▸

Shrimp and Bacon Topping

In a large skillet, fry 6 pieces of bacon until browned and crispy. Remove the bacon from the skillet and drain on paper towels. Chop it into ¼ inch (6 mm) pieces and set aside. In the same skillet, use 3 tablespoons of bacon grease to fry 1 pound (454 grams) of cleaned and peeled shrimp for 2 minutes over medium heat. Mince 1 clove of garlic. Add garlic and 2 teaspoons of lemon juice and continue frying over medium heat for another minute or until the shrimp is cooked. Serve on top of the grits with miso-honey butter.

MISO-HONEY BUTTER ON TOASTED ONIGIRI

Makes 6 onigiri

For the Onigiri

1 cup (240 ml) water

1 teaspoon sea salt

1 tablespoon light sesame oil or toasted sesame oil, and more for the pan

6 cups (1,200 grams) cooked Basic Brown Rice (page 164) or Basic White Rice (page 163), freshly made or a day old

This dish is a spin on honey on toast. When onigiri (Japanese rice balls) are toasted under a broiler or on the grill, they develop a crispy, crunchy crust. They are even better when smeared with salty miso and sweet honey combined to make a wafu compound butter, which is as delicious as it is versatile. I also serve it on crusty bread, I put a dollop on my grits (Dashi Cheese Grits with Miso-Honey Butter, page 45), and I use it to baste roasted vegetables like squash, potatoes, corn, and peppers. If you prefer a savory version, omit the honey.

To make the onigiri, prepare a clean cutting board to work on. Put the water and salt in a small bowl and stir. Use this water to wet your hands so the rice grains don't stick to them while you are forming the onigiri. Line a half sheet pan with parchment paper and brush with sesame oil.

Divide the cooked rice into six equal mounds, one cup each, and place them on the cutting board. To shape the onigiri, wet your hands with salted water. Clap your hands in the air to remove excess water. Transfer the mound of rice to your moistened palm and mold it into a triangular shape. Cup one hand to hold the rice ball. To make a triangular onigiri, press gently with your other hand to create the triangular point, using your index and middle fingers and thumb as guides. Turn the onigiri and repeat a couple more times to give it three corners. The onigiri will be about 1 inch thick. Place the formed onigiri on the oiled parchment paper. Repeat with the remaining rice. Brush the onigiri with a little oil to prevent them from sticking to the paper.

Heat the oven to broil on high. Set the rack 6 inches (15 cm) from the heat source. Broil the onigiri on both sides until crisp and slightly toasted, 5 to 10 minutes on each side depending on the heat. While broiling, cut 6 coins of the compound butter, ⅛–¼ inch thick (3–6 mm). Remove the pan of broiled onigiri from the oven, place a round of butter on top of each, and return to broil until the butter melts, caramelizes, and becomes toasty.

Serve immediately while the onigiri are piping hot. ›

Miso-Honey Butter

Makes ¾ cup (about 160 grams)

1 stick (113 grams) unsalted butter, softened

3 tablespoons (45 grams) white or red miso (Red Miso, page 40, or store-bought miso)

2 tablespoons (42 grams) honey

Mix together the softened butter, miso, and honey, if using, in a small bowl. Use a whisk to thoroughly mix the ingredients until they are fully incorporated and emulsified. Spoon the mixture into the center of a piece of parchment or wax paper. Use the paper to form the butter gently into a log and wrap it. Set in the refrigerator or freezer until firm, then slice off rounds as needed. The miso-honey butter will keep in the fridge for a month.

Variations

Serve the miso-honey butter on hot oatmeal with raisins and toasted flaked almonds. On a hot bowl of rice. On steak. On pancakes.

Add 3–4 tablespoons minced fresh chives to the miso-honey butter along with the honey, mixing until evenly distributed; or 1 tablespoon of fresh jalapeño pepper, minced; or 1 tablespoon of grated yuzu or lemon peel.

MOCHI WAFFLES WITH BLACK SESAME BUTTER

Makes 4 servings

For the Waffle Batter

1¼ cups (190 grams) mochiko (sweet rice flour)

1 cup (120 grams) all-purpose flour

¼ cup (50 grams) cane sugar

1 tablespoon baking powder

¼ teaspoon sea salt

2 large eggs, at room temperature

1½ cups (360 ml) whole milk, at room temperature

1 teaspoon vanilla extract

4 tablespoons unsalted butter, melted

Vegetable oil, for cooking

For the Black Sesame Butter

¼ cup (35 grams) black sesame seeds

¼ cup (50 grams) cane sugar

¼ teaspoon sea salt

¼ cup (55 grams) unsalted butter, softened, or more as needed

These wafu waffles use sweet rice flour in the base. I have tried a variety of mochi waffles, but this one stays gooey even when it's a day old, and you can put it in the oven to crisp it back up. Black sesame butter has a distinctively nutty, aromatic, and earthy flavor. It also has a bitterness that is balanced here with honey and sugar. You can serve this waffle with whipped cream and fruit if you want to make it more decadent and delicious.

———————

Preheat a waffle iron to medium-high.

To make the waffle batter, in a medium bowl whisk together the mochiko, all-purpose flour, sugar, baking powder, and salt.

In a large bowl, combine the eggs, milk, and vanilla extract. Gradually drizzle the melted butter into the bowl, stirring as you go until fully incorporated. You are not trying to aerate the mixture, just blending everything evenly.

Add the dry ingredients to the wet ingredients, folding the batter together using a rubber spatula until just combined. The batter should be thick. Some lumps are okay—stir just enough so there are no dry pockets of flour. Set aside to rest while you make the black sesame butter. Any lumps in the batter should smooth out after leaving it undisturbed for a few minutes.

To make the black sesame butter, place the sesame seeds in a dry frying pan. Lightly toast over medium-low heat, stirring constantly, until aromatic, roughly 2 minutes. Remove from the heat and immediately transfer the sesame seeds to a heat-safe container to cool. (Note: Sesame seeds scorch easily, and with black sesame seeds it is even harder to tell, so err on the side of caution. Sesame seeds may pop and jump while toasting; you can use a pot lid to help keep them in the pan.)

Using a coffee grinder, mortar and pestle, or mini food processor, grind the black sesame seeds to a fine consistency, pulsing and wiping down the sides to ensure even grinding. Transfer the mixture to a small bowl, add the sugar, salt, and butter, and stir well to form a thick paste. If the paste is crumbly, add more butter 1 tablespoon at a time, and blend until it has reached the desired consistency. ›

Mochi Waffles with Black Sesame Butter (cont.)

Cook the waffles. Lightly rub the waffle iron with vegetable oil. Spoon a heaped ½ cup of batter into the center and close immediately. Cook on high or medium-high for about 5 or 6 minutes, until cooked through and golden brown. Repeat with the remaining batter, rubbing the waffle iron with additional oil as needed. Serve immediately with a generous swipe of black sesame butter on top to fill the waffle cavities. The waffles are best eaten fresh. Don't refrigerate. Store the black sesame butter in the fridge. It will keep for 2 weeks.

MAPLE TAMAGOYAKI

Makes 4 servings

5 large eggs

5 tablespoons (75 ml) Kombu and Bonito Dashi (page 20), milk, or chicken broth, at room temperature

2 tablespoons (30 ml) maple syrup

2 teaspoons (10 ml) soy sauce (preferably light-colored usukuchi shoyu), plus more for serving

1½ tablespoons melted butter or untoasted sesame oil

6 ounces (170 grams) Daikon Oroshi (page 5) (optional)

Microgreens, for garnish

Tamagoyaki, classic Japanese omelets, are light and lightly sweet (some store-bought ones are very sweet!) but commonly served as a side dish rather than as a dessert, traditionally with soy sauce and some grated daikon radish. What sets tamagoyaki apart from Western omelets, besides their sweetness, are their beautiful layers. The egg is not scrambled; instead, while cooking, a fork or pair of chopsticks is used to roll it, in stages, into a tube, revealing a swirl pattern when it is cut into slices.

Some people like their tamagoyaki yellow, like a delicate custard. I like mine lightly toasted but soft inside. I've found that using maple syrup instead of cane sugar not only cuts back on the sugary sweetness but also adds caramel and vanilla flavors to the omelet, making it a perfect breakfast.

The traditional rectangular shape is achieved by using a shaped pan called a tamagoyaki-ki, which can be found in Japanese markets or online. You can also use a round, well-seasoned, 9 inch (23 cm) or 10 inch (25 cm) skillet. The omelet will be shaped into an oblong rather than a rectangle, but for homemade tamagoyaki, that is common.

In a medium bowl, combine the eggs, dashi, maple syrup, and 2 teaspoons soy sauce. Whisk the eggs gently, being careful not to overwhip.

Heat a nonstick pan or a well-seasoned cast-iron skillet over medium-high heat. Use a pastry brush or soak a crumpled paper towel in the butter or oil and use it to spread the fat evenly in the pan, keeping the pastry brush or paper towel nearby for later use. Test the pan by putting a few drops of the batter into it; if the pan is hot enough, the batter will sizzle without burning. If the pan is too hot, lower the heat and let the pan cool a bit.

Pour one third of the batter into the pan and cook, spreading the batter quickly and evenly by tilting the pan back and forth. If you see any air bubbles form, use a fork or chopsticks to pierce them.

When the batter begins to set on the bottom, fold the tamagoyaki into thirds. Start by lifting the far end of the egg batter with a fork or chopsticks and rolling it toward you like a jelly roll. ›

Let the rolled egg set for 30 seconds, then push it into one edge of the pan. Re-grease the pan with the paper towel, moving the egg roll around to ensure full contact with the oil. You want to cook it on all sides.

Now pour another third of the egg batter into the pan, making sure to lift the first egg roll with your fork or chopsticks so the batter gets underneath it.

Cook this second batch of batter until almost set, then roll the second omelet over the first, to make layers. Repeat this step one more time with the remaining batter, incorporating the first roll into the second, and the second roll into the third. Transfer the tamagoyaki onto a clean cutting board.

You can use a bamboo mat to further shape the tamagoyaki, if you like. Let the tamagoyaki rest, wrapped, for 3 minutes.

To serve, unwrap the tamagoyaki and slice it crosswise into 1½–2 inch (4–5 cm) pieces. Serve warm or at room temperature with grated radish, soy sauce, and microgreens. Tamagoyaki will keep in the refrigerator for 2 to 3 days.

Variation Add 2 tablespoons grated cheddar cheese and 2 tablespoons chopped fresh chives into the egg batter and proceed with the recipe.

YOGURT WITH SWEET BLACK SOYBEANS, FRUIT, AND TOASTED COCONUT FLAKES

Makes 4 servings

For the Sweetened Black Beans
(makes 3 cups)

10½ ounces (300 grams)
black soybeans
(preferably Tamba black
soybeans)

10 ounces (284 grams)
cane sugar

½ teaspoon sea salt

2 tablespoons (30 ml) soy sauce

8 cups (2 liters) water

To Serve

1 cup (240 ml) plain yogurt

1 cup (200 grams) seasonal fruit,
such as blueberries, strawberries,
blackberries, peaches, loquats,
pineapple, or bananas

½ cup (35 grams) toasted
coconut flakes

Kuromame no amani are black soybeans cooked in sweet syrup and served as one of the good luck dishes for osechi ryori, the traditional Japanese New Year's feast. Simmered in a pot for six to eight hours, the beans transform into lustrous jewels that taste tender, creamy, and nutty like chestnuts. Beans symbolize diligence and healthy living, and I like to keep a jar of kuromame no amani year round. They pair surprisingly well with yogurt or on pancakes like a fruit compote, ice cream, and granola or can be eaten straight with a spoon. These sweet beans also go well with roasted kabocha squash and sweet potatoes, if you want to give your Thanksgiving an extra flair. The broth of the cooked beans is rich in antioxidants, so it's a wholesome dish.

———————

To make the sweetened black beans, rinse the beans in cold water and drain. In a medium pot, preferably cast iron, combine the beans, sugar, salt, soy sauce, and 8 cups water and let the beans soak uncovered on the kitchen counter overnight.

Bring the beans back to a boil over medium heat in the same pot. As soon as they reach the boiling point, lower the heat to a bare simmer. Using a lid that fits inside the pot or a piece of aluminum foil, directly cover the beans. Cook until the beans can be easily squashed with your fingers. Start checking for doneness after 8 to 10 hours. Always keep the beans submerged in the cooking liquid so they remain plump and unwrinkled. If the beans surface, add more water. When they are done, let them rest and cool in the liquid overnight. You will have more beans than you need for this dish. Allow about 3 tablespoons of cooked beans for each serving of yogurt. Save the rest for another occasion.

Serve the beans with yogurt and fresh fruit. Sprinkle with toasted coconut, if you like.

The beans will keep in the fridge for a couple of weeks.

AONORI POTATO PANCAKE
WITH MISO-STEWED APPLES

Makes 6–8 pancakes

2 large russet potatoes, peeled (about 600 grams)

½ yellow onion

¾ teaspoon sea salt

⅛ teaspoon freshly ground black pepper

⅛ teaspoon ground nutmeg

1 egg, beaten

¼ cup (60 ml) neutral oil (such as grapeseed or light sesame oil), or Schmaltz (rendered chicken fat, see Wafu Skillet Chicken Pot Pie, page 175) for frying

3 tablespoons aonori powder

1 batch Miso-Stewed Apples (page 285) or store-bought applesauce, to serve

1 cup (240 ml) sour cream, to serve

In my past life, as a film buyer, Berlin was one of my favorite destinations for both film and food. I attended the Berlin Film Festival in February every year, when the city was freezing cold. I would watch films all day and go to red-carpet events at night, ponder which film(s) to pursue, and then try to make a deal with the producers and agents. I had little time to eat. But then I discovered the gourmet food court at the top of the KaDeWe department store. There was a small restaurant that served a crispy buttery potato pancake with applesauce and sour cream. I would sit at the bar and indulge in this snack while sipping wine and watching the chef dexterously make the pancake right in front of me. It became my getaway place. At home, I wafu this pancake by adding aonori (seaweed flakes), the standard furikake (garnish) used on Buckwheat Okonomiyaki with Eggs and Bacon (page 66). A fried egg on top is also nice. I also make a variation using mentaiko (spicy pickled pollack roe, see Variations below), which is a popular ingredient in wafu pastas and as a filling for onigiris. Mentaiko is like the poor man's caviar. I keep some of these pancakes on standby in my freezer at all times.

To make the potato pancakes, coarsely grate the potatoes into a medium bowl, using a four-sided grater. Transfer the grated potatoes to a cheesecloth or clean dishcloth. Twist and squeeze out as much liquid as you can into a medium bowl. Set aside the squeezed grated potato and let the potato liquid stand for 3 to 4 minutes. Then take a spoon and carefully remove the top layer of the liquid, leaving the white starch at the bottom of the bowl. Add the squeezed grated potato back to the bowl with the white starch.

Grate the onion and combine with the potato mixture. Add the salt, pepper, nutmeg, and beaten egg.

Heat the oil over medium heat in a large well-seasoned cast-iron or nonstick pan. You will know the pan is hot enough when you flick a few drops of water on the surface and it makes a sizzling noise.

For each pancake, pour ⅓ cup of the batter into the hot oil and lightly press with the back of the spoon to spread it out into a round pancake. Cook over medium heat for 4 to 5 minutes on each side, undisturbed, being careful not to burn them. When they are cooked, drain on a paper towel. Do not stack the pancakes, or they will get soggy.

Sprinkle with the aonori and serve immediately with miso-stewed apples (or applesauce) and sour cream.

Variations Add 4 tablespoons of mentaiko, removed from the sac, to the pancake batter. Or add ½ teaspoon Sonoko Curry Powder (page 153) to the pancake batter in place of the ground nutmeg.

MISO CARROT CAKE
WITH STREUSEL TOPPING

Makes one 8 x 8 (21 x 21 cm) inch cake

For the Streusel Topping

½ cup (110 grams) brown sugar

1 teaspoon ground cinnamon

½ cup (60 grams) all-purpose or Sonora flour

6 tablespoons (85 grams) unsalted butter, softened

Pinch sea salt

½ cup (55 grams) walnuts, broken into small pieces

For the Cake

¾ cup (150 grams) cane sugar

8 tablespoons (113 grams) unsalted butter, softened

2 eggs

2 large carrots, peeled and grated (2 cups)

1 tablespoon (15 grams) Red Miso (page 40) or store-bought red miso

1 tablespoon Okinawa Black Sugar (Kokuto) Syrup (page 293) or molasses

1 cup (120 grams) all-purpose flour or Sonora flour

1 teaspoon baking soda

1 teaspoon ground cinnamon

Miso-Honey Butter (page 50), to serve (optional)

This is a moist and not-too-sweet coffee cake that you can enjoy at breakfast and then leave on the kitchen counter to nibble on all day. Here, traditional carrot cake is given a wafu twist with the addition of miso and Okinawa black sugar (kokuto) syrup, which adds a subtle yet pungent nutty caramel flavor.

———————

Preheat the oven to 350°F (176°C) and line an 8 inch square pan with parchment paper.

To make the streusel topping, stir together the brown sugar, cinnamon, and flour. Add the softened butter to the dry ingredients and stir. Chill in the refrigerator while you make the cake batter.

To make the cake, whisk the sugar and butter in a large bowl. Add the eggs, one at a time, and continue mixing. Stir in the carrots, miso, and syrup. Add the flour, baking soda, and cinnamon, and mix until just combined.

Pour the batter into the prepared pan. Add the salt and walnuts to the streusel and mix together. Top the batter with the streusel and bake for 40 minutes or until the center of the cake is set. Serve with miso-honey butter, if you like. The cake will keep in the fridge for 2 to 3 days or in the freezer for a month.

SPICED CURRY PUMPKIN CRUMBLE MUFFINS

Makes 12 muffins

For the Muffins

1¾ cup (210 grams) all-purpose flour

1 cup (200 grams) cane sugar

¼ cup (55 grams) brown sugar

1 tablespoon baking powder

¼ teaspoon sea salt

1 teaspoon ground cinnamon

⅛ teaspoon ground nutmeg

2½ teaspoons Sonoko Curry Powder (page 153) or store-bought Japanese curry powder

1 cup (225 grams) pumpkin puree, canned or homemade

½ cup (114 ml) full-fat coconut milk

½ cup (120 ml) melted coconut oil (use refined for less coconut flavor, use unrefined for a stronger flavor)

2 tablespoons molasses

1 cup (120 grams) chopped walnuts

For the Crumble Topping

¼ cup (30 grams) all-purpose flour

¼ cup (55 grams) brown sugar

¼ cup (18 grams) unsweetened dried coconut flakes

1 teaspoon Japanese curry powder (preferably Sonoko Curry Powder, page 153)

¼ teaspoon sea salt

½ teaspoon ground cinnamon

¼ cup (30 grams) pepitas

2 tablespoons orange zest

3 tablespoons melted coconut oil

6 walnuts, halved

What started out as an experiment with my kitchen assistant Daniela turned into the most fragrant, moist, moderately sweet, and pleasantly spicy pumpkin muffin I've ever had, like a delicious pumpkin pie redolent with warm spices. They have become the vegan muffins that I sell at the farmers market. Aside from being exceptionally delicious, these muffins gave me a real surprise one day during my early-morning drive to the market. I came to a stop with a jerk that made half a dozen muffins, fresh out of the oven and steaming, fly out of the pan and land on the dashboard. I gasped in horror—but like a group of acrobats, they rolled right back into the pan practically unscathed and ready to face the day.

———

Preheat the oven to 400° (204°C) and place the rack in the middle of the oven. Grease or line a 12-muffin tin.

To make the muffins, sift together the flour, sugars, baking powder, salt, cinnamon, nutmeg, and curry powder in a large bowl. Whisk together to combine.

In a medium bowl, whisk together the pumpkin puree, coconut milk, coconut oil, and molasses.

Pour the wet ingredients into the dry and mix until combined. Add the walnut pieces.

Evenly divide the batter among the 12 cavities, filling each about two thirds full.

To make the crumble topping, mix all the ingredients except for the walnut halves together with your hands and sprinkle evenly over all 12 muffins. Place a walnut half on the top of each muffin.

Place the muffin tin on the middle rack and bake for 18 to 22 minutes, rotating once at after 10 minutes, until a toothpick or knife inserted into the center comes out clean. Let the muffins cool on a rack. The muffins are best eaten fresh.

BUCKWHEAT OKONOMIYAKI WITH EGGS AND BACON

Makes 4 pancakes

For the Okonomiyaki

¾ cup (90 grams) all-purpose flour

¼ cup (30 grams) buckwheat flour

½ teaspoon baking powder

¼ teaspoon sea salt

1 egg

1½ cups (360 ml) Kombu and Bonito Dashi (page 20) or water

10 ounces (280 grams) finely shredded green cabbage

1 red bell pepper, sliced into ¼ inch (6 mm) strips

2 tablespoons neutral cooking oil

4 strips raw bacon

For the Toppings

4 eggs, fried

2 tablespoons Japanese mayonnaise, such as Kewpie, or homemade

2 tablespoons Homemade Tonkatsu Sauce (recipe page 197) or store-bought tonkatsu sauce, or to taste

½ cup (4 grams) bonito flakes (omit for vegetarian option)

½ cup (4 grams) crumbled dried nori or aonori seaweed

4 scallions, greens and whites, sliced thinly

The Japanese savory pancake, okonomiyaki, made with wheat flour, eggs, and water and seasoned with tonkatsu or okonomiyaki sauce, is as classic as wafu cooking gets. Back before World War II, someone came up with a thin pancake seasoned with Worcestershire sauce, which was considered Western food—yoshoku—and sold for such an affordable price that people started calling the pancake "Issen Yoshoku" ("One Sen Western Food"—"sen" refers to an obsolete Japanese currency). Cabbage was added as a filler when the Japanese experienced a shortage of flour during the war. Ever since, cabbage has been a defining feature of this pancake, which is now called okonomiyaki. There are other legends, but I like this story the best.

My okonomiyaki is made with a mixture of buckwheat flour and all-purpose flour—along with tons of shredded cabbage and green onions, as is traditional. With fried eggs and bacon on top, this okonomiyaki makes for a very wafu breakfast any time of the day.

To make the okonomiyaki, whisk together the flours, baking powder, and salt in a large bowl. In a medium bowl, whisk the egg and dashi or water. Add the flour mixture and mix until just blended. The batter should be quite thin. Add the cabbage and red peppers to the batter and mix well.

Heat 1 tablespoon of the oil in a 9–10 inch (22–25 cm) nonstick skillet or well-seasoned cast-iron skillet over medium-high heat. Pour ½ cup (120 ml) of the batter into the pan to make a 6 inch (15 cm) pancake. Cook until the bottom is just beginning to brown, about 1 minute.

Place two strips of bacon on top of the pancake and allow the bottom to continue to cook and firm up until golden brown, about 5 to 10 minutes. Once the bottom is golden brown, flip the pancake over, bacon side down. Turn the heat to low and cook until the second side of the pancake is browned, the bacon is thoroughly cooked, and the cabbage and peppers are tender—about 10 to 15 minutes. Repeat until the batter is used up.

To serve, top each pancake with a fried egg and drizzle with mayonnaise and tonkatsu sauce. Sprinkle with the bonito flakes, crumbled nori or aonori, and scallions. Eat while piping hot.

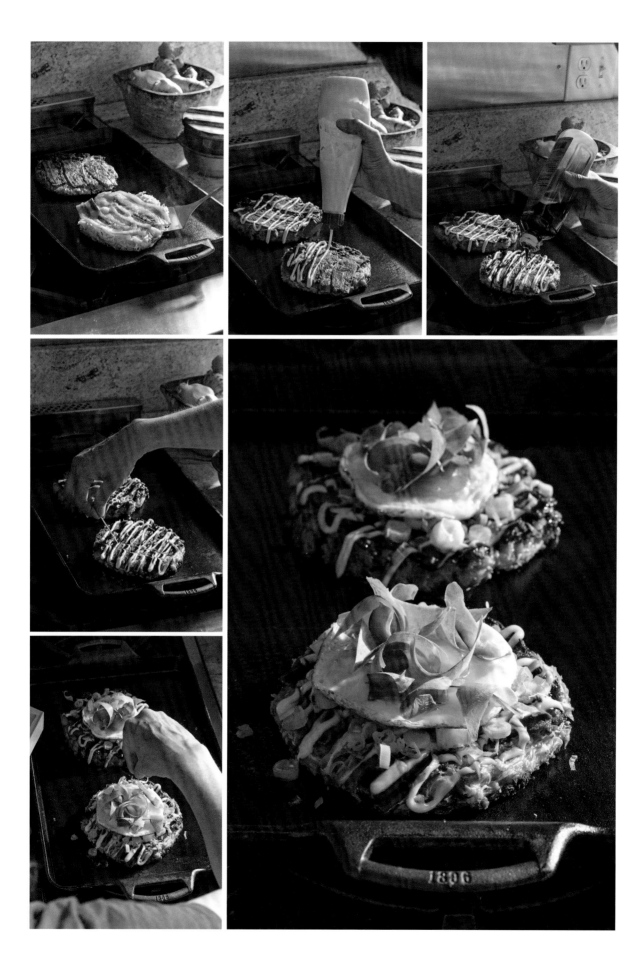

SOUPS

Every Japanese-style soup—from light miso soups to creamy pureed ones—begins with dashi, broth. (Read more about dashi on page 13.) Soups are a great way to express the shun—the spirit of the season—which is an essential part of Japanese cooking. Wafu-ing a soup can be as easy as adding a piece of kombu or a dollop of miso to deepen the umami, but in this chapter I'm sharing a wide spectrum of varieties that showcase the diversity of wafu cooking. You'll find a variety of classic wafu soups—such as Egg Drop Soup with Peas, Tofu, Ginger, and Parmesan Cheese (page 73), an adaptation of a Chinese version (making it a wafu chuka, or simply chuka, a Chinese-style wafu dish)—as well as more modern adaptations like Japanese Italian Wedding Soup (page 85) and Posole Japonesa (page 87), where Western and Japanese flavors are fused together in harmony.

Japanese soups are traditionally served in owan, small bowls, using chopsticks to guide the morsels of food as needed. No spoons are used. Today's wafu soups are more free range. You can serve and eat them however you wish. Sip them or use chopsticks or a spoon.

In this chapter, I've also included a recipe for a yofu soup—Collard Greens and Cabbage Miso Soup with Crispy Bacon (page 79). which is a Western twist on miso soup—so you see that the cultural fusion can go both ways, from East to West or West to East.

CORN SOUP WITH LITTLENECK CLAMS AND LIME

Makes 4–6 servings

6 ears yellow or white corn, husks and silk removed

8 cups (2 liters) water

One 3 x 3 inch (7 x 7 cm) piece dried kombu

6–8 littleneck clams

½ cup (120 ml) sake or white wine

2 tablespoons unsalted butter

2 shallots, chopped

2 garlic cloves, thinly sliced

1 large russet potato, ½ inch (1 cm) dice

Sea salt, to taste

Freshly ground black pepper, to taste

Shichimi pepper, to taste

3 sprigs fresh cilantro, chopped

1 lime, quartered

When corn season arrives in the summer, all my senses go into search mode to find the perfect ear in "shun"—the peak of its flavor. This soup is a wafu riff on corn chowder. The shucked cobs are used to make corn dashi, which is further infused with kombu. Clams provide extra umami and visual appeal, but if you wish to skip them, the soup will still taste delicious. This soup can be enjoyed chilled or warm.

Working one at a time, stand a corn cob upright in a medium bowl and use a sharp knife to scrape off the kernels, making sure to catch the milk from the cobs. Repeat with 4 more cobs. Cut the scraped cobs in half. Set aside.

Put the water and kombu in a large saucepan and bring to a boil over medium-high heat. Remove the kombu (see page 15 for suggestions of ways to use spent kombu). Lower the heat to a simmer and add the whole corn cob and the scraped cobs and cook for 10 minutes. Remove the whole cob and set aside. Continue cooking over low heat for 10 minutes. Turn off the heat and discard the cobs.

Meanwhile, add the clams and sake or wine to a medium pot and bring to a boil. Once boiling, cover with a lid. When the clams begin to open, after about 5 minutes, remove them from the liquid one by one and transfer to a bowl, reserving the cooking liquid. Discard any unopened clams. Reserve the clam shells—you will reinsert the cooked clams in their shells when it's time to serve the soup.

In a large saucepan, melt the butter over medium heat. Add the shallots and garlic and cook, stirring often, until soft and translucent, 8 to 10 minutes. Add the corn kernels and their milk, the potatoes, and the kombu–corn cob dashi and bring to a boil. Lower the heat to a simmer and cook, uncovered, for 10 minutes.

Remove the pot from the stove. Using an immersion blender, puree the soup until creamy. Reheat the soup over medium-low heat. Add the reserved cooking liquid from the clams. Scrape the kernels off the cooked whole corn. Add the cooked kernels to the pot and stir. Season the soup with salt and pepper. Serve warm with shichimi pepper. Return the cooked clams in their shells and put one or two on top of each soup bowl. Garnish with cilantro and lime wedges. This soup is best eaten the same day it is made.

EGG DROP SOUP WITH PEAS, TOFU, GINGER, AND PARMESAN CHEESE

Makes 4 servings

2 eggs

4 cups (1 liter) Chicken Dashi (page 25), Kombu and Bonito Dashi (page 20), or store-bought low-sodium chicken broth

1½ teaspoons potato starch or kuzu, diluted in 1 tablespoon of water or broth

1 teaspoon sea salt, or more to taste

1 teaspoon soy sauce (preferably light-colored usukuchi shoyu), plus more as needed

8 ounces (225 grams) fresh snow peas, strings removed (see headnote)

1 pound (454 grams) tofu (preferably soft kinugoshi type), diced

1 teaspoon peeled and grated ginger

2 scallions, sliced very thinly crosswise

2 tablespoons grated Parmesan cheese or toasted sesame oil for drizzling, for garnish (optional)

Egg drop soup, also known as egg flower soup, is a staple on Chinese restaurant menus. Beaten egg is dropped into a simmering chicken broth, creating delicate ribbons that look like clouds. Kakitama jiru, the wafu adaptation, uses a kombu and bonito dashi and kuzu (a traditional Japanese starch) or potato starch as a thickener, which results in a soup that is lighter and brothier than its Chinese cousin. My own interpretation features snow peas from my spring garden, but snap peas, or even cherry tomatoes, baby turnips, or wakame seaweed, will also work well. My kitchen assistants and I have tried this soup several different ways. Kali likes it seasoned with toasted sesame oil, as it is in China. Tracy likes it with grated Parmesan cheese, to balance out the flavors, and because it reminds her of her grandma's stracciatella—an Italian version of egg drop soup. I include both options here. I like to serve this soup in an owan, a Japanese soup bowl. Bring the bowl up to your mouth for sipping and use the chopsticks to guide the egg flowers. But if you want to eat it from a soup bowl with a spoon, that works, too.

Break the eggs into a small bowl and beat lightly.

In a saucepan set over medium-low heat, bring the dashi or other broth to a boil. Lower the heat to a simmer and add the diluted starch. Stir to combine (this will thicken the broth slightly). Season with salt and soy sauce, to suit your palate.

Add the peas and tofu to the saucepan and continue simmering until they heat through, about 1 minute.

Bring the broth back up to a boil over high heat, then lower the heat again to a simmer. Using a pair of long chopsticks or a ladle, stir the soup in a circular motion and slowly pour the beaten eggs around the perimeter of the pot. Continue to simmer for 30 seconds, undisturbed, until the eggs float to the top and transform into "egg flowers." Swirl the eggs around once before they firm up.

Remove the pan from the heat and pour the soup into individual bowls. Garnish with a pinch of grated ginger and sliced scallions. Add a few droplets of toasted sesame oil or sprinkle with Parmesan cheese, if you like. This soup will keep in the fridge for a couple of days, but it tastes best the day you make it. ›

Wakame Seaweed

Another way to make wafu egg drop soup is to start with Chicken Dashi (see page 25) or store-bought chicken broth and infuse it with wakame, which adds a delicious subtly briny and sweet flavor to the soup. Hydrate 2 tablespoons of cut dried wakame in water for 2 minutes (the seaweed will double in size). Rinse and drain. Combine the hydrated wakame with the dashi and prepare the soup according to the directions above.

Udon Noodles

Before making the soup, cook 1 packet (contains 4 to 5 servings in a packet, 6.5 ounces/188 grams each serving) frozen udon noodles or 1 packet (contains 6 to 8 servings in a packet, 3.5 ounces/100 grams each serving) dry udon noodles following the manufacturer's instructions. Drain and divide the noodles between four soup bowls and pour the hot egg drop soup over them. Garnish with a pinch of grated ginger and sliced scallions. Add either a few droplets of toasted sesame oil and a dash of shichimi pepper or sprinkle with Parmesan cheese.

KABOCHA SQUASH SOUP WITH MISO, CRÈME FRAÎCHE, AND CURRIED PEPITAS

Makes 4 servings

For the Soup

One 2–2½ pound (908–1,135 grams) kabocha squash, cut on the equator and seeded (or butternut squash, cut lengthwise and seeded)

¼ cup (60 ml) extra-virgin olive oil or neutral oil (such as grapeseed or light sesame oil)

1 yellow onion, finely chopped

4 garlic cloves, smashed

1 medium Yukon Gold potato, or potato of your choice, peeled and cubed (about 1 cup)

7 cups (1.65 liters) Chicken Dashi (see page 25) or dashi of your choice

Pinch ground nutmeg

1 tablespoon sake

1 ounce (28 grams) ginger, peeled and finely grated, juice only

¼ teaspoon sea salt

¼ teaspoon freshly ground black pepper

1 tablespoon honey, or more to taste

¼ cup (60 ml) soy milk or whole milk (optional)

3 tablespoons red or white miso, or more to taste (see headnote)

1 sprig fresh parsley or mitsuba leaves, chopped, for garnish

¼ cup (60 ml) crème fraîche, for serving >

Kabocha is a type of squash harvested at the end of summer and kept in storage to ripen for a couple of months, which makes them sweeter. Japanese people "kon kon," tap kabocha with their fingers to check for ripeness. If they sound hollow and muffled, they're ready. Here, the kabocha are made into a divinely creamy soup with a depth of umami that can be credited to the use of miso. If you use red miso, the soup will have a hint of caramel and pungent flavors. In contrast, white miso will add sweetness. Or use a fifty-fifty blend, if you like. Every miso has different levels of saltiness, so don't add all of it at once. Taste and adjust. This soup makes a welcome addition to your fall and winter table and is garnished with curried pepitas, an idea my friend Maya Kaimal, an Indian cookbook author and the founder of Maya Kaimal Foods, gave me. The recipe for curried pepitas makes more than you need, so enjoy the rest as a snack. (If you can't find kabocha, you can use butternut squash as a substitute.)

————————

To make the soup, preheat the oven to 425°F (218°C) and arrange a rack in the center. Line a baking sheet with parchment paper or aluminum foil for easy cleanup.

Slice each squash in half again to make quarters. Rub 2 tablespoons of oil over the flesh of the squash and place the pieces cut side down on the baking sheet. Roast for 40 minutes or until the flesh is easily pierced through with a chopstick or fork. Set aside to cool, then peel the squash and set it aside in a bowl.

In a large Dutch oven or heavy-bottomed pot, warm the remaining oil over medium heat. Sauté the onions and garlic until the onions are translucent but not brown, about 6 to 8 minutes. Add the squash and the potatoes, then add the dashi to cover the vegetables. Bring the mixture to a boil, then reduce the heat and simmer for 15 minutes. Season with nutmeg, sake, ginger juice, salt, pepper, honey, soy or whole milk (if using), and miso. Remove from the heat and puree the pumpkin mixture in the pot with an immersion blender or transfer it to a food processor to puree. Taste and make adjustments with more dashi or water and seasonings. >

**For the Curried Pepitas
(makes 1 cup)**

1 cup (120 grams) hulled,
unsalted pumpkin seeds

1 teaspoon Sonoko Curry
Powder (page 153)

1 teaspoon light sesame oil

½ teaspoon salt

1 teaspoon mirin

To make the curried pepitas, preheat the oven to 325°F (165°C). Set a rack in the middle of the oven. Line a baking sheet with parchment paper. In a medium bowl, combine the pumpkin seeds, curry powder, light sesame oil, salt, and mirin and mix well. Pour the seeds onto the baking sheet and spread them out in a single layer.

Bake for about 10 minutes, moving the seeds around from time to time, until they become slightly brown and crisp. Remove from the oven and cool completely. Store in a container with a tight-fitting lid and eat within a month.

To serve, reheat the soup and garnish with parsley, crème fraîche, and curried pepitas.

COLLARD GREENS AND CABBAGE MISO SOUP WITH CRISPY BACON

Makes 4 servings

4 slices raw bacon

2 tablespoons bacon fat or neutral oil (such as grapeseed or light sesame oil)

½ yellow onion, chopped

1 garlic clove, minced

2 cups (180 grams) chopped green cabbage or napa cabbage (or other winter green, see headnote)

2 cups (90 grams) stemmed and chopped collard greens (or other winter green, see headnote)

5 cups (1.2 liters) Kombu and Bonito Dashi (page 20) or dashi of your choice, or store-bought low-sodium chicken broth

5 tablespoons red or white miso, or more to taste

Sansho pepper, freshly ground black pepper, or shichimi pepper, to taste

½ teaspoon lemon zest (optional)

It never crossed my mind to put collard greens in miso soup until my son, Sakae, suggested we try it one morning when I was visiting him and his wife, Binah, in Seattle. Sakae is an avid gardener. In addition to some rare heirloom vegetables that he starts from seed, he likes to grow collard greens. Though I know collards are highly nutritional and common in southern dishes, they're not something I had cooked with before. Sakae brought out his recipe notebook to take notes (impressive!) while I gave him a lesson on making miso soup. This recipe is a modern spin on miso soup because I sauté the onions in bacon fat before adding the greens. If you want to go the traditional route for making miso, skip the bacon and sautéing. You can use other winter greens like chard, rapini, spinach, escarole, and kale in the place of cabbage, but the collards (and bacon) give it a distinctly southern twist. Finishing the soup with yakumi (herbs and spices) like sansho pepper, freshly ground black pepper, or shichimi pepper and lemon zest brightens and accents this soup and makes it even more wafu.

———————

In a Dutch oven or large saucepan, arrange the bacon in a single layer and cook over medium-high heat until browned on the bottom, 3 to 4 minutes. Flip with tongs and cook until browned on the other side, about 2 minutes. Transfer the bacon to a paper towel–lined sheet tray to drain off the excess fat. Cut the bacon into ½ inch (1.25 cm) strips. Reserve 2 tablespoons of the fat in the Dutch oven.

Reheat the bacon fat (or use a neutral oil, if you don't have enough) in the Dutch oven over medium-high heat. Add the onions and cook until softened, about 3 minutes; then add the garlic and greens and cook until they are softened, about 3 minutes, stirring regularly.

Pour the dashi into the pan and bring to a boil over medium-high heat. Reduce the heat to a simmer and cook for about 10 minutes or until the greens are tender.

Remove a cup of the broth from the pot and combine it with the miso in a small bowl; add it back to the pot and stir to combine. Taste and adjust with more miso, as needed. Turn off the heat. Serve immediately with the pepper of your choice, the crispy bacon chips, and lemon zest, if using, sprinkled on top.

TONJIRU

Hearty Vegetable Miso Soup with Pork

Makes 4–6 servings

One 9-ounce (255-gram) packet konnyaku (see headnote) or one 7-ounce (198-gram) packet shirataki

2 tablespoons toasted sesame oil or vegetable oil

½ pound (227 grams) pork shoulder or pork belly, sliced into ⅛ x 2 inch (3 x 5 mm) pieces

1 yellow onion, coarsely chopped

8 shiitake mushrooms, stems removed, quartered

½ burdock root (4 ounces/ 113 grams), unpeeled and cut diagonally into ¼ inch (6 mm) coins

8 ounces (225 grams) daikon radish, peeled and cut into ¼ inch (6 mm) quarter moons

1 carrot, peeled and cut into ¼ inch (6 mm) coins

6 cups (1.4 liters) Kombu and Bonito Dashi (page 20) or dashi of your choice

1½ tablespoons mirin

5–6 tablespoons Red Miso (page 40) or store-bought red miso, or more to taste

Sea salt, to taste

1 cup (240 grams) cubed tofu

3 tablespoons thinly sliced scallions or chives, for garnish

2 teaspoons peeled and grated ginger, for garnish

Shichimi pepper or freshly ground black pepper, to taste

Legend has it that when the English introduced curry to the Japanese navy, one sailor didn't care for its spicy flavors so he swapped in miso for the curry roux that would have turned the soup into a thick spicy stew. I regard this accidental soup the product of a wafu twist, which resulted in one of Japan's greatest soul foods. You might expect tonjiru to be fatty because it uses pork, but the amount is just enough to add a depth of umami. The soup is a medley of vegetables like daikon radish, burdock, shiitake mushrooms, and carrots, as well as tofu. I also add konnyaku, a jiggly, low-calorie food made from a type of taro potato. Konnyaku might not inspire love at first taste (it is flavorless), but it offers a great chew that is distinctly its own and takes on the flavors of any seasoning you give it. Shirataki noodles, also called miracle noodles, are konnyaku's closest cousin, so you can use those instead. You can finish the soup with a drizzle of chili oil, if you want to spice it up, or with butter if you want to give it a yofu (western in style) twist.

———————

Bring a medium pot of water to a boil over medium heat. If using, blanch the konnyaku for 1 minute. Drain, then slice into 1 x 1 inch (2.5 x 2.5 cm) dice, using a soup spoon to make irregular shapes. If using shirataki, blanch, drain, and slice in the same manner as konnyaku.

In a large saucepan, heat the oil over medium heat and sauté the pork for 2 minutes, until it turns opaque. Put the meat in a small bowl, leaving 2 tablespoons of the oil in the pan to sauté the vegetables. Add the onions and sauté over medium-low heat for another 4 to 5 minutes, until they soften and become translucent.

Add the mushrooms, burdock, daikon radish, carrots, and konnyaku (or shirataki) and continue sautéing over medium heat for 4 to 5 minutes.

Add the dashi and bring to a boil over medium-high heat. Lower the heat and simmer the soup for 15 minutes or until the vegetables are cooked to your desired tenderness. You want them to maintain some firmness. Add the mirin. Remove ½ cup (120 ml) of the broth from the pot and combine it with the miso in a small bowl; add it back to the pot and stir to combine. Taste and adjust the seasoning as desired. Add the tofu cubes and heat over low heat for 1 minute. Serve the soup in individual soup bowls.

Garnish with scallions, ginger, and pepper, to taste.

ONE-POT FRENCH ONION SOUP WITH TOASTED MOCHI

Makes 4 servings

For the Soup

4 tablespoons extra-virgin olive oil

2 tablespoons unsalted butter

4 yellow onions, sliced in half and then crosswise into ¼ inch (6 mm) thick slices

Pinch sea salt, plus more to taste

4 cups (1 liter) Chicken Dashi (page 25) or dashi of your choice

2 garlic cloves, grated

1 teaspoon peeled and grated ginger

2 teaspoons soy sauce

1 bay leaf

Freshly ground black pepper, to taste

For the Mochi Toast

2 tablespoons unsalted butter

4 slices crusty bread, sliced in pieces that will fit (with the mochi) your individual soup bowls

1 cup (120 grams) grated Gruyère cheese, or more to taste

Four 2-ounce (53 gram) pieces unsweetened mochi, fresh or kirimochi, cut into ¼ inch (6 mm) thick discs or rectangles

Sea salt, to taste

Freshly ground black pepper, to taste

1 tablespoon chopped fresh parsley, for garnish

When mochi is toasted, it puffs up like popcorn, but the center stays gooey like melted cheese. The idea of adding it on top of the crusty bread of a French onion soup feels a bit decadent (carb on carb!), but it's irresistible. Cheese was unfamiliar to most Japanese people until the 1950s, but once their diet became more yofu, or Western in style, and cheese became common, they discovered that it tastes wonderful melted on toast. Naturally someone tried it on toasted mochi. You can find fresh or shelf-stable "unsweetened" kirimochi mochi at Japanese markets. That's what you need for this savory delicious soup.

———————

To make the soup, heat the butter and oil in a frying pan over medium-high heat. Lower the heat to medium, add the onions and a pinch of salt, and sauté until onions are translucent, about 5 to 7 minutes. Cover with a lid, lower the heat again, and cook for another 3 to 4 minutes, until the onions start to brown. Open the lid periodically only to turn the onions with a spatula to distribute the heat evenly, about 40 minutes. Remove from the heat.

Put the caramelized onions, dashi, garlic, ginger, soy sauce, and bay leaf in a large saucepan and bring to a boil over medium-high heat. Remove any foam that rises to the surface and lower the heat to a simmer. Season with salt and pepper.

Preheat the oven to broil or a toaster oven to toast. Distribute the heated soup into individual, heat-resistant soup bowls.

To make the mochi toast, butter the slices of crusty bread and place them on a sheet pan in a single layer. Sprinkle with the cheese and broil until the cheese softens, and then place a piece of mochi on top. Broil or toast until the mochi puffs up like popcorn and browns on the edges, about 3 to 4 minutes. You may sprinkle more cheese on top of the puffed mochi and toast again for a minute for a richer finish, if you like. Place the cheesy mochi toast on top of each soup bowl. Finish with salt and pepper and garnish with parsley. Serve immediately before the mochi deflates.

The soup without the toasted mochi will keep in the fridge for 3 to 4 days. Toasted mochi should be eaten right away or it will get hard.

JAPANESE ITALIAN WEDDING SOUP

Makes 6 servings

For the Meatballs

1 pound (454 grams) ground pork

1 yellow onion, grated

1 garlic clove, minced

1 egg

1 tablespoon sake or white wine

1 tablespoon soy sauce

2 tablespoons potato starch or cornstarch, diluted in 2 tablespoons water

½ teaspoon sea salt

¼ teaspoon freshly ground pepper

¼ cup minced fresh parsley

1½ teaspoons minced fresh oregano

½ cup (45 grams) grated Parmesan cheese

For the Soup

2 tablespoons extra-virgin olive oil

½ yellow onion, finely diced

2 garlic cloves, minced

1 large carrot, peeled and diced small

8 cups (2 liters) Chicken Dashi (page 25) or store-bought low-sodium chicken broth

¼ cup (60 ml) sake

1 tablespoon soy sauce

½ head escarole, hearts and outer leaves, coarsely chopped

Pinch sea salt, plus more to taste ›

My great-great-grandfather Herman Sieber was born in Bergamo, Italy, and is buried in Torino, so I consider myself a little Italian. My Italian Swiss cousins in Torino often treat me to wonderful home cooking, and ever since I discovered the good flavor of escarole, which is often used in the Italian minestra maritata, or wedding soup, I have been using it in my own soups. This recipe for meatball and vegetable soup has a wafu twist—by seasoning the meat filling with soy sauce, sake, Parmesan cheese, and oregano, and using potato starch as a binder instead of bread, it is a nod to both my Japanese and Italian heritages. Some Italian families add egg in place of the pasta to give the soup a fluffy texture, like I do in my Egg Drop Soup with Peas, Tofu, Ginger, and Parmesan Cheese (page 73). I love both versions.

Preheat the oven to 425°F (218°C).

To make the meatballs, combine the ground pork, grated onion, garlic, egg, sake, soy sauce, diluted starch, salt, pepper, parsley, oregano, and Parmesan cheese in a medium bowl. Mix the ingredients with your hands until just combined. Do not overmix. Using your hands, form the mixture into meatballs about 1 tablespoon in size, and set them on a parchment-lined sheet pan. You will get about 40 meatballs. Bake on the middle rack for 20 minutes, until they are lightly browned and nearly cooked.

To make the soup, set a large pot over medium heat, add the oil, and sauté the onions and garlic until softened, about 3 minutes. Add the carrots and sauté for another 2 to 3 minutes. Then add the dashi, sake, and soy sauce to the pot and bring to a boil. Lower the heat to a simmer and add the meatballs, one at a time. Simmer until the meatballs are cooked through, about 5 to 7 minutes. Add the escarole, cover with the lid, and simmer for another 10 minutes.

In the meantime, bring a small saucepan of water to a boil over high heat. Add a pinch of salt and the acini di pepe or other small pasta. Lower the heat to a simmer and cook until al dente. Rinse with cold water, drain, and set aside. ›

½ cup (50 grams) acini de pepe
or other small pasta
(such as orzo)

Freshly ground black pepper,
to taste

1 teaspoon finely zested
lemon peel

Grated Parmesan cheese, to serve

Crusty bread, to serve (optional)

Just before serving the soup, add the cooked pasta to the pot. Season with salt, pepper, and lemon peel. Serve with grated Parmesan and crusty bread, if desired.

Variation Substitute eggs for the pasta. In a small bowl, whisk 2 eggs and 2 tablespoons grated Parmesan cheese. Just before serving, slowly pour the egg mixture into the simmering soup in a circular motion. Let the eggs set for about 1 minute before stirring. Season with salt, pepper, and lemon peel. Serve immediately.

POSOLE JAPONESA

Makes 4–6 servings

For the Soup

16 ounces (454 grams) dried hominy (I use Rancho Gordo brand, but any other will work just fine)

4 pounds (1.8 kilograms) pork butt, cut into 2 x 2 inch (5 x 5 cm) chunks

1 tablespoon sake

3 tablespoons soy sauce

Sea salt, to taste

For the Pork Bone Dashi

2 pounds (908 grams) pig trotters

3 pounds (1.3 kilograms) pork bones (neck, shanks, or legs)

2 chicken backs

1 yellow onion, cut in half

5 garlic cloves, left whole

1 bay leaf

5 x 5 inch (13 x 13 cm) piece kombu

5 dried shiitake mushrooms, hydrated in 4 cups (1 liter) water for 1 hour or overnight, soaking liquid reserved

2 leeks, cut lengthwise in half and then into thirds

1 carrot, peeled and cut into chunks

1 tablespoon peeled and sliced ginger

2 dried Japanese or Mexican chili peppers

1 teaspoon whole black peppercorns

4 cups (32 grams) bonito flakes ›

I spent many of my formative years in Mexico City, which is where I first encountered posole—a rich brothy soup made with pork, hominy, and red chilies, and garnished with shredded cabbage, scallions, radishes, and lime. When my kitchen assistant Ruben and I started talking about making a wafu-ed version, I realized that the basic broth recipe calls for pork bones, so I used my ramen broth recipe (which also uses pork bones, dried shiitake mushrooms, kombu, and bonito flakes) as the launching pad. We also mixed up the accoutrements to include napa cabbage and shiso leaves. Serve with fresh tortillas or tortilla chips.

To make the soup, soak the hominy overnight. Strain and set aside.

To make the dashi, blanch the pig trotters, pork bones, and chicken backs in boiling water for 2 minutes, then drain and rinse them in cold water and set them aside. (This blanching method is commonly used in Japan to remove impurities and odors from meats.)

In a stock pot, add the onions, garlic, bay leaf, kombu, and shiitake mushrooms with the soaking liquid, leeks, carrots, ginger, chili peppers, peppercorns, and blanched meat. Fill with water to cover the ingredients by 2 inches (5 cm) and bring to a boil. Then lower the heat and simmer for 2 hours. Periodically skim off any foam that floats to the surface. Strain the dashi through a fine mesh strainer, discarding the solids and reserving the stock.

Return the warm dashi to the stock pot. Use cheesecloth or a nut milk bag as a sachet to hold the bonito flakes. Add this to the stock and let steep for 2 minutes. After 2 minutes, remove the sachet and discard. Your dashi is now ready.

To make the adobo sauce, char the onions and garlic cloves in a skillet or comal until browned but not scorched on all sides. Set it aside. Rehydrate the deseeded guajillo and ancho chilies in hot water for 20 minutes, reserving the liquid. In a blender, blend the rehydrated chilies, charred onions and garlic, fresh oregano, and the vinegar into an unctuous liquid, not too soupy and not like a paste. Add some of the reserved chili water if the mixture is too dense, to ensure that all the ingredients are well blended. Strain the adobo mix through a fine mesh strainer and add it to the completed dashi. ›

For the Adobo Sauce

2 medium yellow onions, halved

3 garlic cloves,
peeled and left whole

10 dried guajillo chilies,
deseeded

10 dried ancho chilies, deseeded

2 tablespoons chopped
fresh oregano

2 tablespoons rice wine vinegar

To Serve

Warm tortillas

For the Garnishes

Sliced red or purple radishes

Napa or or other cabbage

Minced white onion

Sliced shiso leaves or cilantro

Dried Mexican oregano

Diced avocado

Quartered lime

Add the hominy and the pork butt pieces to the adobo and broth mixture along with the sake and soy sauce. Simmer for 2 hours or until the hominy is tender and the pork butt cooks through until almost melting as if shredded. Add salt to taste.

Serve the pozole in a bowl with warm tortillas. Add your desired garnishes. It keeps in the fridge for 3 to 4 days.

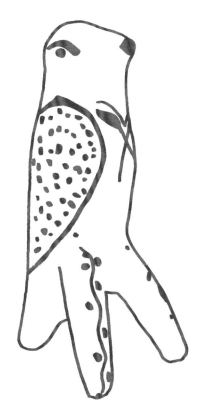

PLANTS AND VEGETABLES

Japan has a strong vegetarian tradition, dating back to the seventh century. For more than twelve hundred years, practically the entire population was vegetarian or pescatarian. The land (less than three quarters the size of California and 70 percent mountainous) is too limited to raise cattle, and due to Buddhist scripture, eating meat was banned for centuries. It wasn't until the mid-nineteenth century that Japanese people began to open to Western ways, slowly introducing meat into their diets. I grew up during this transitional period in the seaside city of Kamakura. Our family diet consisted mostly of local vegetables, fruit, rice, and catch of the day. The tofu vendor would toot his small brass horn to announce his coming; the local farm lady would regularly visit our doorsteps carrying a basketful of fresh daikon radish, spinach, scallions, flowers, natto, and rice, and always take the time to tell us about what was "shun," the Japanese term for seasonal offering, when the fruits and vegetables are at the peak of their flavor. These people were just as entertaining to me as the paper puppet master/storyteller who would set up his makeshift theater on the street corner.

These days, I am a happy omnivore, though I eat mostly vegetables during the week. I have a small urban patch where I grow a variety of vegetables, beans, herbs, flowers, and a dozen fruit trees (oro blanco, yuzu, Meyer lemon, sudachi, Santa Rosa plum, Mexican lime, kumquat, mission fig, pomegranate, satsuma tangerine, Fuyu persimmon, and curry tree). I also work as a vendor at a farmers market. I let the shun be the guide and inspiration for my cooking.

There are many wafu dishes in which meat or seafood are cooked with vegetables. Here, I will focus primarily on vegetables and vegetarian dishes alone, but be prepared to see dashi used as a seasoning, and a sprinkle of bonito flakes on top of vegetables. These are umami accents that enhance the flavor of a dish. If you prefer a vegan diet, you can use a vegetarian dashi and dried nori or toasted sesame seeds for sprinkling.

Because of Japan's long history of eating mostly plants, this chapter is bigger than the others. It is divided into three parts: Salada (Salad-ish Dishes), Vegetables and Beans, and Pickles.

Salada

Salad-ish Dishes

We begin with salada—salads. Salada, as a whole, are not traditionally Japanese. While Japanese people have come to love salad-*ish* dishes in many forms, they don't put them all in one category as they are in the U.S. Traditionally, vegetables are eaten raw or briefly blanched and served with a light dashi-infused soy or vinegar dressing or tossed with Surigoma (Ground Toasted Sesame Seeds) (page 6). Oil is seldom used. When I was young, salada was considered yoshoku—Western—dainty and precious. Japanese salada didn't look anything like the salads I would encounter in the United States when my family moved to America again, this time to Los Angeles during the early 1970s.

One of my first jobs was working as a server at the salad station at Pasadena Cafeteria. I felt like I was seeing every food in America. Remembering all the salad names by heart in English was a tongue twister: Ambrosia, Shrimp Louie, Waldorf, Caesar, Green Jello with Cottage Cheese and Pineapple, Chinese Chicken Salad, and House Salad with your choice of Italian, Thousand Island, Ranch, and Blue Cheese dressings. These salads were creamy, meaty, and sumptuous, and I soon loved them, too. I would sometimes sneak into the walk-in with a large spoon and snack on a mouthful of Shrimp Louie and Green Jello.

Fifty years later, I live not far from where Pasadena Cafeteria used to be. American salads look so different today. They have become fresher, more seasonal, diverse, and less processed, with beautiful heirloom varieties of leafy greens, tomatoes, cucumbers, squashes, root vegetables, and herbs. My love of salads has evolved, too. I often make a big salad for a family meal, using the vegetables and edible flowers I grow in my garden or buy at the farmers market. My salad dressings often get a wafu tweak—with fermented seasonings, furikake, and yakumi.

CAESAR SALAD WITH AONORI CROUTONS AND BONITO FLAKES

Makes 4 servings

For the Croutons

½ loaf crusty bread, cut into ¾ inch (2 cm) cubes with crusts (about 3 cups)

2 tablespoons olive oil

2 teaspoons aonori powder

Pinch sea salt

Freshly ground black pepper, to taste

For the Dressing
(makes about 1 cup/240 ml)

1 egg yolk

¼ teaspoon Japanese mustard or Dijon mustard

3 tablespoons Classic Ponzu Sauce (page 36) or Quick Ponzu Sauce (page 36) or store-bought ponzu sauce

1 small garlic clove, grated

2 filets anchovy, drained

1 tablespoon rice vinegar or lemon juice

2 tablespoons Kombu and Bonito Dashi (page 20) or water

Sea salt, to taste

Freshly ground black pepper, to taste

⅓ cup (80 ml) light sesame oil

¼ cup (60 ml) extra-virgin olive oil

2 tablespoons finely grated Parmesan cheese

For the Salad

1 head radicchio or 3–4 heads little gems, torn into bite-sized pieces

½ cup (4 grams) bonito flakes, for garnish (optional)

The dressing in this Caesar salad has a wafu tweak: ponzu sauce and bonito join the traditional anchovies and Parmesan cheese. What you end up with is umami heaven. I toss the salad leaves with croutons that are dusted with an aonori powder, giving them a depth of flavor with oceanic notes.

To make the croutons, preheat the oven to 400°F (204°C). Place the cubed bread in a medium bowl. Drizzle with the olive oil and massage with your hands until the bread is lightly coated in oil. Arrange the oiled bread evenly across a baking sheet. Bake until golden and crisp all the way through, 4 to 7 minutes. Toss halfway through for even color. Just before serving the salad, sprinkle the croutons with aonori, salt, and pepper.

To make the salad dressing, add the egg yolk, mustard, ponzu sauce, garlic, anchovies, rice vinegar, dashi, salt, and pepper to the bowl of a blender. Using a medium-low setting, blend the ingredients to make a puree. Once thoroughly combined, keep the blender going and slowly add the oils, starting drop by drop, gradually increasing to a fine, steady stream. Continue blending until you have fully added both the neutral oil and the olive oil. Add the Parmesan, blend to combine, and taste. Adjust to taste with additional salt or up to 2 tablespoons more oil. Keep in mind that adding more acid will loosen your dressing and adding more oil will thicken it.

To serve, place the radicchio or little gems in a large bowl, and drizzle evenly but lightly with dressing to begin. Toss to combine, taste, and add more dressing if desired, then toss again. Place the dressed radicchio on a large platter and garnish with the seasoned croutons and a light sprinkle of bonito flakes, if using.

CRUDITÉS AND CRACKERS WITH TOASTED MISO

Makes 6 servings

2 tablespoons buckwheat groats, toasted (optional)

2 tablespoons red or white miso

2 tablespoons finely chopped walnuts

2 tablespoons finely chopped chives or scallions

1 tablespoon mirin

1 teaspoon cane sugar (optional)

½ teaspoon lemon, lime, or yuzu zest

Seasonal vegetables such as cherry tomatoes, Romanesco broccoli cut into bite-size florets, Persian cucumbers, rainbow carrots, purple radishes, to serve

Crackers of your choice, to serve

Yaki miso, or toasted miso, served with crudités and crackers is one of my favorite preludes to a wafu meal when I have people over. You'll find the traditional version served in artisanal soba shops. It is miso seasoned with mirin, walnuts, buckwheat groats, chives, and citrus rind, and served like a dip on a wooden paddle. Among soba connoisseurs, it is considered "iki"—"the thing to do"—to sip sake and poke at the yaki miso with a pair of chopsticks as a prelude to the soba. The term "iki" was originally used by the merchant class of Edo (Old Tokyo) to describe someone who had refined manners and taste. My paternal grandmother was an iki person, from the way she wore her kimono, the way she talked, and the way she treated people. Serving yaki miso with crackers and crudités and wine or sake is the modern wafu approach. It's kind of an iki thing to do.

———————

Preheat the broiler to 500°F (260°C). Line a baking sheet with aluminum foil.

In a small bowl, combine the buckwheat groats, if using, miso, walnuts, chives or scallions, mirin, sugar, if using, and citrus zest.

Spread a small mound on the foil. Broil on the center rack until the surface is lightly toasted, about 2 minutes. Serve warm with crackers and a crudités platter. It will keep stored in the fridge for 3 days.

KITCHEN NOTE In soba restaurants, the miso is smeared on a wooden rice paddle before being broiled. If you want to do this, be careful not to start a fire. Wrap foil around the handle of the rice paddle while you are broiling the miso. Use oven mitts to handle the hot paddle.

CHICORY AND PERSIMMON SALADA WITH YUZU DRESSING

Makes 4 servings

1 large or 2 small heads frisée
(curly endive)

1 radicchio or treviso,
or a mixture of both

¼ fennel bulb

1 ripe and firm Fuyu persimmon
or chocolate persimmon
or honeycrisp apple,
peeled, seeded, and sliced into
½ inch (1.25 cm) wedges

1 ounce (28 grams) Manchego
or Parmesan cheese,
shaved (optional)

Fennel fronds, for garnish
(optional)

For the Yuzu Dressing

¼ cup (60 ml) rice vinegar

2 tablespoons minced shallot

1 yuzu or lemon, zested,
plus 2 tablespoons juice

½ teaspoon cane sugar

½ teaspoon sea salt,
or more to taste

5–6 tablespoons extra-virgin
olive oil or light sesame oil

Freshly ground black pepper,
to taste

There is a Japanese proverb that says peaches and chestnuts take three years to bear their first fruit, and persimmons take eight. This is to remind us to be patient because good fruit is the result of hard work and preparation. And indeed, it took eight years for my Fuyu persimmon tree to yield fruit. Now, they give me so much I struggle to use it all, which is how I came up with this recipe. The jammy sweetness of the persimmons combined with fresh and mildly bitter and crispy chicory varieties (such as frisée, Radicchio Rosa, and treviso) makes for a splendid midwinter salad. If you have trouble finding Fuyu persimmons, honeycrisp apples work just as well. Shave on some Manchego cheese for umami and extra texture, if you like.

Wash and dry the frisée and radicchio. If the leaves are large, tear or slice them into bite-sized pieces; otherwise, leave them whole. Slice the fennel bulb into pieces about ⅛ inch (3 mm) thick.

To make the dressing, combine the rice vinegar, shallots, yuzu or lemon zest and juice, sugar, and salt in a small bowl. Let stand for 4 to 5 minutes. Slowly drizzle in the olive oil, one tablespoon at a time, using a whisk to stir. Taste and make adjustments with additional salt and pepper.

In a large bowl, combine the frisée, fennel, radicchio, and persimmons. Add the dressing and toss to coat. If using, shave the cheese into thin pieces, about 2 inches (5 cm) long, and use to garnish the salad. Garnish with fennel fronds, if you wish. Serve immediately.

Variation Add ¼ cup toasted walnuts for a meaty crunch.

SHELLED BEANS AND TOMATO SALADA WITH SHISO VINAIGRETTE

Makes 4 servings

For the Salad

1 pound (454 grams) fresh shelling beans, shucked

1 teaspoon sea salt

1 bay leaf

1 garlic clove, peeled and left whole

½ yellow onion, chopped

1 sprig fresh thyme

Extra-virgin olive oil, for drizzling

Four heirloom tomatoes (about 1 pound/454 grams total)

For the Shiso Vinaigrette

20 fresh shiso leaves, stems removed (about 2 cups; see headnote)

1 shallot, minced

1 garlic clove, minced

½ teaspoon cane sugar

1 tablespoon lemon or yuzu juice

1½ tablespoons rice vinegar

1 tablespoon usukuchi shoyu (light-colored soy sauce), or to taste

½ cup (120 ml) extra-virgin olive oil

Sea salt, to taste

Freshly ground black pepper or ground sansho pepper, to taste

I'm always excited to see fresh shelling beans at the farmers market in Los Angeles. I cook them in a pot with herbs and garlic until they are tender, and I like to combine them in this salad with heirloom tomatoes, served with fragrant wafu shiso vinaigrette dressing. Shiso is similar to basil but mintier in flavor. You can find it all year round in Japanese markets, and it's also easy to grow at home. I add a little soy sauce as a kakushiaji—a hidden flavor agent—to give the salad another layer of umami. If you cannot find shiso, you can use other herbs, like basil, cilantro, and parsley, for this dressing.

To make the salad, combine the beans, salt, bay leaf, garlic clove, onions, and thyme in a medium saucepan. Add enough water to cover the beans and bring to a boil over medium-high heat. Lower the heat and simmer for 25 to 35 minutes. (Cooking time will depend on the size and variety of the beans.) Keep the beans submerged in the water. I like to put a lid on top (small enough to fit inside the pot to rest on top of the beans) to keep the beans submerged. Replenish with more water as needed. When they are done, remove from the heat and drizzle with olive oil.

Cut the tomatoes into bite-sized pieces.

To make the salad dressing, blend the shiso, shallots, garlic, sugar, lemon or yuzu juice, rice vinegar, shoyu, and olive oil in an immersion blender until pureed. Season with salt and freshly ground pepper. The vinaigrette will keep in the fridge for a couple of days but is best made fresh.

Toss the beans with the tomatoes and the shiso vinaigrette. Season with salt and pepper to taste, if needed.

SHAKI SHAKI SALADA WITH PONZU DRESSING

Makes 4 servings

For the Ponzu Dressing

2 tablespoons Classic Ponzu Sauce (page 36) or Quick Ponzu Sauce (page 36) or store-bought ponzu sauce

¼ cup (60 ml) extra-virgin olive oil or light or dark sesame oil

½ teaspoon sugar (optional)

Sea salt, to taste

Freshly ground black pepper, to taste

For the Parsnip Chips (optional)

1 large parsnip (4 ounces/113 grams)

Vegetable oil, for frying

Sea salt, for sprinkling

For the Salad

¼ cup (9 grams) dried cut wakame

8 ounces (240 grams) daikon radishes, peeled and julienned into 2 inch (5 cm) matchsticks

2 Persian cucumbers or 1 Japanese cucumber, peeled or unpeeled, sliced into ⅛ inch (3 mm) coins, crosswise

10 ounces (283 grams) leafy salad greens (romaine, mizuna, little gem, oak leaf)

1 dozen cherry tomatoes, halved

For the Garnish

2 tablespoons Surigoma (page 6) (optional)

The Japanese have a number of quirky phonetic expressions to describe pleasant textures. "Shaki shaki!" is one of those expressions. It applies specifically to certain vegetables and fruits, like radishes, carrots, apples, and pears, that are crispy and juicy in texture. You can't say it about the fried parsnips that I use in this salad as a garnish, even if they are crispy; they would be "pari pari." What is not shaki shaki or pari pari is the wakame seaweed, which gives a soft texture (no special phrase for that!), color, and flavor. Wakame is nutritiously rich, so adding it to any salad is a wafu boost to your health. Add the dressing at the table so everything stays shaki shaki. The parsnip chips are extra work, so they're optional. They can be eaten as a snack or used as toppings to make your salads and vegetables look beautiful.

To make the dressing, in a small bowl, combine the ponzu sauce and oil and mix well. Taste and make adjustments with sugar (if using), salt, pepper, and oil. You can make the dressing ahead of time. You may have more salad dressing than you need for this dish; it will keep it in the fridge for 4 to 5 days.

Meanwhile, if making the parsnip chips, trim the ends of the parsnip and shave it with a peeler into thin strips about 3 inches (7.6 cm) long. Add enough oil to a small cast-iron or heavy-bottom skillet to fill it one third of the way, about 1½ inches (3 cm) in depth, and heat the oil to 350°F (176°C). Deep-fry the parsnip in the heated oil without overlapping the slices. Let the parsnip cook, undisturbed, allowing the air bubbles to subside. When the edges of the parsnip are lightly browned, after about 2 minutes, flip them to the other side and continue cooking for 1 minute more or until lightly browned. Remove from the oil and let drain on paper towels. Repeat with the remaining parsnip. The parsnip chips will crisp up as they cool. Sprinkle with salt and set aside. The chips are best made last minute and served while crisp and fresh.

To prepare the salad, in a small bowl, hydrate the wakame in 1 cup water for 5 minutes to soften. Drain and squeeze out any excess moisture. In a large bowl, combine the daikon, cucumber, salad greens, tomatoes, and wakame. When ready to serve, garnish the salada with surigoma and the parsnip chips, if using. Serve the ponzu dressing on the side and let people dress their own salada.

CRUSHED TATAKI CUCUMBERS WITH CHUKAFU DRESSING

Makes 4 servings

6 Persian cucumbers
or 4 Japanese cucumbers

1 dried red chili pepper,
seeds removed and sliced
thinly crosswise (optional)

2 tablespoons toasted sesame oil

2 tablespoons soy sauce

2 teaspoons mirin

2 teaspoons rice vinegar

1 teaspoon cane sugar

1 teaspoon Surigoma
(page 6)

These cucumbers look a bit like someone accidentally stepped on them. That's because they are crushed by hand rather than cut with a knife. The rough, uneven surface allows the cucumber to soak up the sauce while still giving you a great crunch. If you don't want the spicy taste, omit the red chili pepper or use mild peppers instead. This was my mother's specialty. She wafu-ed a classic Chinese recipe by adding mirin, which adds sweetness and umami to the dressing but is not as intense as cane sugar. Any traditional Chinese dish that has been wafu-ed is called chukafu. My mother crushed the cucumbers with a wooden pestle, and we kids would often help. She would make a large bowlful, and they were so good they would disappear in no time.

Slice the cucumbers in half lengthwise. Break each half into bite-sized pieces with your hands, each about 2–3 inches (5–7.6 cm) wide. The pieces should be uneven in size and not smooth. Transfer to a serving bowl or platter.

In a small bowl, combine the chili pepper (if using), sesame oil, soy sauce, mirin, rice vinegar, and sugar and mix with a small whisk or fork.

Add the sauce to the cucumbers and toss. Let it rest in the fridge for 5 to 10 minutes before serving. Garnish with freshly toasted sesame seeds.

Variation Add wakame seaweed. Hydrate ¼ cup (9 grams) of dried cut wakame seaweed in 1 cup water for 5 minutes. The wakame will double in size. Drain and squeeze any excess moisture from the wakame, and add it to the cucumbers.

CITRUS, CARROT, AND DAIKON SUNOMONO

Makes 4 servings

1 pound (454 grams) daikon radishes, peeled and julienned into 3 inch (7.6 cm) long pieces

1 carrot, peeled and julienned into 3 inch (7.6 cm) long pieces

½ teaspoon sea salt

2 pink grapefruit or other citrus (like cara cara orange or Page mandarins)

2 large oro blanco grapefruit or other grapefruit

1 cup (240 ml) freshly squeezed grapefruit juice

½ teaspoon honey (optional)

6 fresh shiso leaves or basil leaves, plus more for garnish

2 teaspoons toasted sesame seeds or Grapefruit Furikake (page 8), for garnish

Extra-virgin olive oil, to serve (optional)

Sea salt, to serve

Freshly ground black pepper, to serve

This is a winter fruit sunomono—a vinegared dish—using a few varieties of grapefruit and oranges. The oil-free sunomo dressing is classic wafu, but the use of citrus (sometimes right off the oro blanco grapefruit tree in my garden) is not something you will find in Japan. Shiso leaves are added for a brightening accent, and daikon radishes and carrots are sliced into matchsticks to add color and a crispy, or shaki shaki, texture. The juice of the tangy and sweet oro blancos is used as the dressing (freshly squeezed grapefruit juice will also work). You can drizzle on some olive oil, if you like, to make it more salad-ish. I prefer to toss this sunomono at the table so the wedges stay pretty.

Soak the julienned daikon and carrots in a bowl of cold water with the ½ teaspoon salt for 10 minutes. Drain.

While the carrots and daikons are soaking, prepare the citrus into supremes by removing the peel and membranes.

Combine the grapefruit juice with the honey, if using, to make a dressing.

Combine the crispened daikon and carrot with the citrus and shiso in a bowl. Pour the dressing over and toss gently to combine. Garnish with sesame seeds or grapefruit furikake and shiso or basil leaves. Drizzle with olive oil and season with salt and pepper at the table, if you like.

CAULIFLOWER, DAIKON, CHERRY TOMATO, AND BEAN SALADA WITH ONION VINAIGRETTE

Makes 4 servings

For the Onion Vinaigrette

¼ cup (60 ml) mirin

¼ yellow onion, grated

2 tablespoons freshly squeezed lemon juice

¼ cup (60 ml) dark or light sesame oil

¼ cup (60 ml) rice vinegar

½ teaspoon cane sugar

1 teaspoon soy sauce, or to taste

½ teaspoon sea salt, or to taste

Freshly ground black pepper, to taste

For the Salad

½ pound (227 gram) daikon radish, peeled and cut into ¼ inch (6 mm) quarter moons

1 head cauliflower, cut into bite-sized florets

10 string beans, trimmed and cut into thirds, crosswise

6 cherry tomatoes, halved

Furikake, Surigoma (page 6), or shichimi pepper, to garnish

This colorful medley of vegetables is served with a homemade version of a vinaigrette that you'll find in many Japanese restaurants. It's similar to a classic French vinaigrette but with the addition of soy sauce, for umami, and grated onion, for sweetness. The vegetables in this salad benefit from an overnight marinade, but if you want to serve it right away, it's still delicious.

———

To begin, heat the mirin for the dressing in a small pot over medium-low heat to cook off the alcohol, about 1 minute. The mirin may ignite, so keep an eye on it. Remove from the heat and let cool.

While the mirin cools, prepare the salad. Bring plenty of water to a boil in a large saucepan. First, add the daikon and cook for about 1 minute. It should still be on the firm side. Transfer the daikon to a bowl with a ladle. Add the cauliflower florets and string beans to the pan and cook for 2 minutes. Drain and move to the bowl with the daikon.

While the vegetables are hot, finish making the dressing. Combine the heated mirin, grated onion, lemon juice, sesame oil, rice vinegar, sugar, soy sauce, salt, and pepper in a small bowl and mix well. Taste and adjust the seasonings. Pour the dressing over the vegetables immediately and let marinate for 1 hour or up to overnight.

Garnish with furikake, surigoma, or shichimi pepper just before serving. The dressed salad will keep for 3 to 4 days in the fridge.

POTATO SALADA

Makes 4 servings

For the Salad

1¼ pounds (565 grams) red potatoes (about 3), cut into 1 inch (2.5 cm) chunks

Sea salt

2 medium carrots, peeled and cut into ¼ inch (6 mm) thick slices

2 scallions, thinly sliced into rounds

For the Dressing

¼ cup (60 ml) plus 2 tablespoons Japanese mayonnaise (preferably Kewpie)

1 tablespoon rice vinegar

1 tablespoon lemon or lime juice, or to taste

2 teaspoons soy sauce, or to taste

½ teaspoon cane sugar, or to taste

To Finish

Sea salt, to taste

Freshly ground black pepper, to taste

Fresh parsley, for garnish

The flavors in this potato salad make it quite different from the American version. You can try adding a teaspoon of nerigoma (Japanese-style tahini) (page 6), miso, yuzu or lemon zest, and wasabi to the dressing for extra flavor.

Place the potatoes in a medium pot and add water to cover by 2 inches. Add a pinch of salt. Place over medium-high heat, bring to a boil, reduce the heat to medium-low, and cook until the potatoes are cooked through but still firm, 10 to 15 minutes. Drain and let cool.

In a medium pot, bring water to a boil over medium-high heat. Have a bowl filled with ice and water ready. Add a pinch of salt to the boiling water, then add the carrots and cook until they are al dente, about 3 minutes. Drain and transfer to the ice-cold water to cool. Drain and set aside.

To make the dressing, combine the mayonnaise, vinegar, lemon or lime juice, soy sauce, and sugar in a small bowl. Taste and adjust the flavors as needed.

In a serving bowl, combine the potatoes, carrots, and scallions and toss with the dressing. Taste and season with salt and pepper. Garnish with parsley and serve.

Vegetables and Beans

Due to a combination of Buddhist practices and limited access to meat, Japan was a mostly vegetarian country for almost twelve hundred years. It wasn't until the 1950s that meat began to be widely available.

As a result, Japanese cooking is largely plant based—not necessarily vegetarian or vegan (because of the presence of fish in many dishes), but very much focused on vegetable, bean, and seaweed dishes.

My grandmother used to say, if the fish is super fresh, make sashimi. If the fruit is ripe, enjoy it straight. So, if something is fresh and ripe in my garden, I eat it raw right off the vine. But some vegetables are just better cooked, such as root vegetables like daikon radish, beets and turnips, and winter squashes, which lend themselves to cooking with heat, to become more tender or sweeter or less bitter.

Because plant-based cooking was the norm in Japan for so long, cooks there embrace not only vegetables but also beans of all sorts—soybeans, black soybeans, adzuki beans, lima beans, and more. Soybeans, along with rice, first came to Japan from China via the Korean Peninsula hundreds of years ago, and quickly became the two key sources of nourishment in the Japanese diet. No wonder soybeans are called Meat of the Fields, for their high protein, mineral,

and vitamin content. While rice is the most consumed cereal grain in Japan, it is deficient in the essential amino acid lysine, which plays an important role in improving the immune system and absorbing calcium in the body. Soybeans, however, contain enough of all nine, so eating them together is more wholesome. And, of course, rice and soybeans are fermented together to make miso, one of the pillars of wafu cooking.

Soybeans are also made into tofu, which comes in many varieties—kinugoshi dofu (soft), momen dofu (medium firm), firm, extra firm, deep-fried, grilled—most of which you can find in Asian grocery stores. I use kinugoshi dofu and momen dofu tofu in my everyday cooking. You will find tofu used throughout this chapter, such as in Spinach with Shira-ae (Sesame-Tofu Sauce) (page 112) and my Crispy Tofu with Dipping Sauce (page 125).

The seasonings for my vegetables and tofu use basic dashi and condiments. See the Wafu Flavors chapter beginning on page 1 for more details. Most of the dishes in this chapter are easy to prepare. In general, serve hot things hot, cold things cold, but many dishes will also taste delicious at room temperature. I like serving everything family style, so the presentation for the most part is very informal and friendly.

BLOOMSDALE SPINACH WITH HONEY GOMA-AE DRESSING

Makes 4 servings

Pinch sea salt, plus more to taste

1 bunch spinach, Bloomsdale if in season

1 teaspoon soy sauce, divided

3 tablespoons Surigoma (page 6)

1 tablespoon tahini

1 tablespoon honey

1 teaspoon miso

Goma-ae sauce is a traditional wafu sauce made with surigoma (ground toasted sesame seeds) seasoned with soy sauce and cane sugar. For a modern wafu twist, I add a little honey, miso, and tahini. Grinding whole sesame seeds to make surigoma works best using a mortar and pestle. The hand work gives fresher and better flavors since you have more control over releasing the seeds' oil. But if you don't have the equipment or time to make it yourself, use tahini instead. Blanched mizuna, green beans, kale, okra, and peas also work well with this sauce. One thing to remember: Do not toss the vegetables in the sauce until just before serving, or it will get watery and dilute the flavor.

Bring a medium saucepan of water to a boil over high heat. Add a pinch of salt to the water. Blanch the spinach for 1 to 2 minutes, until it's bright green; then drain and transfer to a bowl of ice-cold water for 2 minutes. Drain and press out excess water. Cut the blanched spinach into bite-size pieces if needed. Season with ½ teaspoon of the soy sauce. Toss gently to combine.

In a medium bowl, combine the surigoma with the tahini, honey, miso, and the remaining ½ teaspoon soy sauce. Taste and make adjustments. You can make the sauce in advance and keep it refrigerated, but freshly made tastes best.

Just before serving, toss the spinach with the sauce. Serve chilled or at room temperature.

Spinach with Shira-ae (Sesame-Tofu Sauce)

This sauce is made with surigoma mixed with pureed tofu. Begin by cooking the spinach as directed. Wrap ½ block (6 ounces/175 grams) soft tofu in a paper towel or dishcloth. Place the wrapped tofu on a cookie sheet, then put a cutting board on top for 20 minutes to press out the excess water. Change the towel if it gets too wet. Puree the pressed tofu in an immersion blender or a food processor until it is creamy and blend it with 3 tablespoons ground sesame seeds or tahini, 2 teaspoons soy sauce, and 2 teaspoons cane sugar or honey. Taste and add a pinch of salt, if needed. Combine with the cooked spinach.

BABY BOK CHOY OHITASHI

Makes 4 servings

1 cup (240 ml) dashi (preferably Kombu and Bonito Dashi, page 20)

2 tablespoons soy sauce (preferably light-colored usukuchi shoyu)

2 tablespoons mirin

½ teaspoon of sea salt

1 pound (454 grams) baby bok choy, if large, cut in half lengthwise and half crosswise

Bonito flakes, toasted sesame seeds, or dried nori seaweed strips, for garnish

"Ohitashi" literally means "lightly soaked," but it also refers to a leafy green vegetable dish that is blanched and soaked in a seasoned dashi or simply drizzled with soy sauce at the table. Spinach is classic wafu ohitashi. For this recipe, I wafu-ed baby bok choy, which is a tender Chinese green that tastes somewhere between spinach and napa cabbage. You can make ohitashi with non-Japanese vegetables and mushrooms—asparagus, beet greens, escarole, swiss chard, kale, or spinach. Tomatoes work, too. If you want to add some extra umami, drizzle some sesame oil or extra-virgin olive oil to make it into a salada.

You can garnish it with dried nori strips, toasted sesame seeds, or bonito flakes, but otherwise the vegetable is left alone. My grandmother, who lived to be 102, loved the spinach ohitashi made by Ito-san, her loyal housekeeper of more than fifty years. Every week, Ito-san would clean the house and make my grandmother a bowl of spinach ohitashi. When I heard from my grandmother that Ito-san had stopped working for her, the first thing I thought of was the bowl of ohitashi.

I love to eat ohitashi as a palate cleanser. The dashi marinade gives it a subtle oceanic flavor.

Make the marinade. In a medium saucepan set over medium-low heat, bring the dashi, soy sauce, and mirin to a boil. Remove from the heat and let cool. Refrigerate. You can make the marinade a day in advance and keep it in the refrigerator.

Prepare an ice bath in a medium bowl.

In a large saucepan, bring 1 quart of water and the salt to a boil. Blanch the bok choy until tender, 1 to 2 minutes. Remove from the heat and drain. Transfer the greens to the ice bath for 10 seconds. Drain and wring out the water from the greens, bunching them up with your hands. If you have a bamboo sushi mat, roll the greens in the mat and press to remove excess water. Unroll the mat and cut the greens into 1½–2 inch (4–5 cm) pieces and transfer them to a lidded container. If you don't have a bamboo mat, just use your hands to gently shape the greens.

Pour the marinade over the bok choy and gently tilt the container so the marinade reaches all over. Cover with the lid and refrigerate for 30 minutes and up to 4 hours. Prolonged soaking will discolor the greens and make them taste less fresh. To serve, transfer the cut greens into a small bowl and garnish with bonito flakes, toasted sesame seeds, or dried nori seaweed strips.

KINPIRA GOBO

6 ounces (170 grams) burdock, unpeeled, hairs removed (about 1 burdock)

1 teaspoon rice vinegar

2 teaspoons butter

1 tablespoon light sesame oil

1 medium carrot, unpeeled and julienned into matchsticks, about 2 inches (5 cm) long

Kombu Dashi (page 15) or Bonito and Kombu Dashi (page 20) or water, as needed

2–3 tablespoons Basic Shoyu Tare (page 32)

1 teaspoon cane sugar (optional)

1 tablespoon red wine

1 dried red chili pepper, seeded and chopped

1 tablespoon toasted white or black sesame seeds

Makes 4 servings

Stir-frying vegetables is a technique that originally comes from China, but in this recipe burdock and carrots are lightly caramelized in shoyu tare, a combination of soy sauce, mirin, and sugar, for a distinctly Japanese flavor. They are given a further yofu—Western—twist with the addition of butter and red wine. You can swap in julienned parsnips, celery, bell peppers, green beans, potatoes, eggplant, and even vegetable peels. Burdock is a long root that has been used as food medicine in Asia since ancient times. If you see any hairy roots, trim them off with a knife. Do not peel it, because the flavor is all in the peel. See the process pictures for guidance on how to prepare it (page 117). It's like sharpening a pencil with a knife (if you remember those days!). Serve this as a side dish or mix it into rice. If you want protein, add a fried egg or bacon on top.

With a sharp knife, make vertical cuts into the burdock root, about 4 inches (10 cm) long from the end. Then shave the cut end of the burdock as if you were sharpening a pencil by hand. Rotate the end as you go. When you can't shave any more, make more vertical cuts into the root, and repeat. The shaved pieces will be about 2 inches (5 cm) long. Combine the rice vinegar with 4 cups water in a bowl and let the burdock shavings soak for 10 minutes; this is to prevent them from going brown. Drain well and set aside.

Heat the butter and oil in a frying pan over medium-high heat. Add the burdock and carrots and stir-fry for 3 to 4 minutes or until the burdock and carrots are tender. You can add a splash (1–2 tablespoons) of dashi or water, if you want to quicken the cooking process. Season with the shoyu tare, sugar (if using), red wine, and chili pepper. Continue stir-frying until slightly caramelized. Remove from the heat and garnish with toasted sesame seeds. Serve warm or at room temperature.

KITCHEN NOTE Kinpira Gobo is a classic bento entry. Save the leftovers for Tomorrow's Bento (page 310).

BRAISED GINGER
DAIKON RADISH

Makes 4 servings

2 tablespoons toasted sesame oil

2 tablespoons extra-virgin olive oil or neutral oil (such as grapeseed or light sesame oil)

1 ounce (28 grams) fresh ginger, peeled and julienned

1½ pounds (680 grams) daikon radish, peeled and sliced into batons, 2½ x ¾ x ¼ inches (6.3 x 2 x ½ cm) in size

1 teaspoon dried chili flakes

2 tablespoons soy sauce

2 tablespoons mirin

½ cup (120 ml) water

Lemon zest, to garnish

Stir-frying in a wok is the quintessential Chinese way of cooking. I am the first in my family to own a wok, and I swear by it. Stir-frying results in tender-crisp vegetables that retain more nutrients than when they are boiled. It also creates wok hei, the flavor resulting from the caramelization of sugars and smoking oil in a super-hot wok. With shoyu tare, the basic seasoning of equal parts soy sauce and mirin, and sesame oil in hand, I can turn any vegetable into a delicious wafu dish. This braised daikon radish tastes so meaty that when you cut into the caramelized root, it feels like you are eating a piece of steak. This dish can be served warm or at room temperature.

In a wok or large sauté pan, heat both oils over high heat. When the oil is hot, stir in the ginger and cook until fragrant, about 30 seconds.

Add the daikon batons and continue stir-frying, about 9 minutes, turning them over every 3 minutes to allow them to lightly caramelize.

Reduce the heat to medium and add the chili flakes, soy sauce, mirin, and water and bring to a boil. Cover with a lid, lower the heat to a simmer, and continue cooking, turning them every 2 minutes, until the liquid is nearly gone and the daikon is firm but cooked all the way through, about 5 minutes. Serve warm or at room temperature, garnished with lemon zest.

Variation Garnish the dish with bonito flakes and toasted sesame seeds.

ROASTED CAULIFLOWER WITH YUZU KOSHO, GARLIC, AND VINEGAR

Makes 4 servings

For the Cauliflower

2 pounds (900 grams) cauliflower, trimmed and cut into ½ inch (1.25 cm) thick florets

3 tablespoons olive oil, or more as needed

3 garlic cloves, minced

½ teaspoon sea salt

¼ teaspoon freshly ground black pepper

3 tablespoons chopped fresh parsley, to garnish

For the Yuzu Kosho Sauce

2 tablespoons Kombu Dashi (page 15) or water

3 tablespoons rice vinegar

1 tablespoon soy sauce

1 tablespoon Yuzu Kosho (page 10) or store-bought yuzu kosho

¼ teaspoon cane sugar

¼ cup (60 ml) extra-virgin olive oil, or more as needed

Sea salt, to taste

Freshly ground black pepper, to taste

Yuzu kosho is a spicy fermented condiment made with three ingredients: fresh yuzu, chilies, and sea salt. It is served to spice up sashimi, yakitori, ramen, and hot pots. It works surprisingly well with roasted vegetables—a modern wafu take that I have only seen in the past decade or so. Here, cauliflower is pan seared and briefly roasted and served with a spicy yuzu kosho sauce and finished with chopped fresh parsley and a drizzle of olive oil. If you don't have a large enough skillet to accommodate all the florets in a single layer, sear them in two batches, and then transfer them to a parchment-lined sheet pan to finish roasting in the oven.

———————

Preheat the oven to 500°F (260°C).

Place the cauliflower in a large mixing bowl. Add the olive oil, garlic, salt, and pepper and gently toss until evenly coated.

Heat a large cast-iron skillet over medium heat. Put the cauliflower pieces in the hot skillet in a single layer and toast, undisturbed, until they start to caramelize on the edges, about 3 minutes. Transfer the skillet to the middle rack of the oven and toast for another 4 to 5 minutes, undisturbed. Turn one piece of cauliflower to see if it's browned before turning the rest. Turn the cauliflower with a spatula and cook the other side until browned and caramelized on the edges, about 4 to 5 minutes.

Meanwhile, make the sauce. Combine the dashi or water, vinegar, soy sauce, yuzu kosho, sugar, and olive oil and mix well. Taste and adjust the seasoning as necessary.

Remove the skillet from the oven. Combine the cauliflower with the dressing. Taste and adjust the seasoning with salt and pepper, as needed. Transfer to a platter, garnish with chopped parsley, and serve warm.

Variations Finish with ½ teaspoon Sonoko Curry Powder (page 153) or with Grapefruit Furikake (page 8).

PAN-ROASTED BABY BEETS, CARROTS, TURNIPS, AND ORANGE WITH LEMON-MISO YOGURT

Makes 4 servings

For the Miso-Yogurt Sauce

½ cup (120 ml) plain yogurt

2 teaspoons Surigoma (page 6)

1 tablespoon white miso

½ teaspoon honey

2 teaspoons freshly squeezed lemon juice

Freshly ground black pepper, to taste

Sea salt, to taste

For the Vegetables

1 pound (454 grams) baby carrots, peeled and halved lengthwise if large, or use whole

1 pound (454 grams) baby beets with leaves, unpeeled, halved or quartered, if large

1 pound (454 grams) baby turnips, unpeeled, halved or quartered, if large

3 tablespoons minced garlic (optional)

1 orange (such as cara cara, naval, Page, or Valencia varieties), skin on, sliced into ¼ inch (6 mm) rounds

2 tablespoons olive oil

¼ cup (60 ml) Kombu Dashi (page 15)

Sea salt, to taste

Freshly ground black pepper, to taste

This colorful winter wafu salad is a crowd pleaser during the holidays or a nice weeknight dish. I use the leaves of the beets in the mix, too, which adds to the beauty. The miso acts as a kakushiaji, a secret wafu ingredient that enhances the tangy yogurt with a nutty, lemony, and sweet umami.

———————

Make the sauce first. Combine the yogurt, ground sesame seeds, miso, honey, and lemon juice. Add black pepper and salt to taste. Store in the fridge.

Preheat the oven to 500°F (260°C). Place a large cast-iron skillet on the middle rack and heat the skillet until it is very hot, about 15 minutes.

To prepare the vegetables, in a medium bowl, toss the carrots, beets, turnips, garlic (if using), and orange slices with the olive oil.

Wear oven mitts to pull the skillet out of the oven. Add the carrot mixture to the hot skillet and return it to the center rack. Roast until the vegetables and the orange slices soften and brown, 5 to 7 minutes, turning only once with a spatula. Brown the other side for 5 to 7 minutes. Remove from the oven.

Carefully add the dashi to the hot skillet and stir to combine. Return the skillet to the oven to finish cooking. Allow the liquid to be absorbed. Lightly season the roasted vegetables with salt and pepper.

Pour the miso sauce onto a serving platter and spread it evenly on the plate. Place the vegetables on top of the sauce. Serve immediately.

CRISPY TOFU WITH DIPPING SAUCE

Makes 4 servings

For the Crispy Tofu

1 block (1 pound/454 grams)
momen dofu
(medium-firm tofu), drained

½ teaspoon sea salt

2 cups (480 ml) neutral high-heat
oil (such as canola, grapeseed,
or peanut oil)

3 tablespoons all-purpose flour

3 tablespoons potato starch
or tapioca starch

For Serving

8 ounces (230 grams)
daikon radish, peeled

1 tablespoon peeled ginger

2 scallions,
sliced thinly crosswise

4 tablespoons bonito flakes

½ teaspoon shichimi pepper

½ batch Basic Dipping Sauce
(Tsuyu or Tsukejiru)
(page 35) or soy sauce

Tofu was introduced from China and adopted by Japanese cooks centuries ago. This classic wafu tofu dish, also called Agedashi Dofu, is topped with a yakumi of either grated daikon radish (see Daikon Oroshi, page 5), chopped scallions, grated ginger, shichimi pepper, or bonito flakes—or with a combination of a few or all. Here the tofu is deep-fried to a crisp and served with a sauce made of tsuyu or tsukejiru (dipping sauce). Tofu comes in many varieties. In this recipe, I use medium-firm tofu, also called momen dofu.

Lightly salt the tofu on both sides and let it stand on a clean cutting board for 15 minutes. This step removes excess moisture from your tofu before frying. Drain the water and wipe the tofu with paper towels. Cut the tofu into ½ inch (1.25 cm) squares.

In the meantime, make the garnishes. Grate the daikon (preferably using oroshiki, a Japanese grater) by moving it against the grater in a circular motion. Lightly press the grated daikon to get rid of excess juice. Set aside in a small bowl. Do the same with the peeled ginger and add the grated ginger to the grated daikon. Have the grated daikon and ginger, sliced scallions, and bonito flakes on standby. When the tofu fries up, you will spoon or sprinkle these on top.

When you are ready to fry, heat the oil to 350°F (176°C) in a small cast-iron frying pan or Dutch oven. Add enough oil to fill to about 1 inch (2.5 cm).

Whisk together the flour and starch in a medium bowl until thoroughly combined. One at a time, place a tofu square in the bowl and evenly and lightly coat it on all sides.

Divide the tofu squares into four batches and fry them one batch at a time, until crispy and brown, about 3 to 4 minutes on each side, turning them over halfway through. Place your fried tofu on a flat surface lined with a clean dry dish towel or paper towel to allow any excess oil to drain away. Continue working in batches until all the tofu is fried.

Serve the tofu immediately with the garnishes and dipping sauce.

Variation As a salad topping, sprinkle red pepper flakes or shichimi pepper on your crispy tofu and add it to your salad.

CHARRED CABBAGE WITH DASHI, CRUSHED RED PEPPER FLAKES, AND VINEGAR

Makes 4–6 servings

1½ pounds (680 grams) small green cabbage (1 head)

3 tablespoons neutral oil (such as grapeseed, canola, or light sesame oil)

¼ cup (60 ml) dashi of your choice

2 tablespoons Teriyaki Sauce (page 33) Basic Shoyu Tare (page 32), or soy sauce

1 teaspoon rice vinegar, or more to taste

Red pepper flakes, to serve

Green cabbage is not indigenous to Japan. It wasn't cultivated there until the late nineteenth century, mainly for Westerners. But when tonkatsu—breaded and fried pork cutlet—was introduced to the country, shredded cabbage became its essential companion. I love cabbage, especially charred. The smell of cabbage caramelizing takes me right back to yakisoba noodles and okonomiyaki pancakes—typical Japanese street food for which generous amounts of cabbage are always used. The cabbage wedges in this dish are seared in a cast-iron skillet until they are tender and charred and taste like sweet caramel. I further wafu this dish with a splash of dashi seasoned with shoyu tare to give it even more umami flavors. You can drizzle it with La-yu (Spicy Chili Oil) (page 258) and furikake instead of the pepper flakes, if you like more kick.

Remove any wilted leaves from the cabbage and cut head into eight 2 inch (5 cm) thick wedges, leaving the core intact.

In a large cast-iron skillet, heat the oil over medium-high heat. Add the cabbage wedges and cook until the cabbage is floppy and deeply charred on all sides, 6 to 8 minutes per side. When you get the desired color on the cabbage, add the dashi, teriyaki sauce, and rice vinegar and cook until the sauce is thickened, about 2 minutes. Remove from heat.

Place the charred cabbage on a platter and pour the warm sauce over it. Serve immediately with crushed red pepper flakes.

KABOCHA, EGGPLANT, AND PEPPERS WITH GARLICKY OKAKA SAUCE

Makes 4–6 servings

2 pounds (908 grams) kabocha squash, unpeeled, sliced into 1½ inch (3.8 cm) wedges

6 tablespoons toasted sesame oil, divided

2–3 green and yellow peppers (such as bell, Anaheim, or poblano), seeded and sliced into ½ inch (1.25 cm) pieces

2 Japanese eggplants, sliced lengthwise and cut into ½ inch (1.25 cm) pieces, diagonally

3 garlic cloves, minced

2 tablespoons Basic Shoyu Tare (page 32) or Teriyaki Sauce (page 33)

1½ cups (12 grams) bonito flakes, divided

The combination of soy sauce and bonito—also known as okaka—adds a very nice umami kick. It is one of the most popular onigiri fillings. I never thought of using it for anything other than onigiri until I tried okaka on my roasted vegetables. So delicious. It's wafu meets yofu (Western in style), since Japanese cooks don't do much in the way of roasting. You can either mix the bonito flakes into the sauce or use them as a garnish—or do both, as I do here.

———————

Preheat the oven to 425°F (218°C).

Toss the kabocha wedges with 2 tablespoons of the sesame oil on a baking sheet lined with parchment paper.

Place on the middle rack of the oven and roast. After 20 minutes, toss the peppers and the eggplants with 2 tablespoons of the sesame oil, add to the baking sheet, and combine with the kabocha. Continue baking for 20 minutes. Test the vegetables' doneness with a toothpick. If it goes in smoothly, they are done. If not, continue to cook until desired tenderness is reached.

In a medium frying pan, heat the remaining 2 tablespoons of sesame oil over medium-low heat. Fry the minced garlic until slightly toasted, about 1 minute. Remove the pan from the heat, add the soy sauce and 1 cup of the bonito flakes, and stir until combined.

Toss the warm sauce with the roasted vegetables. Serve immediately, sprinkling the remaining bonito flakes on top, if you like.

Variation Substitute the vegetables with a medley of 2 yellow summer squash and 2 zucchini cut into bite-sized pieces and 1 cup of okra, stems trimmed.

STEAMED EGGPLANT SALADA WITH GINGER, SESAME, AND SCALLIONS

Makes 4 servings

4 Japanese eggplants

For the Dressing

1 tablespoon fish sauce

2 teaspoons soy sauce (preferably light-colored usukuchi shoyu)

2 tablespoons rice vinegar

1 teaspoon cane sugar, or more to taste

2 tablespoons toasted sesame oil

1 tablespoon water

Juice of 1 lime or ½ lemon, to taste

2 teaspoons minced ginger

Ground sansho pepper or freshly ground black pepper, to taste

Sea salt, to taste

For the Garnish

1 tablespoon Surigoma (page 6)

1 cup (25 grams) daikon sprouts or other micro sprouts

1 hot or medium-hot chili pepper, deseeded and sliced thinly

2 scallions, sliced thinly

Here is a wafu eggplant salad that is served with a light fish sauce dressing and lots of yakumi—grated ginger, lemon zest, and sansho pepper. Though less well known than Thai and Vietnamese fish sauces, Japanese fish sauces like shottsuru, ikanago, and ishiru are regional specialties that are enjoying a revival. Fish sauces differ in their potency and saltiness due to their varying fishy ingredients and the method of fermentation, but they are interchangeable in this recipe. If you can't find any fish sauce, just use soy sauce.

———

Prepare a steamer basket. Add 1 inch (2.5 cm) of water to the bottom of a saucepan or pot and then place the steamer basket on top. Bring the water to a boil.

Trim the eggplants and cut them in half crosswise. Then slice each half into batons about 3 x ½ inch (7.5 x 1.25 cm). Put the sliced eggplant in the steamer basket in a single layer so the pieces don't overlap. Steam for 10 to 15 minutes, until they are tender. Use a toothpick to test doneness. Remove from the steamer and transfer to a plate to cool. You can steam the eggplant in the morning and keep it in the refrigerator until the evening.

To make the dressing, combine the fish sauce with the soy sauce, rice vinegar, sugar, sesame oil, water, lime or lemon juice, ginger, and ground sansho or black pepper in a small bowl. Whisk and taste. Adjust with salt, as needed. Set aside.

Just before serving, arrange the eggplant on a platter and pour the dressing on top. Garnish with sesame seeds, daikon sprouts, chili peppers, and scallions. Serve immediately.

MUSHROOM DASHI RISOTTO

Makes 4–5 servings

8–10 cups (1.8–2.3 liters) Kombu and Bonito Dashi (page 20), dashi of your choice, or a combination of dashi and chicken broth

1 tablespoon olive oil

4 tablespoons butter, divided

1 small yellow onion, finely diced

1 sprig fresh thyme

1 cup fresh mushrooms (such as shiitake, oyster, or enoki, or a mix), trimmed and sliced thinly, about ⅛ inch (3 mm) thick

2 garlic cloves, minced

2¼ cups (450 grams) arborio rice (approximately 2 handfuls per person plus a handful for the pot)

½ cup (120 ml) sake

Sea salt, to taste

Freshly ground black pepper, to taste

1 cup (170 grams) peas, fresh or frozen

2 tablespoons heavy cream (optional)

¼ cup (22 grams) freshly grated Parmesan cheese, plus more for serving

1 cup (8 grams) bonito flakes

Risotto reminds me of ojiya, a Japanese porridge. While Japanese porridge is cooked in seasoned dashi, risotto takes a few more steps to toast the raw grains of rice in fat and then simmer the rice with broth and a little wine, until it is cooked and creamy, yet still has some bite. I'd always found it a bit complicated, but watching my friend Francesca, who was born and raised in Milan, make it, I changed my mind. We didn't have chicken broth around, so we put together a kombu and bonito dashi to give it a wafu twist and finished it with Parmesan cheese and a garnish of bonito flakes, for another layer of umami. It was delicious!

Heat the dashi in a large pot and keep it at a simmer.

In a medium heavy-bottomed saucepan, heat the olive oil and 2 tablespoons of the butter over medium-low heat. Add the onions and sauté until soft and translucent. Be careful not to brown or burn the onions. Combine the sprig of thyme, mushrooms, and garlic. Continue sautéing over medium-low heat until the mushrooms and garlic soften, about 2 to 3 minutes.

Add the rice, increase the heat to medium, and stir until coated with the oil and butter, about 1 minute. Add the sake to the pot to deglaze, stirring until fully absorbed by the rice. Now, gradually add the dashi to the pot, two ladlefuls at a time (1–1½ cups/240–360 ml), to just cover the rice, replenishing the pot as the dashi is absorbed, and then stir to combine.

Lower the heat to a simmer and stir continuously while adding more dashi as it is absorbed by the rice. Stirring will help release the starch and give the risotto its creaminess. As the rice cooks, add less broth and continue cooking until rice is al dente. Season with salt and pepper to taste. Add the peas and continue cooking until the peas are cooked but remain bright in color.

Once the rice is cooked, remove the woody stem of the thyme sprig, turn off the heat, and add the remaining 2 tablespoons butter, the cream, if using, and the Parmesan cheese. Stir to combine.

Serve it immediately in bowls, topped with bonito flakes and additional Parmesan cheese. Another lesson that Francesca taught me is "Risotto never waits," so let's follow the Italian way.

DAIZU HUMMUS WITH BEETS

Makes 2 cups (480 grams)

1 cup (170 grams) cooked soybeans (page 139), cooking liquid reserved

1 large beet, roasted, peeled, ¾ roughly chopped, ¼ finely diced into cubes (approximately ¼ inch/6 mm)

½ cup (120 grams) tahini or homemade nerigoma (Japanese-style tahini) (page 6) or store-bought

1 lemon, zested and juiced (about 3 tablespoons juice)

2 small garlic cloves, smashed

½ teaspoon kosher salt

2 teaspoons soy sauce

⅓ cup (80 ml) olive oil, plus more for serving

One day, my kitchen assistant Kali and I were exploring ways to use cooked soybeans (leftovers from our miso-making workshop), and she suggested we make hummus, swapping in soybeans for the usual chickpeas and adding a little soy sauce. It came out just as nutty, creamy, and beany but with a distinct flavor of its own. The addition of pureed beets makes it even prettier and sweeter. I serve it with pita bread.

———————

In the bowl of your food processor, combine the soybeans, roughly chopped beet, tahini or nerigoma, lemon zest and juice, garlic, salt, and soy sauce. Begin blending, and with the motor running, gradually stream in the olive oil. Blend until completely smooth. Add 2 tablespoons soybean-cooking liquid (or water) as needed to loosen the puree and allow the mixture to blend properly.

Remove the hummus from the food processor and serve immediately, topped with the remaining finely diced beet and a generous drizzle of olive oil. Daizu hummus can be stored in the refrigerator in a sealed container for up to 5 days. It is delicious alongside crudités, spread on a piece of toast, or with flatbreads, salads, and dips.

Plain Daizu Hummus with Natto and Scallions

Omit the beets and kosher salt. Before serving, combine 3 tablespoons high-quality natto (preferably NYrture's New York Natto or MegumiNATTO based in Sonoma) with 1 teaspoon of soy sauce and stir to combine. Top the plain hummus with the soy-sauced natto and a sprinkle of thinly sliced scallion greens.

CRISPY ASPARAGUS TEMPURA

Makes 4 servings

10 large stalks green asparagus

1 egg

¾ cup (180 ml) ice-cold water, plus more as needed

1 cup (115 grams) cake flour

3 cups grapeseed or rice bran oil, for frying

1 lemon, cut into wedges

Sea salt, to taste

This tempura follows the traditional wafu method of frying that Portuguese traders first taught the Japanese four hundred years ago. But instead of the traditional dipping sauce, I often serve it with lemon and sea salt. Besides asparagus, you can fry a variety of vegetables—eggplant, zucchini, carrot, okra, or shiso. You can also fry seafood—shrimp, oysters, or scallops—using this batter. Make sure that the water is ice-cold and the oil is at its optimum frying temperature of 340°F (170°C). Use the metric setting on your digital scale for accuracy when measuring the water and flour.

You can, of course, serve this with the traditional Basic Dipping Sauce (page 35). Daikon Oroshi (Fresh Daikon Radish Sauce) (page 5) and grated ginger are delicious on the side as well.

To prepare the asparagus, peel the lower half of the skin with a peeler. Then cut the asparagus in half.

In a medium bowl, combine the egg and the ¾ cup of water. Whisk until combined. Add the flour and draw a figure eight in the batter with the whisk four times to combine. Do not overmix the batter. Some flour should remain unincorporated.

In an 8 inch (20 cm) cast-iron skillet, add enough oil to reach about 1¼ inch (3 cm) in depth. Heat the oil to 350°F (176°C) and maintain this temperature, using a digital thermometer to check. Deep-fry the asparagus pieces, five at a time, until crispy, about 1 minute, turning once with long chopsticks or tongs. Transfer to a paper towel–lined sheet pan. Deep-fry the remaining asparagus.

Serve immediately with lemon wedges and salt.

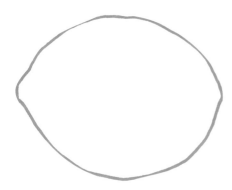

Pickles

Pickles play a very special role in Japanese cuisine. They announce the season, reset the palate, and aid in digestion, and some are even believed to bring good luck! They pair well with everything, especially with rice. They are ancient and regional, and use a variety of mediums to preserve foods—like salt, miso, soy sauce, shio koji, vinegar, and sugar. Pungent and hot spices like ginger, garlic, wasabi, chili pepper, sansho pepper, and kombu are used to brighten or deepen the umami of the pickle.

In this section, I share an assortment of wafu pickled vegetables (although Japanese cooks also pickle seaweed, tofu, eggs, meats, seafood, nuts, and grasshoppers like inago no tsukudani). Many are adaptations of Western, Chinese, and Korean pickles that are easy and quick to make at home, including recipes for water kimchi and root vegetable pickles that I make for the Hollywood Farmers Market, where most of my ideas for pickling come from. Whenever I see vegetables in their shun—their peak—I want to preserve their flavors to enjoy later.

GOOD LUCK PICKLE WITH LOTUS, DAIKON, CARROTS, GREEN BEANS, KONNYAKU, AND SOYBEANS

Makes six 1 pint (568 ml) jars

Special Equipment

6 sterilized 1 pint (568 ml) mason jars

For the Pickles

⅓ cup (66 grams) dried soybeans (optional), hydrated in a quart of water overnight

8 ounces (225 grams) konnyaku, drained (optional)

8 ounces (225 grams) daikon radish, peeled and sliced into ¼ inch (6 mm) wedges

1 medium carrot, peeled and sliced into ¼ inch (6 mm) coins

8 ounces (225 grams) lotus root, peeled and sliced into half moons, or coins if the root is small

4 dried shiitake mushrooms, rehydrated in 2 cups water and sliced into ¼ inch (6 mm) pieces (the soaking liquid can be saved and used as dashi or to make miso soup)

20 green beans, trimmed

For the Pickling Brine

6 cups (1.4 liters) water

2½ tablespoons (35 grams) sea salt

½ cup (120 ml) rice vinegar

2½ tablespoons (30 grams) cane sugar

1 teaspoon soy sauce

I call this the good luck pickle because it's made with root vegetables like daikon radishes, carrots, and lotus root. It's a classic wafu pickle. I included this recipe so you can make it for New Year's, like I do, to bring good luck. Root vegetables symbolize groundedness and stability. The inclusion of a lotus root is particularly auspicious, because the holes of a sliced lotus root are believed to give you perspective, and the shape of the sliced root will remind you of a wheel that puts you in forward motion. Some of these beliefs, as well as the base seasoning of soy sauce, originate from ancient China. The Japanese took these beliefs and foods and combined them with their own ingredients, like konnyaku—a wobbly, rubbery jelly made from a type of taro potato. You can skip it, if you think it's too weird, but konnyaku is a good source of fiber and considered food medicine in Japan. Cooked soybeans, which are also in this pickle, are a rich source of protein. They bring good luck because beans symbolize productivity. This pickle makes a nice holiday gift, and keeps in the fridge for one month.

———————

If using soybeans, boil the hydrated beans in a pot with plenty of water, skimming off any foam that rises to the surface. Cook until they are tender and squashable. This will take 4 hours in a simmering pot or 20 minutes in a pressure cooker. (Follow the manufacturer's instructions for cooking beans.) Drain and bring to room temperature. Set aside.

If using konnyaku, cut it into 2 x ¼ inch (5 cm x 6 mm) batons. Bring a medium pot of water to a boil and blanch the konnyaku for a couple of minutes to remove the odor. Drain and set aside.

To make the brine, combine the 6 cups water, salt, rice vinegar, sugar, and soy sauce in a large pot and bring to a boil over medium-high heat. Add the daikon, carrots, lotus root, mushrooms, and green beans and cook for 1 minute. Turn off the heat and transfer everything, including the cooking liquid, to a large bowl. Add the cooked soybeans and the konnyaku, if using, to the brine. Let stand for 1 hour. Drain. Transfer the vegetables evenly between the mason jars.

The pickles will keep in the refrigerator for 1 month.

NAPA CABBAGE PICKLE WITH KOMBU, LEMON, AND CHILI

2¼ pounds (1 kilogram)
napa cabbage

1 tablespoon (14 grams) sea salt

One 2 x 2 inch (5 x 5 cm) piece
(10 grams) dried kombu

2 dried Japanese,
Calabrian, Mexican,
or Indian chili peppers, seeded

Peel from ¼ lemon, slivered

1 tablespoon Surigoma
(page 6) (optional)

Soy sauce, for serving (optional)

Makes about 4 servings

Napa cabbage pickles are Chinese in origin. From China they were brought to Japan via the Korean Peninsula. Koreans make kimchi, and the Japanese make a variety of pickles using napa cabbage, one of which is a quick pickle called hakusai-no-asazuke. My salt-based lemony wafu pickle is a modern version of the classic hakusai-no-asazuke, made during the winter when napa cabbage is sweet, young, and crispy. The addition of kombu deepens the umami. My Korean friend Katy, who makes a delicious kimchi, tells me where she's seen the nicest napa and I follow her trail to get them before it disappears, which is always rather quickly. I give my napa cabbage a sunbath before I put it in the pickling bin. This releases the excess moisture in the cabbage, and concentrates its "amami"—sweetness. Nothing tastes better under the sun! Napa cabbage can vary in size and weigh between 2 and 6 pounds (1 to 3 kilograms). To determine the amount of salt needed for pickling, it's best to weigh the cabbage on a metric digital scale. The amount of salt to use for pickling is about 2 percent of the weight of the cabbage. So if the cabbage weighs 2¼ pounds (1 kilogram), use 20 grams of salt, which is about 1 tablespoon. You can add other vegetables, like baby beets and carrots, if you like.

———————

Wash the cabbage and discard the outer leaves. Slice the cabbage into quarters. If you can, put it out in the sun for 4 hours. Rinse briefly under running water.

Put a cabbage wedge in the bottom of a medium bowl or pickling container, and generously sprinkle salt over it.

Break the strip of kombu into six pieces and slice the chili peppers into thirds. Place two pieces of the kombu and two pieces of the peppers on top of the cabbage wedge. Layer another wedge on top of the first at a right angle and continue to layer salt, peppers, seaweed, and cabbage. Sprinkle the lemon peel slivers on top.

Put pressure on the pickles by applying a weight about twice the weight of the cabbage. I usually put a flat plate or lid on top of the pickle and then several cans or a clean rock.

Let it stand in the refrigerator or a cool place. In 6 hours the moisture in the cabbage should be released and enable the cabbage to pickle in its own brine. If you don't see any brine rising, you need to add more weight or more salt. Remove the pressure after 6 hours and let the pickles stand for another 8 hours in the refrigerator or a cool place.

To serve, rinse the pickles under water. Chop coarsely or slice into strips. Sprinkle with surigoma, if you wish. Slice the kombu into thin strips and sprinkle on top of the cabbage. Serve with soy sauce, if you like.

It keeps in the refrigerator for 1 week.

Variation Add 2 peeled and thinly sliced beets like Chioggia beets and 1 peeled and julienned carrot to the napa cabbage before you begin pickling.

WATER KIMCHI IN SUMMER MELON BRINE

Makes 4–6 servings

6 large napa cabbage leaves, cut crosswise into 2 inch (5 cm) pieces

2 tablespoons salt, or more to taste, divided

4 cups (1 liter) water

One 2 x 2 inch (5 x 5 cm) piece kombu

One 5 pound (2.2 kilograms) watermelon or honeydew

1 teaspoon gochugaru (Korean chili powder), or more to taste

2 ounces (55 grams) ginger, peeled and grated, juice only

2 garlic cloves, grated

2 large Asian pears (1⅓ lbs or 600 grams total) or apples (honeycrisp, cameo, Fuji)

1 pound (454 grams) daikon radish or baby turnips and their tender stems

4 Persian cucumbers

⅓ cup (80 ml) rice vinegar, or more to taste (or apple cider vinegar)

1 tablespoon Shio Koji (page 38), or more to taste

Freshly ground black pepper, to taste

3 scallions, trimmed and halved lengthwise

Juice from 1 lemon

3 cups (720 ml) ice cubes

4 tablespoons toasted pine nuts, for garnish (optional)

When summer arrives, this is my go-to energizer dish. It is a fermented Korean pickle that I wafu with kombu dashi and shio koji, so you get the probiotic benefits. Water kimchi isn't just a pickle. You can drink it like soup or eat it with cold somen noodles. I was talking with my friend Katy, who owns a dry cleaning shop in my neighborhood. She is always letting me taste her kimchi and shares her family stories, so my dry cleaning stop always takes much longer than it should. But she is such a joy to talk to. The latest idea she gave me was using watermelon juice or 7Up to make the water kimchi brine. If you use honeydew or watermelon juice, the pickling agent is naturally sweetened, so no sugar is needed. It's also really pretty. I haven't made water kimchi with 7Up yet—that sounds too wild for me.

In a large bowl, combine the napa cabbage and 1 tablespoon of salt and massage the salt into the cabbage. Add 4 cups of water and the kombu, and let stand while you prepare the other vegetables and fruit.

Cut the watermelon or honeydew in half and scoop out the fruit, removing the seeds as you go. Put the fruit, gochugaru, ginger juice, and garlic in a food processor or blender and puree. Pour through a fine mesh strainer. You should have 4–5 cups of spicy drinkable melon juice.

Slice each pear or apple into eight wedges. Remove the cores and slice each wedge crosswise into ⅛ inch (3 mm) slices. Peel the daikon or turnips and slice into quarters lengthwise. Slice each wedge crosswise into ⅛ inch (3 mm) slices. Slice the cucumbers crosswise into ⅛ inch (3 mm) pieces. Add the pear or apple, daikon, and cucumbers to the bowl of napa cabbage and kombu brine.

Add the spicy melon juice, remaining 1 tablespoon of salt, rice vinegar, shio koji, and pepper, and mix well. Taste and make adjustments if necessary. Top with scallions. Let stand for 2 hours to overnight in the fridge.

Just before serving, add the lemon juice and ice cubes and stir the mixture. Serve the water kimchi in individual cereal or soup bowls. Garnish with toasted pine nuts and serve immediately. It will keep in the fridge for 4 to 5 days. ›

Variations

If you don't have access to fresh watermelon or honeydew melon juice, use 2 quarts water combined with ¼ cup sugar instead, or more to taste.

You can serve the water kimchi with somen noodles: Cook 1 pound (454 grams) somen noodles and shock in ice-cold water. Serve these noodles in iced water on the side with the water kimchi or drop them in the water kimchi and slurp!

BABY TURNIP, APRICOT, AND CHILI PICKLE

Makes 4 servings

For the Pickle

5 Japanese baby turnips

1½ teaspoons sea salt or kosher salt

2 cups (480 ml) water

3 dried apricots, cut into ¼ inch (6 mm) thick slices

1 teaspoon toasted sesame seeds, for garnish

½ teaspoon yuzu or lemon zest, for garnish

For the Amazu Dressing

6 tablespoons rice vinegar

2 tablespoons cane sugar

½ teaspoon sea salt

5 tablespoons water

One 2 x 2 inch (5 x 5 cm) piece dried kombu

1 dried red chili pepper, seeded and sliced into ⅛ inch (3 mm) rings

This is a refreshing sweet-and-sour pickle that you can nibble on as a snack or have with curry rice or as a side dish with your grilled foods. It's a good luck pickle we eat on New Year's and throughout the year. This pickle finds its roots in China, and I give it a wafu twist with yuzu and kombu. You can also use the amazu dressing to pickle young ginger, daikon, cucumber, and radishes.

If the turnips are young and fresh, and their skins are not bruised, there's no need to peel them. Otherwise, peel the turnips. Cut them into quarters. Combine the salt and water in a bowl. Transfer the turnips to the brine, put a plate on top to press the turnips down, and let stand for 20 minutes at room temperature. Drain the brine. Gently squeeze any excess moisture out of the turnips with your hands.

Meanwhile, prepare the dressing. In a large bowl, combine the rice vinegar, sugar, salt, water, kombu, and chilies and stir well.

Add the turnips and the apricots to the dressing. Put a plate on the turnips to press them down again, and let stand for 1 hour at room temperature.

Garnish the turnip and chili pickles with toasted sesame seeds and yuzu or lemon zest. Store the pickles, in their brine, in the fridge. They will keep for 3 days.

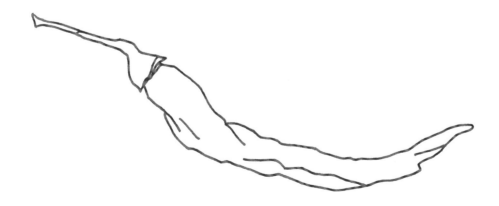

UMEBOSHI

Pickled Ume Plums

Makes about 2 dozen

Special Equipment

Small spray bottle

One 12 x 16 inch (30 x 40 cm) plastic bag without handles

Ceramic, enamelware or plastic jar, sterilized

6.6 pounds (3 kilogram) stone (or can) that fits on top

Craft paper (paper bag)

Kitchen twine

For the Umeboshi

4½ pounds (2 kilograms) yellow ripe but firm and unbruised ume plums (preferably kaga ume)

¼ cup (60 ml) shochu (Japanese grain liquor) or clear distilled spirit (35 percent alcohol)

7 ounces (200 grams) sea salt (10 percent of the weight of the plums)

3½ ounces (100 grams) koori zato (Japanese rock sugar) or cane sugar

Japanese cooks have been pickling ume plums to make umeboshi since ancient times. Umeboshi were originally introduced to Japan by the Chinese as food medicine and now enjoyed as a condiment that enhances a dish and aids in digestion. The traditional umeboshi is very salty and sour—it will make your mouth pucker. This recipe is a modern wafu version. I added a little honey and koori zato, a Japanese rock sugar, to give the sour plums a mild and subtly sweet flavor, but it's still salty enough to make your mouth pucker.

Ume plums are not like your sweet Santa Rosas, damsons, or greengages—they are inedible unless you turn them into a pickle. Every year, in the late spring, I touch base with Penny at Nicholas Family Farms in Fresno, California, to say hello and find out how her ume plums are doing. Penny's family grows marvelous fruit, including a variety of stone fruit and grapes. They have several dozen ume trees that produce tons of plums. Penny learned how to make umeboshi from a Japanese American farmer friend. She brings ume plums and umeboshi to the farmers market and also ships around the country. The ume season is short, and these plums are finicky to grow. Bad weather like hail can damage their delicate skin, so my umeboshi production varies from year to year. The plums turn from pale green to yellow with a blush of red as they ripen. The green umes make a crunchy umeboshi. The riper, more fragrant umes produce a softer umeboshi. It's a matter of preference. Enjoy umeboshi with rice, add it to your salad dressings, or nibble on it with green tea. When making umeboshi, I weigh everything on a metric digital scale for accuracy.

Using a toothpick, gently remove the small brown stems from the ume. Rinse the ume and discard any blemished or bruised fruit, as they can start to grow mold.

Soak the ume in water overnight to remove bitterness. The next day, drain the ume and pat dry with a towel. Place the ume in a large bowl and spray the stem end with the shochu, using the small spray bottle. Sprinkle and gently rub the salt over the ume using your hands.

Place the salted ume in the plastic bag. Add the koori zato (Japanese rock sugar) or the cane sugar on top. Twist the top to close the bag and put it › in the container. Place a weight directly on the top of the bagged ume (you can use a few cans of tomato sauce or a rock). The weight will press the ume inside the plastic bag and extract the brine. Cover the container with craft paper and tie a string around it to hold the paper in place. Leave it in a cool, dark place.

After a couple of days, check the jar. You should start to see the brine that is being extracted from the ume. The brine should cover the ume. If you don't see any brine, you may need to add a couple more tablespoons of salt and 1–2 pounds more weight. Gently turn the ume in the plastic bag so they get an even coating of brine. Twist the top of the bag and return the ume to the container. Once the ume is submerged in the brine, remove the weight and leave the bagged ume in the container for a month in a cool place.

After a month, take the ume out of the bag and reserve the brine/vinegar in a jar. This vinegar is called umezu, and it makes a wonderful base for salad dressings. Spread the ume on bamboo mats and place them in the sun. You can cover them with a screen to keep the bugs out. Dry them for 3 days in a row or until the surface of the fruit turns slightly white. The plum vinegar in the pickling container should also get time in the sun, about the same amount of time as the plums.

At the end of each day, place the sunbathed ume back in the jar with the sunbathed plum vinegar, and bring the ume back out the next day. After 3 days, place the plums in a clean jar and store the umeboshi and the vinegar in separate containers in a cool, dark place. The plums can be eaten after 10 days or so, but it is good to wait for a few months to a year or longer for better flavor. The traditional umeboshi is made with a much higher salt ratio of 18–20 percent of the weight of the ume, which allows for a much longer shelf life than modern umeboshi. Centenarian umeboshi exists in the form of shriveled crystals. I have a collection of several small jars of my late grandmother's umeboshi that date back to the 1960s that I treasure. Store-bought umeboshi should be eaten within 3 to 6 months.

Variation You can enhance the color and flavor of umeboshi with red shiso leaves. You will need about 1 pound (400 grams) fresh red shiso leaves, which is equivalent to 20 percent of the weight of the ume plums. Rub 1 tablespoon (15 grams) of salt into the leaves, massaging them until a dark (blackberry-like) juice is extracted. Squeeze and discard the liquid. Add the shiso leaves to the umeboshi container. It will turn the umeboshi and the brine red. The red shiso makes an excellent furikake. Dry the pickled red shiso leaves in the sun or a dehydrator. When the leaves are fully dried, finely grind them in a spice grinder or with a mortar and pestle. Store the furikake in a container with a tight-fitting lid, where it will keep for up to 3 or 4 months. Sprinkle the furikake on rice or salads.

YOUNG GINGER PICKLE

Makes 1 pound (454 grams)

For the Pickles

4 cups (1 liter) water

1 pound (454 grams) young ginger, peeled

Scant teaspoon sea salt

For the Pickling Solution

1½ cups (360 ml) Kombu Dashi (page 15)

1½ cups (360 ml) rice vinegar

¼ cup (50 grams) cane sugar or honey

1 teaspoon sea salt

Young ginger pickle, called gari at sushi bars, is a classic wafu pickle. Ginger originated in India and made its way to Japan via China in the third century, and was first used as medicine and later turned into a versatile condiment that brightens so many dishes. Its pickling solution is made wafu with kombu dashi and rice vinegar. I serve these pickles with various curries (see the Curries and Stews chapter, beginning on page 151) and with Chilled Spicy Ramen Salad with Egg, Chashu Pork, Tomatoes, and Cucumbers (page 251), as well as with sushi, grilled meats, and seafood. It's a nice palate cleanser.

––––––––––

Bring the 4 cups water to a boil in a medium pot set over medium-high heat. Cut the ginger along the grain into very thin slices (about ¹⁄₁₆ inch/ 2 mm). A Bernina cutting tool can be a useful tool for slicing, but if you don't have one a knife works fine. Toss the sliced ginger with the salt. Let it stand for 5 minutes. Rinse it under running water and then blanch the ginger in the boiling water for 1 minute. Drain and let cool to room temperature.

To make the pickling solution, combine the kombu dashi, rice vinegar, sugar, and salt in a small saucepan. Set the pan over medium heat and warm until the sugar is dissolved. Stir in the ginger. Remove the pan from heat. Let the mixture marinate for at least 2 hours before eating. Store the cooled pickled ginger in the marinade in the refrigerator, where it will keep for up to 1 month.

CURRIES
AND STEWS

Curries and stews are now quintessentially
Japanese dishes, but they didn't arrive in
Japan until the late nineteenth century, when
Europeans introduced the practice of eating
meat, along with onions, tomatoes, corn, and
potatoes. Aromatic spices—like turmeric, cloves,
and cinnamon, which are essential for making
curries and stews—had already been brought
to Japan from Persia, India, and China via the
spice and silk routes centuries before the arrival
of English curry powder, but they were still
regarded as precious and medicinal. My mother
and grandmother only kept a handful of spices—
red chili pepper, shichimi pepper, sansho pepper,
ginger, and wasabi—in their kitchen cabinets,
and they used them sparingly.

Curry finds its origin in India (though they
don't call their dishes curry, per se, but rather
have regional names for each recipe), where it
was adapted by the British and then introduced
to Japan in the late nineteenth century as
yoshoku, a Western food. The Japanese have
further transformed the British version into
something that can be called their own, using a
variety of tweaks with wafu flavors like dashi, soy
sauce, and sake.

Classic Japanese-style curry is thick like a stew
and has mostly relied, for decades, on factory-
made curry roux, a beloved flavor and convenient
for the busy cook. But that's starting to change.
I've started blending, grinding, and blooming
spices to make my own Japanese curry powder,
and further enhanced my spice knowledge with
a trip to the south of India, where I stayed with
the family of Asha Shivakumar, author of *Masala
& Meatballs*. It gave me a deep appreciation for
how they use spices and a new perspective on
how deeply Japan is connected to India.

I love stews as much as I love curry. While
the British are credited with introducing
curry to Japan, the French brought their own
distinctive stews. In the late nineteenth century,
French chefs were employed in Japan to work at
high-end official venues, including the official
imperial banquets where they served classic
French food to foreign and Japanese dignitaries.
As Japanese people became accustomed to the
idea of eating meat and adopted Western table
manners, they began to change what they could.
The classic wafu stew Quick Amakarani Beef
and Shirataki Stew (page 169) shows one way
in which the Japanese palate first adapted to

the widespread introduction of beef. Tonkatsu is a wafu adaptation of côtelette—fried meat. When meat first started to become common in Japan, some diners broke their plates trying too hard to cut the meat with a knife and a fork, so someone figured out that if the meat was precut and served with chopsticks, it would be so much easier to eat. Then there is Dry Curry Omuraisu (page 165), a cross between British, Indian, and French ingredients and culinary traditions that came together as a wafu dish.

Other dishes in this chapter, like Wafu Skillet Chicken Pot Pie (page 175) or Anne's White Bean Chili (page 173), are my wafu interpretations, adding seasonings like dashi, soy sauce, and miso, but not so changed from their original forms as to become something else; you can still identify their origins. We call this kind of wafu-ing kakushiaji—secret seasoning.

SONOKO CURRY POWDER

Makes about ½ cup

Whole Spices

1 tablespoon brown or black mustard seeds

One 2 inch (5 cm) piece cinnamon stick, broken into small pieces

1 bay leaf

2–3 cardamom pods

1 tablespoon coriander seeds

1 tablespoon fennel seeds

1 tablespoon cumin seeds

1 teaspoon fenugreek seeds

½ teaspoon whole cloves

1½ teaspoons black peppercorns

⅛ teaspoon allspice berries

Other Ingredients

¼ dried shiitake mushroom

One 1 x 1 inch (2.5 x 2.5 cm) piece dried kombu

Ground Spices

1 teaspoon sweet paprika

1 tablespoon ground ginger

1 tablespoon turmeric

1 teaspoon cayenne pepper, or more to taste

Pre-pandemic, I learned a life-changing skill: how to blend spices and make curry powder. I began tinkering with spices in my kitchen, and soon went from not knowing anything about them to having huge buckets of them delivered directly from India. They completely took over my second bedroom; even my towels and pillowcase turned yellow from turmeric. Indian spice experts like Sana Javeri Kadri of Diaspora Co. and Maya Kaimal of Fine Indian Foods helped me get a small cottage spice business going, and soon I was selling my own curry powder. I am forever grateful for the community I discovered in my search for something more sustainable and delicious.

Nowadays, many Indian, Pakistani, and other South Asian friends come to my curry workshops to eat my curry and prepare curry bricks to store in their freezers, so when they return from their travels or they are too busy to cook, they just pop them into broth with some veggies and make curry. It gives me a bit of a relief to know that we are finally doing justice to their beautiful spices and opening a whole new chapter for Japanese curry, beyond the bastardized version that the British introduced to Japan.

If you go to Japan today, you will find wafu curries available in many forms—spice curry (curries made from whole spices rather than factory-made roux), soup curry, dry curry (fried rice with curry), curry noodles, curry pan (milk bread rolls filled with curry), and curry pasta, to name a few. Curry powder has become a standard wafu flavor, and throughout this book, you will find dishes that call for a sprinkling.

————————

In a dry medium skillet, toast the whole spices over low heat until fragrant and the mustard seeds just begin to pop, about 2 minutes. Stir often and be careful not to burn. Remove the spices from the heat and set aside to cool.

Place the dried shiitake and kombu into a spice grinder and grind on high for about 30 seconds or until pulverized. Remove them from the grinder and sift into a bowl through a fine mesh strainer.

Place the toasted whole spices in the spice grinder and grind on high for 30 seconds to 1 minute. Shake and tap the grinder a couple of times to ensure that all spices are pulverized. Sift them into the same bowl as the mushroom and kombu.

Add the ground spices to the bowl, and combine with fork. Store in an airtight container in a cool, dry place. Use within a year.

SONOKO CURRY SIMMER SAUCE

Makes 2 cups (480 ml)

4 tablespoons unsalted butter, ghee, or coconut oil

1 yellow onion, minced

2 garlic cloves, minced

1 tablespoon minced fresh ginger

3 tablespoons all-purpose flour (or mochiko, sweet rice flour)

1 tablespoon Sonoko Curry Powder (page 153)

1 small ripe tomato, chopped coarsely

2 tablespoons sake

½ teaspoon sea salt, or more to taste

1 tablespoon soy sauce, or more to taste

1 chili pepper (togarashi, Kashmir, or ancho), seeded and minced (optional)

Freshly ground black pepper, to taste

2½ cups (600 ml) dashi of your choice or low-sodium store-bought broth of your choice

1 teaspoon rice vinegar

½ teaspoon honey (optional)

I grew up as part of a generation of Japanese cooks introduced to instant curry roux by the advent of television. Since Japanese people use spices sparingly in their cooking, no one had a clue what curry powder or curry roux was made from, but that didn't seem to bother most cooks. What mattered was that it tasted good. I started using instant curry roux because it was convenient and my family loved it, but as a home cook who celebrates natural ingredients I felt like a hypocrite. Times are changing, though. Now in Japan, you will find not only the standard Japanese curry (karei raisu) but also variations that don't rely on the store-bought roux, which mostly contains artificial flavor enhancers, food coloring, palm oil, and preservatives. This curry simmer sauce provides you with a foundation for using natural ingredients and being creative. It's mild but can be adjusted to suit your palate and creativity. Make it spicier by adding more cayenne pepper or other hot peppers, dry or fresh. Add a splash of vinegar or citrus juice like lemon or honey if the sauce needs more brightness, or honey for sweetness. This will depend on the acidity and sweetness of the tomato. Make it soupier by adding more dashi or thicker by cooking it down so it's more like a stew in consistency. The two curry recipes that follow make use of this sauce.

In a medium saucepan, heat the butter over medium-high heat until melted. Add the onions and sauté until soft and slightly caramelized, about 10 to 15 minutes. Add the garlic and ginger and continue cooking over medium-low heat for 5 minutes. Sprinkle the flour into the pot with the softened aromatics, stir to coat evenly, and increase the heat to medium. Stirring regularly, allow the butter and flour mixture to turn a light cream color but not brown, about 3 to 4 minutes. Scrape the bottom of the pot to reincorporate any bits that are sticking. Turn off the heat, sprinkle in the curry powder, stir to combine, then continue.

To the pot, add the tomato, sake, salt, soy sauce, chili pepper, if using, and black pepper. Stir to incorporate. The mixture will turn thick, almost like a paste at this stage. Return the pot to medium-low heat and gradually add in 2 cups (480 ml) of the dashi, ½ cup (120 ml) at a time, stirring as you go, until it has all been incorporated. Continue to heat, stirring occasionally, bringing the pot up to a boil, then reduce to a simmer. Allow to simmer until thickened enough to coat the back of the spoon, about 15 minutes. Add ½ cup (120 ml) of the remaining dashi or more until the desired thickness.

Use an immersion blender to puree the sauce. Taste and add the rice vinegar and honey, if using, adjusting the amounts as desired. Acidity and sweetness vary in tomatoes, so I like to taste and add the rice vinegar and honey at the end.

The simmer sauce can be used as a base for meat, seafood, and vegetable curries.

It will keep in the fridge for 3 to 4 days or in the freezer for up to 3 months.

KITCHEN NOTE Save freezer space and make what I call "curry bricks" because they look like bricks. (And because I like to think that by cooking with natural and responsibly sourced ingredients, we can help restore our planet brick by brick, one curry pot at a time!) In a small saucepan, melt 3 tablespoons butter over medium heat, then add 3 tablespoons flour (rice or all-purpose) and stir to combine. Continue heating over medium, stirring for 3 to 5 minutes, until the mixture is paste-like in texture. Turn off the heat, stir in 1 tablespoon of Sonoko Curry Powder (153) or other Japanese curry powder, pour into a small heat-safe container, cover, and store until ready to use. Curry bricks will keep in the fridge for up to 1 month or in the freezer for up to 4 months. When you're ready to make a simmer sauce, sauté your onions, garlic, and ginger in just 1 tablespoon of melted butter in a medium saucepan until soft, just golden brown, and aromatic. Add tomatoes, sake, salt, soy sauce, chili pepper, if using, pepper, broth, and honey all at once. Stir to combine, then drop in your premade curry brick, let it melt and dissolve, then proceed with immersion blending. Adjust your sauce with more broth, a splash of vinegar, or other seasonings before serving.

SHRIMP AND TOMATO CURRY WITH MIXED GRAINS

Makes 3–4 servings

For the Mixed Grains

1¼ cup (225 grams) white rice

¼ cup (50 grams) mixed whole grains (brown rice, buckwheat, quinoa, millet, wheat berries, or even adzuki beans)

1¾ cups (400 ml) water

For the Curry

4 tablespoons neutral oil (such as grapeseed or light sesame oil), divided

1 pound (454 grams) large shrimp, peeled and deveined (about 12 pieces)

1 medium yellow onion, chopped

1 medium tomato, cored and cut into ¼ inch (6 mm) dice

5 ounces (140 grams) fresh mushrooms (such as oyster, shimeji, or shiitake caps), thinly sliced (oyster and shimeji mushrooms can be torn by hand)

1 serrano or other spicy chili pepper, seeds removed, thinly sliced (optional)

½ cup (60 ml) dashi of your choice or water, divided

1 batch Sonoko Curry Simmer Sauce (page 154)

For the Garnish

1 carrot, peeled and julienned

½ teaspoon sea salt, divided

¼ teaspoon cane sugar

1 lime or lemon, cut into wedges

1 dozen cherry tomatoes, sliced in half

1 sprig fresh cilantro, leaves only

¼ cup Surigoma (page 6) (optional)

Japanese curry is a weekly staple in most Japanese homes. This version highlights juicy shrimp paired with tomato and relies on my basic curry simmer sauce—made with Japanese curry powder and a blend of spices and herbs—for that warm, umami-rich flavor. Japanese curry is always served with a tasty, pickled condiment like the cucumber and radish pickles that I suggest in this recipe, but anything from the Pickles recipe section (beginning on page 137) would work well.

———————

In a medium bowl, rinse the rice and other grains or beans under cool running water for about 30 seconds. Then drain the water completely using a fine-mesh strainer. Combine the grains and the 1¾ cups (400 ml) water in a heavy-bottomed 3 quart (3 liter) pot with a tight-fitting lid. Let the rice soak in the water for at least 1 hour and up to overnight.

Put the same pot on the stovetop, uncovered, over medium heat and bring to a boil with the water bubbling around the rim of the pot. This will take about 8 minutes. Cover, decrease the heat to the lowest possible setting, and cook, without lifting the lid to peek, for 17 minutes. Remove from the heat and, without opening the lid, let the rice rest for 10 minutes. Remove the lid and gently fluff the rice with a rice paddle or wooden spoon. Replace the lid and allow it to rest for another 5 minutes. The rice will keep fresh for 1 day. It will harden if you refrigerate or freeze it. Japanese cooks use the microwave or a steamer to soften hardened rice.

To make the curry, heat 2 tablespoons of the oil in a medium saucepan set over medium-high heat. Add the shrimp and cook until they just begin to turn pink and opaque, about 2 minutes. Remove the shrimp from the pan and set aside.

Add the 2 remaining tablespoons of oil to the pan, add the onions, and cook over low heat until softened and caramelized, about 15 minutes. Add the tomatoes, mushrooms, and chili pepper (if using) and simmer for 10 minutes. Add ¼–½ cup dashi or water, as needed, if you like a soupier curry sauce.

Add the simmer sauce and increase the heat to medium-high. Bring to a boil. Once boiling, lower the heat of the simmer sauce, add the shrimp, and cook for 3 to 4 minutes. You can thin the curry with the remaining water or more dashi as needed. ▸

To prepare the garnishes, rub the shredded carrots with ¼ teaspoon of the salt and the sugar. Let stand in a small bowl for 5 minutes. Squeeze out excess water and squeeze on some lime juice. Serve as a quick pickle.

Place the sliced cherry tomatoes in a bowl and serve straight or with a sprinkle of the remaining salt.

Serve the curry with the mixed grains and garnish with sliced cherry tomatoes, carrot pickle, lime wedges, and cilantro. Sprinkle with surigoma, if you like.

EGGPLANT KATSU CURRY WITH A SEVEN-MINUTE EGG

Makes 3–4 servings

For the Curry

3 cups (720 ml) rice bran oil, peanut oil, grapeseed oil, or light sesame oil

1¼ pounds (560 grams) Japanese or Chinese eggplants (3–4 eggplants)

½ teaspoon sea salt

Freshly ground black pepper, to taste

For the Egg Batter

1 scant cup (114 grams) cake flour plus ¼ cup for dusting the eggplant

1 large egg, beaten

1 scant cup ice-cold water

2 cups (180 grams) panko breadcrumbs

For Serving

1 batch Sonoko Curry Simmer Sauce (page 154)

Kombu Dashi (page 15) or water

8 ounces (230 grams) shredded cabbage, chicory, lettuce, arugula

½ lemon or lime, cut into wedges

1 batch Basic White Rice (page 163) or Basic Brown Rice (page 164)

¼ cup chopped fresh parsley, cilantro, or chives, for garnish

4 radishes, sliced into ⅛ inch (3 mm) coins

Homemade Tonkatsu Sauce (page 197) or store-bought tonkatsu sauce (optional)

4 Seven-Minute Eggs (see page 265) (optional)

This eggplant katsu is perfect for non-meat eaters. It's a variation of Katsu Curry (Pork Cutlet with Curry Sauce) (see the end of this recipe), tender and meaty inside and crispy outside. I discovered that coating the eggplant in a tempura batter and finishing it with panko crumbs does the trick. I also serve the fried eggplants as an appetizer or side dish with curry sauce, tonkatsu sauce, or soy sauce to dip them in, and some lemon wedges.

———————

To make the eggplant cutlets, pour the oil into a 2 quart (2 liter) cast-iron Dutch oven or heavy-bottomed pot. The oil should be about 1½ inches (3.5 cm) deep. Heat over medium heat until the oil reaches 350°F (176°C). Maintain the temperature by checking it with a thermometer.

Trim off the stems of the eggplants and cut each eggplant crosswise into 1 inch (2.2 cm) pieces. Salt and pepper the cut side and let stand in a bowl for 10 minutes. Then wipe off the moisture with a paper towel or clean dishcloth.

Line up three medium shallow bowls. Place ¼ cup of flour for dusting the eggplant in one. Combine the egg and water in the second, stir with a whisk, add the scant cup of cake flour to the bowl, and whisk four or five times. Do not overmix. Place the panko in the third bowl. Take one piece of eggplant and dip it first into the flour. Give it a pat with your hands and then dip it into the egg batter and shake to remove any excess. Finally, dip the battered eggplant into the panko to generously coat. Set it on a sheet tray. Repeat with the remaining pieces of eggplant.

You are now ready to start frying. Test the temperature of the oil by dropping in a few panko crumbs. If the crumbs sizzle up instantly but do not burn, the temperature is right for frying. Add three pieces of eggplant to the oil and cook for 3 to 4 minutes, until they are lightly browned on one side. Flip and fry for another 3 to 4 minutes, until lightly browned on the second side. The timing will depend on the thickness of the eggplant and the temperature of the oil. Test for doneness by taking one eggplant out of the oil when it is lightly browned on both sides and do a toothpick test or slice it in half to check doneness. You want your eggplant katsu to be tender but not mushy. Drain the fried eggplant on a paper › towel–lined sheet tray to remove excess oil. Continue working in batches to fry the remaining eggplant.

To serve, heat the curry sauce in a medium saucepan over medium-low heat until it begins to simmer, about 3 to 4 minutes. Add ¼–½ cup of dashi or water, as needed, if you prefer a soupier curry sauce.

Serve the eggplant cutlet over the shredded cabbage with the lemon or lime wedges, heated curry sauce, and a bowl of fresh-cooked rice on the side with a sprinkle of fresh herbs. Garnish with sliced radishes and serve with tonkatsu sauce, if you wish. (Purists don't use it, but I've included it anyway because my kitchen assistants love it.) For a slightly richer dish, add one seven-minute egg to the top of each serving.

Katsu Curry

Pork Cutlet with Curry Sauce

Trim the fat around the edges of 4 pork chops (about 1½ pounds/ 680 grams). Pound the pork chops with a meat mallet to slightly flatten them and rub with salt and pepper. You are now ready to start frying. Line up three small shallow bowls: one with ¼ cup flour, one with 2 beaten eggs, and one with 3 cups of panko. Take one pork chop and lightly flour it on both sides, patting to remove excess flour. Dip the chop into the egg mixture, then coat it generously with panko. Repeat with the remaining chops. Follow the eggplant recipe for frying the chops. The chops will take 3 to 4 minutes on each side. Cook until lightly brown on both sides. Test for doneness by taking one chop out of the oil and slicing it; it should not be pink inside. Be careful not to overcook the chop. Your cutlets will continue to cook after they are removed from the oil. Slice the chop crosswise about ¾ inch/2 cm thick and serve over shredded cabbage, the lemon or lime wedges, tonkatsu sauce, and curry sauce.

BASIC WHITE RICE

Makes about 5 cups (600 grams)

1½ cups (300 grams)
medium-grain or
short-grain white rice

1¾ cups (400 ml) water

Put the rice in a fine mesh strainer and rinse under cold running water for about 30 seconds. Drain the starchy water completely. Combine the measured water and rice in a heavy-bottomed 2 quart pot with a tight-fitting lid. Let the rice soak in the water for at least 30 minutes and up to overnight.

Put the pot on the stovetop, uncovered, over medium heat and bring to a boil with water bubbling vigorously around the rim of the pot. This will take about 7 minutes. Cover, decrease the heat to the lowest possible setting, and cook, without lifting the lid to peek, for about 15 minutes.

Remove from the heat and, without opening the lid, let the rice rest for 15 minutes. Remove the lid and gently fluff the rice with a rice paddle or wooden spoon. Replace the lid and allow the rice to rest for another 5 minutes.

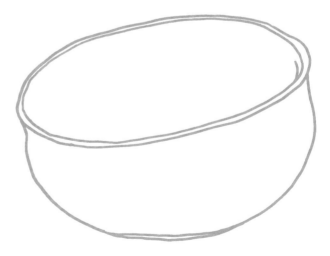

BASIC BROWN RICE

Makes about 5 cups (600 grams)

1½ cups (300 grams) short-grain
or medium-grain brown rice

2½ cups (600 ml) water

¼ teaspoon sea salt

Put the rice in a fine mesh strainer and rinse under cold water for 30 seconds. Drain the water completely.

Combine rice, measured water, and salt in a heavy-bottomed 2 quart pot with a tight-fitting lid. Let the rice soak at room temperature for 6 hours or up to overnight.

Put the pot on the stovetop, uncovered, over medium heat and bring to a boil with the water bubbling rigorously around the rim of the pot. This will take about 7 minutes. Cover, decrease the heat to the lowest setting, and cook, without lifting the lid to peek, for about 40 minutes.

Remove from the heat and, without opening the lid, let the rice rest for 15 minutes. Remove the lid and gently fluff the rice with a rice paddle or wooden spoon. Replace the lid and allow the rice to rest for another 5 minutes.

DRY CURRY OMURAISU

Makes 4 servings

For the Dry Curry

2 tablespoons vegetable oil

1 tablespoon butter

½ yellow onion, cut into ¼ inch (6 mm) dice

2 chicken thighs, skin on, cut into ½ inch (1.25 cm) dice

1 tablespoon Sonoko Curry Powder (page 153) or store-bought Japanese curry powder, plus more to taste

1 green bell pepper, cut into ¼ inch (6 mm) dice

1 cup corn (150 grams) kernels (fresh or frozen)

½ cup (85 grams) peas (fresh or frozen)

½ teaspoon sea salt, plus more to taste

Freshly ground black pepper, to taste

3 tablespoons ketchup, or more to taste

1 tablespoon soy sauce, or more to taste

1 batch freshly cooked Basic White Rice (page 163) or Basic Brown Rice (page 164)

For the Omuraisu

8 eggs, divided

¼ cup (60 ml) whole milk or heavy cream, divided

1 teaspoon sea salt, divided

4 tablespoons neutral oil

Ketchup, for serving

Sprig of fresh parsley, for garnish

Dry curry gets its name because it is not saucy like regular Japanese curry, which descended from British-style curries. It is delicious on its own but even better as omuraisu, with the curry wrapped in an omelet. I provide both versions below.

Omuraisu is not something I make at home a lot, but my kitchen assistant Kali kept saying we should make it, so we did, and it turned out that Kali was the best omuraisu maker, so she gets credited for this pretty and delicious version.

——————

To make the dry curry, heat the oil and butter in a frying pan over medium-high heat. Add the onions and sauté until softened, about 2 minutes. Add the chicken and continue sautéing for 3 minutes. Lower the heat, add the curry powder, and mix it evenly into the meat mixture. Then add the green peppers, corn, and peas. Season with salt, ground pepper, ketchup, and soy sauce.

Add the rice all at once and stir-fry to rapidly combine with the meat mixture.

(If you are serving as a dry curry, rather than as omuraisu, transfer the rice to individual plates or bowls.)

If you are making omuraisu, whisk together 2 eggs, 1 tablespoon of milk, and ¼ teaspoon of salt in a small bowl. Heat an 8 inch nonstick frying pan over medium-low heat with 1 tablespoon of oil, using a paper towel to wipe out the excess. Add the egg mixture to the frying pan in an even layer. Gently stir the batter to create small curds, being careful not to leave any holes or gaps in the egg in the pan. The heat should be low enough that you have time to move the curds and settle the runny egg back into any holes. Place 1 cup of still-piping-hot chicken dry curry in the center of the still slightly runny omelet. The rice should be shaped like a long narrow oval, with slightly pinched ends. With the omelet still soft, gently fold the two empty sides over the length of the rice to meet in the top middle.

Now, here comes the tricky part: gently slide the stuffed, folded omelet to one edge of the frying pan and carefully turn it out onto a serving plate. You want to flip it over as you turn it out, so the seam on top ends up underneath. With the omelet still hot, you can use a clean kitchen towel to gently mold and shape the omelet to your liking to be more › symmetrical and taut. Drizzle the top with ketchup, garnish with a sprig of parsley, and serve immediately. Repeat three more times, with the remaining eggs.

KITCHEN NOTE Quick cucumber pickles go very well with this curry fried rice. To make them, slice 2 Persian cucumbers crosswise into ⅛ inch slices. Rub with a mixture of ½ teaspoon salt and ½ teaspoon cane sugar. Let stand for 5 minutes. Discard excess water. Squeeze on some lemon or lime juice and sprinkle with toasted sesame seeds, if you like.

QUICK AMAKARANI BEEF AND SHIRATAKI STEW

Makes 2–3 servings

One 7 ounce (190 gram) package shirataki noodles, drained

1 tablespoon neutral oil (such as grapeseed or light sesame oil) or butter

1 medium yellow onion, sliced into ¼ inch (6 mm) pieces

1 pound (454 grams) thinly sliced beef (sukiyaki thin; see Kitchen Note)

3 cups (720 ml) Kombu Dashi (page 15) or Dried Shiitake Mushroom Dashi (page 22)

¼ cup Teriyaki Sauce (page 33) or more to taste

1 teaspoon cane sugar (optional)

1 dried chili pepper, seeded and sliced thinly

1 egg yolk per serving, to serve (optional)

Beef was one of the first Western foods to be distinctly wafu-ed by Japanese cooks, when it was introduced in the late nineteenth century, so this is a dish that dates back more than a century. Since most Japanese people had been vegetarian or pescatarian for eons, meat and animal fat took a lot of getting used to. Japanese cooks tamed the meat, tenderized it, and made it taste more familiar with traditional seasonings like soy sauce, mirin, sake, and sugar. One of those dishes evolved into sukiyaki—a hot pot cooked at the table with seasoned beef, shirataki, tofu, scallions, and greens. It is served with a raw egg, which is used to coat the seasoned meat like a sauce. This recipe is like sukiyaki but quicker to assemble for an easy weeknight meal. Shirataki noodles, also called miracle noodles, are rubbery in texture and made from a fiber that comes from a tuber called konjac, a plant that is similar to yam and taro. Shirataki doesn't have much flavor on its own, but it takes on the flavor of ingredients cooked with it: spicy, oily, sweet, and salty.

––––––––––––

In a medium saucepan, bring a good amount of water to a boil. Add the shirataki and blanch for 1 minute. Drain and chop the noodles roughly into 3 inch (7.6 cm) pieces and dry with a paper towel.

In a frying pan, heat the oil or butter over medium heat. Sauté the onions until they become soft, about 3 to 4 minutes. Add the beef and continue sautéing for 2 minutes; add the shirataki to the pan. Then add the dashi, teriyaki sauce, and cane sugar, if using, and bring the liquid to a simmer over medium-low heat for 15 minutes. Add the dried chili. Taste and make adjustments with more dashi and teriyaki sauce, as needed.

Serve right away, with the raw egg yolk on top of the heated stew, if you want.

KITCHEN NOTE Common cuts used for Amakarani include thinly sliced flank steak, sirloin steak, and ribeye, as well as thinly sliced pork. They are cut about 1/16–1/8 inch (1.5–3 mm) thin. They can be found in Asian markets.

FIVE DAL MASALA

Makes 4 servings

1 cup (190 grams) five dal mix or mung dal

4 cups (1 liter) water

½ small white or yellow onion, diced

1 teaspoon minced fresh ginger

2 tablespoons ghee or butter

½ teaspoon whole black mustard seeds

½ teaspoon whole cumin seeds

1 dried red chili (Kashmiri or togarashi)

2 garlic cloves, thinly sliced

2 teaspoons Sonoko Curry Powder (page 153)

2 small tomatoes, cut into 1 inch (2.5 cm) dice

1 tablespoon soy sauce

½ teaspoon sea salt, or more to taste

7 ounces (198 grams) firm tofu, diced into 1 inch (2.5 cm) cubes

2 tablespoons roughly chopped fresh cilantro, for garnish

1 batch Basic White Rice (page 163), or flatbread to serve

Lime wedges, to serve

When I first began teaching Japanese curry–making workshops, I was surprised at the number of Indian people who came. Meena Pennington is an Indian chef and cooking teacher who showed me how to temper spices, a process that really enhances the flavor of a dish. This recipe is inspired by her Five Dal Masala (five types of split mung beans) but wafu-ed with Japanese curry powder, soy sauce, and tofu. It is a hearty dish that can accommodate additional vegetables, like spinach and mushrooms. The flavor of this stew improves when you let it sit overnight in the fridge.

———————

Rinse the five dal mix in a bowl until the water is clear.

In a large saucepan, combine the rinsed dal, the water, onions, and ginger and bring to a boil over medium-high heat. Lower the heat to a simmer and cook until the dal is soft and mushy, about 30 to 45 minutes, and set aside.

Heat the ghee or butter in a large wok or Dutch oven over medium-high heat, then add the black mustard seeds, cumin seeds, and red chili. Wait for the mustard seeds to swell and begin to pop. Add the sliced garlic and stir until it just begins to brown lightly, then add the curry powder and stir for about 1 minute. Add the tomatoes and stir quickly. You want to coat the tomatoes, but you do not want the pieces to break down into a paste. The red chili is there to add a mild smoky flavor and is not for eating, so remove before serving. Add the cooked dal to the wok and add soy sauce and salt, to taste.

Stir the tofu into the dal and cook until the tofu is warmed through, 2 to 3 minutes.

Sprinkle with chopped cilantro and serve with rice and lime wedges.

ANNE'S WHITE BEAN CHILI

Makes 6–8 servings

3 cups (540 grams) dried cannellini beans, soaked overnight in enough water to cover by 3 inches (7 cm)

3 teaspoons sea salt, divided

2 bay leaves

¼ cup (60 ml) extra-virgin olive oil

1 yellow onion, diced

2 yellow bell peppers, cut into ½ inch pieces

1 chili pepper such as jalapeño or Anaheim, seeded and sliced crosswise, ¼ inch (6 mm) thick

2 pounds (908 grams) pork shoulder roast, cut into 1 inch (2.5 cm) chunks

3 garlic cloves, minced

2 teaspoons chili powder

2 teaspoons cumin

1 tablespoon soy sauce

¼ cup (60 ml) sake

1 teaspoon freshly ground black pepper

1 teaspoon dried basil

1 teaspoon dried oregano

1 teaspoon dried thyme

1 teaspoon coriander

½ teaspoon cayenne pepper

19 ounces (560 grams) pureed tomatillos, fresh or canned

1 cup diced green jalapeño or Fresno chilies

5 cups (1.2 liters) Chicken Dashi (page 25) or store-bought chicken broth

1 cup fresh cilantro leaves

1 cup sliced green onions

Every Christmas Eve for nearly a decade, my friends Anne and Roger would invite us to their house in Venice (California, not Italy) for their famous white bean chili, made with pork, beans, and tomatillos. I was in charge of making the cornbread (see recipe on the following page), which always made me a little nervous, as it was the key accompaniment. But with practice, my cornbread improved over the years. Anne is my most constructive critic when it comes to all things American. One year, she asked me to take over the cooking and handed me the recipe for her chili. Like I always do, I tweaked it a bit to make it secretly wafu by adding dashi, soy sauce, and sake. Anne and Roger thought my chili was fabulous, so it is here to stay, and I can say that it is truly Japanese American.

————————

Drain the cannellini beans. Place them in a large pot with enough cold water to cover by 3 inches. Add 1 teaspoon of salt and the bay leaves and bring to a boil over medium-high heat. From time to time, skim off any foam that collects on the surface. Reduce the heat and cover the pot with a lid. Simmer for 3 hours, until the beans are tender and they can be squashed between two fingers. (This can be done 1 to 2 days in advance and the beans can be stored in the fridge.)

Heat the oil in a stock pot set over medium heat, and sauté the onions, bell peppers, and chili peppers for 10 minutes. Add the pork, garlic, chili powder, cumin, soy sauce, sake, black pepper, basil, oregano, thyme, coriander, cayenne pepper, and the remaining 2 teaspoons of salt. Continue cooking over medium heat until the onions take on a golden-brown color, about 12 minutes. Add the pureed tomatillos, green chilies, and dashi. Cover and simmer for 1 hour.

Add the cooked beans with their juices to the chili. Return to a simmer until heated through, about 10 minutes. Taste and make adjustmets as needed with salt, black pepper, and soy sauce. Serve with fresh cilantro and green onions. ❯

Cornbread

6 tablespoons unsalted butter, melted, divided

1 cup (135 grams) Sonora flour (heirloom wheat flour) or all-purpose flour

1 cup (180 grams) yellow cornmeal (preferably Anson Mills)

5 tablespoons (62 grams) cane sugar

1 teaspoon sea salt

3 teaspoons (12 grams) baking powder

½ teaspoon baking soda

1½ cups (360 ml) buttermilk

1 large egg

Sorghum syrup or Miso-Honey Butter (page 50), for serving

This is a quintessentially American bread with southern roots, made in a cast-iron skillet. In order to achieve its coarse, open crumb and natural sweetness, I blend two heirloom flours: freshly milled cornmeal from Anson Mills and Sonora wheat flour from our local Tehachapi Grain Project. I serve this bread with miso-honey butter, or I drizzle it with sorghum syrup made by Chelsea Askew, a farmer friend who lives in Tennessee. Sorghum syrup is slightly tangy in taste, which makes you wonder if it's a distant cousin of miso.

———————

Preheat the oven to 400°F (204°C). Butter a 10 inch cast-iron skillet using 1 tablespoon of the melted butter. Set aside.

In a medium bowl, whisk together the flour, cornmeal, sugar, salt, baking powder, and baking soda.

Make a well in the middle of the dry ingredients and add the remaining 5 tablespoons of melted butter, along with the buttermilk and the egg. Mix with your hands until the batter comes together and there are only a few lumps.

Pour the batter into the skillet and bake in the middle rack for 20 to 25 minutes, rotating halfway through. You will know it's done when a toothpick comes out clean when inserted in the center. For a browner top, for the last 3 minutes of cooking, turn the oven up to a broil and, keeping a close eye, broil for 2 to 3 minutes or until the top is golden brown. Serve warm with a drizzle of sorghum syrup or with miso-honey butter.

WAFU SKILLET CHICKEN POT PIE

Makes 6 servings

For the Chicken Filling

5 tablespoons (45 grams) all-purpose flour

1 teaspoon sea salt, divided

1 pound (454 grams) boneless chicken thighs, skin on

2 tablespoons neutral oil (such as grapeseed or light sesame oil), divided

2 tablespoons unsalted butter, divided

1 garlic clove, sliced thinly

1 medium yellow onion, cut into 8 wedges

1 medium carrot, peeled and sliced into ¼ inch (6 mm) coins

2 stalks celery, cut into ¼ inch (6 mm) slices

3 ounces (88 grams) mushrooms of your choice, sliced into ¼ inch (6 mm) pieces or trimmed and separated

1 small yellow summer squash or zucchini, cut into ¼ inch (6 mm) coins

2 cups (480 ml) Chicken Dashi (page 25), Kombu Dashi (page 15), or low-sodium chicken broth

¼ cup (60 ml) whole milk

2 tablespoons white miso, or more to taste

2 teaspoons soy sauce

Freshly ground black pepper, to taste

½ cup (85 grams) peas (fresh or frozen)

¼ cup fresh parsley, chopped ›

Stew—always chicken and vegetable, never beef, which was exorbitantly expensive—was standard on the menu at my junior high school in Tokyo. When my family moved to Los Angeles from Tokyo, I was introduced to chicken pot pie. It reminded me of the creamy chicken stew from my school days, except for the crust, so here's a recipe that combines the two. My wafu chicken pot pie is made with skin-on chicken thighs, so the chicken fat rendered from searing the meat serves as a flavor base in addition to the butter, milk, miso, and dashi. I use the pie crust recipe in this book, but you can use store-bought pie crust if you like. My recipe makes two pie crusts, so you can use half for this recipe and freeze the other half for future use.

———————————

To make the chicken filling, combine the flour and ½ teaspoon of salt in a medium bowl, add the chicken, and toss well to coat.

In a 10 inch skillet, heat 1 tablespoon of oil and 1 tablespoon butter over medium heat. Add the chicken thighs, skin side down, and cook just until the skins are lightly brown, about 5 minutes. Add the garlic slices and cook for 1 minute without disturbing the chicken. Turn the thighs and garlic once and cook on the meat side for 1 minute. The chicken will not be fully cooked at this time, but don't worry, it will cook when combined with the vegetables.

Remove the chicken and garlic from the skillet and transfer to a cutting board to cool. Discard the garlic if it is brown. Turn the chicken meat side up and dice into 1 inch (2.5 cm) pieces. Set aside.

In the same skillet, use 2 tablespoons of the rendered chicken fat to sauté the onions over low heat. You can add an additional tablespoon of butter and oil as needed to sauté the onions until they soften, about 5 minutes. Then add the carrots and celery and continue sautéing for another 5 minutes. Add the mushrooms and squash and cook for 5 minutes or until they are softened.

Add the diced chicken and dashi, bring to a simmer over medium-low heat, and cook until the chicken is cooked through and the stew thickens, about 5 to 7 minutes. Add the milk and miso and stir. Taste and make adjustments with soy sauce and pepper. Continue simmering for ›

Wafu Skillet Chicken Pot Pie (cont.)

For the Pie Crust

½ pie crust recipe from
Miso Apple Pie (page 281)

10 minutes. Add the peas and parsley and stir to combine. Taste and make adjustments with remaining salt, soy sauce and pepper. Remove from heat and cool completely while you prepare the crust. You can make the filling ahead and keep it refrigerated for 5 days or frozen for 1 month until ready to use.

When you're ready to bake the pie, preheat the oven to 375°F (190°C) and set the rack in the middle of the oven.

On a floured surface, roll out the disc of pie dough (using half of the dough—freeze the other half) into a circle. If you are using a 10 inch skillet, roll out the dough to about 11 inches so it fits. Lay the dough over the filling in the skillet. Cut 3 slits on the top of the dough to allow steam to vent. Crimp the edges to seal. Put the pie in the freezer for 10 minutes. Remove from freezer and lightly brush the top of the pie dough with the beaten egg.

Bake pie for 50 to 60 minutes or until the crust is golden brown. Remove it from the oven and allow it to cool for 10 minutes before serving.

KITCHEN NOTE For the pie crust, and for all baking, I strongly recommend that you measure by weight and not volume. It is best practice to follow the gram measurements here.

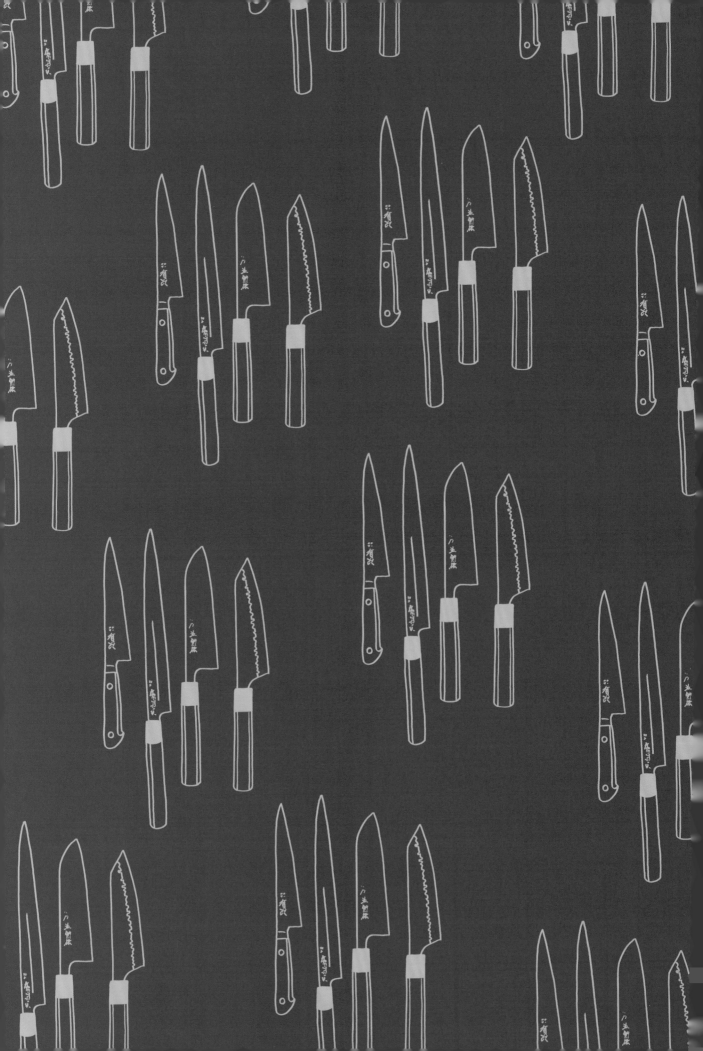

SEAFOOD

I spent a good part of my 1960s childhood
in the city of Kamakura, situated on Sagami Bay,
which is bounded by the Pacific Ocean on the
east coast of Japan. I grew up eating a lot of good
seafood caught by the local fishermen: mackerel,
sardines, yellowtail, barracuda, squid, and
turban shells. I took frequent walks to the beach
with my grandmother at dawn to buy directly
from the fishermen, and she and my mother
showed me how to prepare fish in a variety of
classic wafu ways. As a child, my favorite fish
was aji, Spanish mackerel, which I love in all
its preparations: in sashimi; macerated in rice
vinegar and served on seasoned rice; grilled with
salt; dry-brined (himono); and deep-fried with
a crispy panko crust or tempura batter. I never
got tired of eating aji because it was always so
fresh. On special occasions, like birthdays and
New Year's, we were treated to bigger fish like
tuna and salmon (a whole salmon makes a good
luck New Year's gift) or nigiri-style sushi, hand-
molded by a sushi chef and delivered to our
house.

Many years have passed since my days in
Kamakura. I have made Los Angeles, another
coastal city bounded by the Pacific Ocean, my
home. I still feel connected to Japan through the
ocean. When I have fish and seafood in mind, I
am in pursuit of the freshest, most sustainable
seafood, whenever possible.

My number one sources for information
about seafood are Claire Ito of Riviera Seafood
Club—a seafood company in Los Angeles that
Claire co-owns with her three siblings, and that
is committed to selling responsibly sourced
seafood—and her marine biologist father, Rex
Ito of Primetime Seafood. Rex and Claire are
incredible resources on the environmental
impact of seafood, a subject that's important to
me as a home cook. The U.S. imports 90 percent
of its seafood, of which 60 percent is raised
using aquaculture. Having grown up eating wild
fish, this is a statistic that surprised me. But
talking with Rex and Claire, I feel optimistic;
especially when they mentioned polyculture as
one way to move toward sustainable farmed fish.
I had only heard the term "polyculture" used
by organic farmers and agronomists. Broadly
speaking, monoculture means only planting one
type of crop for maximum yield and efficiency,
whereas polyculture is raising a variety of crops,
either together or by rotation, to restore the
health of the soil. The same is happening in
aquaculture. The regenerative farming of pacu in
Argentina is a good example of this. The pacu is
an Amazonian omnivorous cousin of the piranha

and commonly eaten in Brazil and Argentina. Pacu are released into rice fields after harvest, and they chew through the decaying plants, which cleans the fields and naturally fertilizes the soil. When pacu grow big enough, they are harvested to eat. It's a win-win situation for farmers and fisheries—and for us. Pacu are not widely available in the United States yet, but the Itos are working to make this happen soon.

Thanks to the work of Claire, Rex, and others, we are starting to see more varieties of high-quality fish at the market, both wild and farmed.

In this chapter, I share some of my favorite wafu fish recipes—both classic and modern. The less you fuss with fresh fish, the better. Grilled spotted prawns and mackerel—or pacu, if you can find it—is simply seasoned with sea salt and freshly ground pepper and served with a shiso salsa verde (page 190). My filet of salmon is marinated in shio koji (fermented koji salt); it's a simple rub, but it tenderizes, concentrates the flavors, and gives the salmon a miso-like umami. My snapper recipe (page 198) is perfumed with ginger, scallions, sake, and butter and is an ode to my mother. And recipes like Marine Striped Bass Crudo with Plums (page 183)—a dish that takes us from California to Mexico to Japan on the same plate—represent the cultural exchange that is happening in food today.

MARINE STRIPED BASS CRUDO WITH PLUMS

Makes 2–4 servings

¼ cup extra-virgin olive oil

2 tablespoons usukuchi shoyu (light-colored soy sauce)

2 teaspoons lemon juice

½ pound (227 grams) sashimi-grade striped sea bass or Thai snapper filets, skin removed and reserved (optional; see Kitchen Note)

3 plums, sliced into ⅛ inch (3 mm) wedges

1 jalapeño pepper, seeded and sliced crosswise into ⅛ inch (3 mm) pieces

2 chives, cut into ½ inch (1.25 cm) strips

1 large Umeboshi (page 147), seeded and mashed into a paste, or flaky sea salt (such as Maldon)

Toasted sesame seeds or crumbled grilled fish skin (optional; see Kitchen Note)

The first time I tried crudo, I thought it was an Italian take on sashimi, because they are both made with super-fresh sashimi-grade fish. But apparently crudo is not derived from sashimi—it finds its origins in Italy and Spain. Sashimi is served simply, with soy sauce or sea salt and yakumi, like wasabi paste or grated ginger, on the side. Crudo, on the other hand, is dressed with olive oil, lemon juice, herbs, and flaky sea salt. Perhaps crudo is a bit more relaxed than sashimi. Whatever the difference, usuzukuri—the wafer-thin-cut method of sashimi (see box)—works well for both.

In a small bowl, combine the olive oil, soy sauce, and lemon juice, and mix well. Set aside.

Cut the fish filet wafer thin, using the usuzukuri method (see box). Arrange the slices in a circular pattern on a chilled plate. Garnish with plum wedges.

Top with the dressing, garnish with the jalapeño and chives, and dot with umeboshi paste or sprinkle with salt, to taste. Sprinkle with toasted sesame seeds or crumbled grilled fish skin and serve immediately.

KITCHEN NOTE You can make a crispy, delicious chip using the discarded skin of the fish. Baste it with some olive oil, put it on aluminum foil, and grill it until the skin turns brown and crispy. Raise it from the pan or grill with a spatula. Crumble and sprinkle over the crudo. Eat right away.

Usuzukuri (Wafer-Thin-Cut) Method

You can use this method with firm fish such as striped bass, Thai snapper, and flounder. Place the filet lengthwise on a clean cutting board. The narrow end should be facing toward you. Tilt the knife toward the thick part of the filet and slice as thinly as possible, drawing the knife from base to tip in one single motion, cutting across the grain.

CEVICHE

Makes about 4–6 servings

1 pound (454 grams) very fresh sashimi-grade skinless fish filets, cut into ½ inch (1.25 cm) cubes or slightly smaller (you can use rock cod, snapper, halibut, striped bass, flounder, halibut, mahi-mahi, or even scallops)

1 small red onion, chopped into ¼ inch (6 mm) dice

¾ cup (180 ml) freshly squeezed lime juice

¾ cup (180 ml) freshly squeezed lemon juice

¼ cup (60 ml) freshly squeezed orange juice

1 small tomato, cut into ¼ inch (6 mm) dice

1 Persian cucumber, cut into ¼ inch (6 mm) dice

2 jalapeño, serrano, or habanero (very spicy!) peppers, stemmed, de-seeded, and minced

¼ cup fresh shiso or cilantro, leaves and soft stems, chopped, plus more reserved for garnish

1 tablespoon light sesame oil or olive oil

1 ounce (28 grams) ginger, to make 1 teaspoon grated ginger juice

2 teaspoons usukuchi shoyu (light-colored soy sauce)

Freshly ground black pepper, to taste

Sea salt, to taste

½ ripe avocado, pitted, peeled, and cut into ¼ inch (6 mm) cubes, to garnish

Tortilla chips, for serving

When I was growing up, my family took trips down to Baja California every summer. There was plenty of good seafood to catch and eat, especially as ceviche. Years later, I had Peruvian ceviche in Lima when I was there teaching Japanese home cooking to the Morioka family. They took me to El Encuentro Otani, a cevicheria run by a Japanese-Peruvian chef. He was in his eighties but still went to the fish market every morning to pick out the freshest fish himself. I asked him what the secret of his longevity was, and he smiled and answered me in Japanese, "Shigoto"—"work"—and then he pointed to the open can of beer next to the kitchen counter. Work and beer. The ceviche was fresh and delicious, served with choclo (large corn), corn nuts, plantains, and sweet potatoes, as is traditional in Peru. I heard that Chef Otani passed away, but now his son, Jose Luis, is in charge. My ceviche is a wafu riff on both the Mexican and Peruvian traditions, using soy sauce and ginger juice as part of the seasoning and shiso as a fresh garnish. I salute Chef Otani with some beer and ceviche.

Mix the diced fish with the onions and citrus juices in a medium bowl and refrigerate to marinate and "cook" for 30 minutes to an hour, stirring gently every 15 minutes.

Combine the tomatoes, cucumbers, peppers, shiso, and sesame or olive oil with the fish. Season with the ginger juice, soy sauce, and black pepper. Taste and adjust with salt as needed. Serve the ceviche in a bowl or platter and garnish with avocado and more shiso and serve with tortilla chips.

TUNA CRUDO CHIRASHI SUSHI

Makes 3–4 servings

For the Tuna
1 pound (454 grams) sashimi-grade tuna

2 teaspoons sake

1 tablespoon mirin

2 tablespoons soy sauce

¼ cup (60 ml) olive oil

1 ounce (28 grams) ginger, to make 1 teaspoon grated ginger juice

For the Rice
Basic White Rice (page 163)

For the Sushi Vinegar
¼ cup (60 ml) rice vinegar

2 tablespoons (25 grams) cane sugar

2 teaspoons sea salt

For the Garnishes
2 ounces (56 grams) ginger, peeled and minced finely

¼ cup toasted sesame seeds, divided

12 fresh shiso leaves, or parsley

2 cups (50 grams) mitsuba leaves or micro sprouts (such as daikon radish, chives, basil, or beets)

1 sheet dried nori seaweed, cut into ⅛ x 2 inch (3 mm x 5 cm) strips (keep in a airtight container until ready to use)

1 lemon, sliced thinly crosswise (optional)

This recipe is inspired by tekone sushi from the Mie region, along the Pacific coast. Tekone, meaning "to mix by hand," is derived from the simple recipe busy fishermen used for making sushi with tuna, or other meaty sashimi-grade fish like bonito, where the filet of fish is briefly marinated in a soy-mirin tare. Here, I make a modern wafu version of tekone sushi by adding olive oil to the tare. The tuna crudo is served on top of sushi rice scattered with sesame seeds, herbs, and minced ginger. It's finished with nori—just before serving, so the nori strips remain crispy. It's a colorful and joyful dish that can be enjoyed all year round.

On a clean cutting board, slice the tuna sashimi into ¼ inch (6 mm) pieces, across the grain, following the hirazukuri method (page 187).

Combine the sake and mirin in a small pot. Bring the mixture to a boil over low heat and cook for about a minute. Remove from heat and let cool. Add the soy sauce, olive oil, and ginger juice and stir. Put the sashimi in the soy-mirin mixture for 10 minutes. Cover with a paper towel and keep in the refrigerator.

Transfer your freshly cooked rice into a large bowl or handai (wooden rice tub).

While the rice is resting, make the sushi vinegar. Combine the rice vinegar, sugar, and salt in a small bowl and mix with a whisk until the granules are dissolved. Combine the freshly cooked warm rice with the sushi vinegar. Tilt the paddle or rubber spatula at an angle to gently toss and mix the rice, being careful not to squash the grains. Add the minced ginger, 3 tablespoons of the sesame seeds, and the shiso leaves and mix gently to combine. Spread the seasoned sushi rice onto a serving platter.

Remove the tuna from the marinade and arrange on the seasoned rice. Garnish with mitsuba leaves, the remaining sesame seeds, nori, and lemon slices, if using. Serve immediately. For the best flavor and freshness, sushi should be eaten right away and not refrigerated.

Variation Add sliced avocado and cooked asparagus, cut into 2 inch (5 cm) pieces, after the tuna has been added.

Slicing Sashimi

Hirazukuri (the basic cut): This technique can be used on any type of fish. It is a rectangular cut, which makes slices measuring from ⅜ inch (1 cm) to ½ inch (12 mm). Put the filet lengthwise on a clean cutting board. The narrow end of the filet should be facing toward you. Draw the knife from the end closest to you to the tip in one single motion, slicing through the filet without much pressure other than the weight of the knife. Slice each piece about ⅜ inch (1 cm) thick. The firmer the fish, the thinner it can be cut. Soft-fleshed fish such as tuna should be cut rather thick, about ½ inch (12 mm). Occasionally wipe the knife with a well-wrung damp cloth to remove the fish oil.

GRILLED SEAFOOD WITH SHISO SALSA VERDE

Makes 6 servings

For the Shiso Salsa Verde (makes about 1 cup/240 ml)

1 cup (18 grams) fresh shiso leaves

1 cup (18 grams) fresh basil or parsley, leaves only

2 tablespoons capers

4 anchovy filets, drained

1 garlic clove

¾ cup (180 ml) extra-virgin olive oil

½ lemon zest, or more to taste

½ teaspoon red pepper flakes, optional

Sea salt, to taste

Freshly ground pepper, to taste

For the Seafood

2¼ pounds (1.2 kilograms) assorted seafood (such as halibut, cod, mahimahi, swordfish, pacu filet with skin on, whole mackerel, scallops, spotted shrimp in their shells, or other seafood of your choice—allow about 4–6 ounces per person)

¼ cup (60 ml) extra-virgin olive oil

Sea salt, to taste

Freshly ground black pepper, to taste

Chopped fresh parsley, for garnish (optional)

Lemon juice, freshly squeezed, to serve

Grilled seafood in Japan is traditionally served with a simple garnish (see Yakumi and Furikake, page 3), like grated ginger, grated daikon radish, shiso leaves, a squirt of lemon, or wasabi. The salsa I use in this recipe works in a similar way, emphasizing and celebrating the fish. I like to grill the fisherman's catch—whatever fresh I can get from the local fishmonger—sardines, Spanish mackerel, mahimahi, swordfish, cod, halibut, or whatever else. I was pleasantly surprised with pacu, which my friends Rex and Claire introduced me to. It has a well-balanced robust taste and fat that is perfect for grilling, but if you can't find any, ask your fishmonger to recommend a good fresh fish for the grill.

To make the salsa verde, place the herbs, capers, anchovies, and garlic on a cutting board and mince. Add the chopped mixture to a small bowl and add the olive oil, lemon zest, and red pepper flakes, then season with salt and pepper to taste. Adjust the ingredients to suit your palate.

To grill the fish, start by preheating your barbecue grill or grill pan. Brush one side of the fish lightly with olive oil. Sprinkle with salt and pepper. Place the fish skin side down on the grill. Brush the second side with olive oil.

Cook the fish for about 2 to 4 minutes. Cooking time will depend on its size and thickness. Use a wide spatula to turn the fish over and cook for an additional 2 to 4 minutes. Cook just until you can pull the flesh apart at the thickest point with a fork and flake easily.

Transfer the cooked fish to a plate. Sprinkle with chopped parsley, if using, and drizzle with lemon juice. Serve with the shiso salsa verde.

KITCHEN NOTE Binchotan charcoal is a porous Japanese charcoal that is best suited for grilling seafood and meat like chicken because of its high heat output, long burning time, and clean burn. Allow the charcoal to burn until it's covered in a thin layer of ash before you begin grilling.

SALMON CHIRASHI SUSHI WITH AVOCADO, GRAPEFRUIT, AND HERBS

Makes 4 servings

For the Dry-Brined Salmon

12 ounces (340 grams) fresh salmon, skin on

2 tablespoons sake

1½ teaspoons sea salt

1 tablespoon neutral oil (such as grapeseed or light sesame oil)

For the Sushi Vinegar

¼ cup (60 ml) rice vinegar

2 tablespoons (25 grams) cane sugar

2 teaspoons sea salt

For the Rice

Basic White Rice (page 163)

For the Garnishes

2 ounces (56 grams) ginger, peeled and minced finely

¼ cup toasted sesame seeds, divided

12 fresh shiso leaves, minced (optional)

1 ruby grapefruit, cut into supremes

2 Persian cucumbers, sliced crosswise ⅛ inch (3 mm) thick

1 avocado, pitted, peeled, quartered, and thinly sliced crosswise ¼ inch (6 mm) thick

5 sprigs fresh mitsuba, leaves only (if not available, use shiso, parsley, cilantro, or basil)

Young Ginger Pickle (page 149) or store-bought pickled ginger, for serving

1 sheet dried nori seaweed, cut into matchstick strips (keep in a ziplock bag until ready to use)

Avocado, citrus, and salmon are not commonly used in traditional sushi, but in this modern wafu California recipe, the ingredients shine. Chirashi sushi is scattered like a rice salad instead of molding the rice into bite-sized pieces, nigiri style. Grilled salmon flakes and other toppings, like avocado, cucumbers, grapefruit wedges, toasted sesame seeds, ginger, shiso, and mitsuba—a Japanese three-leaf herb that tastes like a cross between parsley and celery—turn this sushi into a colorful and festive dish. Mitsuba is available year round at Japanese grocery stores and is easy to grow in your garden. If you can't find mitsuba, use fresh parsley, shiso, cilantro, or basil.

For this chirashi, I dry-brine the salmon. I love dry-brined fish. In fact, if there is one thing I miss seafood-wise from Japan, it is the dry-brined fish from Kamakura, where the local fishermen set up racks full of himono, butterflied mackerel dipped in seawater and left in the sun to dry—a dry-brine method called tempi-boshi (sun-dried). Salting fish and letting it air-dry in a cool, well-ventilated place removes excess moisture and concentrates the umami. When I passed the fishermen's storefronts as a child on my way to school, the silvery fish shimmered in the morning light and gave off a pleasant oceanic smell. You can get a similar result at home by dry-brining the fish in the fridge overnight. The salting can be adjusted according to your taste. This recipe is salted amajio style, which is on the lower side, and it is the saltiness that most Japanese people prefer for dry-brining fish. If you want a saltier salmon, increase the salt from ½ teaspoon to 1 teaspoon for each 4 to 6 ounces of salmon filet.

If you don't have time to dry-brine, use smoked salmon instead (see variation below).

The day before you plan to serve this dish, prepare the salmon. First marinate the salmon in the sake in the fridge for 1 hour. After 1 hour, pat the salmon dry with a paper towel. The sake tenderizes the fish and removes any fishy odors.

Line a baking sheet with a paper towel and season the salmon with the salt on both sides. Let the fish rest, skin side up, on the baking sheet. Refrigerate uncovered for 8 to 24 hours. ›

Take the salmon out of the fridge and bring it to room temperature. The fish should feel dry on the surface. Pat the fish with a paper towel if you see any excess moisture.

Preheat the broiler. Baste the fish with oil and place it skin side down on a half sheet pan covered with aluminum foil. Place the fish under the broiler and cook until the meat is opaque and it's slightly toasted on top, about 10 to 15 minutes, depending on the thickness of the filet. Cook just until you can pull the flesh apart at the thickest point with a fork and flake easily.

Remove from heat and let cool. Flake the salmon and transfer it to a small bowl.

Make the rice vinegar mixture. Combine the rice vinegar, sugar, and salt in a small bowl and mix with a whisk until the granules are dissolved. Combine the freshly cooked hot rice with the sushi vinegar mix. Tilt the paddle or rubber spatula at an angle to gently toss and mix the rice, being careful not to squash the grains. Add the minced ginger, 3 tablespoons of the sesame seeds, and minced shiso leaves, if using, and mix gently to combine. Spread the seasoned sushi rice on a serving platter.

Arrange the flaked salmon on the bed of rice. Decorate the rice with grapefruit supremes, cucumbers, avocado, mitsuba leaves, and the remaining sesame seeds. Divide into four bowls. Serve with pickled ginger on the side. If desired, sprinkle the sushi rice with nori just before serving.

Variation Use smoked salmon instead of dry-brined salmon: Put 12 ounces smoked salmon in a dry nonstick frying pan over medium-low heat. When the bottom of the filets turn opaque, flip them over to the other side and cook until they are opaque. Transfer filets to a bowl. Use a fork or your hands to turn them into flakes. Sprinkle on sushi rice and follow the instructions above to make chirashi sushi.

FISH AND LOTUS CHIPS

Makes 4 servings

3 cups (720 ml) oil for deep-frying (peanut, canola, or light sesame oil), or enough oil to fill the pot, about 1¼ inches (3 cm)

For the Lotus Chips

1 lotus root, about 4 inches (10 cm) long, peeled and sliced crosswise into ⅛ inch (3 mm) thick rounds

½ teaspoon sea salt

For the Fish

1 cup (150 grams) rice flour or all-purpose flour

1 egg, beaten

2 cups (180 grams) panko breadcrumbs

1½ pounds (680 grams) fresh rock cod, haddock, halibut, or other firm-fleshed white fish, cut into four pieces

1 teaspoon sea salt

To Serve

Lemon wedges

½ pound (227 grams) cabbage to make about 5 cups finely shredded cabbage

Homemade Tonkatsu Sauce (page 197) or store-bought tonkatsu sauce

Wasabi Tartar Sauce (page 197)

Panko gives a no-miss light and crisp crust—and a wafu twist—to fish and chips. Panko is different from Western breadcrumbs because it is made with crustless white bread, which absorbs less oil and gives you a crunchier crust. In Japan, ebi furai (panko-fried shrimp) and kaki furai (panko-fried oysters) are the typical fried seafood you will find in yoshoku, vintage Japanese-style Western restaurants. Here, I use rock cod, one of the freshest, cheapest, and tastiest fish that is available locally year round in Southern California, where I live. If you don't have local white fish available, use cod, halibut, pollack, sole, or sea bass, which are all meaty and retain their moisture when fried. Or you can use shrimp or oysters.

The "chips" in this recipe are freshly cut lotus root. If you have trouble finding fresh lotus root, potato, sweet potato, parsnip, carrot, and burdock all make good chips. I use one pot to fry the batter-less lotus chips first and then the fish. Authentic Japanese fish and chips are usually served with store-bought tonkatsu sauce, but I often like to serve them with a wafu tartar sauce, which is prepared with hard-boiled eggs, mayonnaise, wasabi, and soy sauce in the mix. Either way, shredded cabbage and a wedge of lemon or lime are essential accompaniments. The chips can also be served on their own as an appetizer.

Heat the oil in a deep fryer, a large heavy pan, or a Dutch oven over medium-high heat until the temperature reaches 325°F (165°C).

To make the lotus root chips, blot the sliced lotus root with paper towels to remove excess water. Deep-fry the lotus roots in small batches, about 4 to 5 pieces at a time to avoid overcrowding. Fry each batch for 2 to 3 minutes, until lightly browned on both sides. Use a slotted spoon to scoop them from the oil and transfer them to a paper towel–lined sheet pan to remove excess oil. Sprinkle them with ½ teaspoon salt while they are hot, and set aside.

To make the fish, first set up your workstation: Place the flour in a small bowl for dredging, add the beaten egg to another small bowl for dipping, and add the panko to another small bowl for coating.

Blot the fish with paper towels to remove excess moisture. Use 1 teaspoon salt to season the fish on both sides. Dredge all sides of the fish in the ➤

flour and pat to remove the excess. Dip the fish into the egg to coat all sides, allowing some of the excess to drip off. Finally, dip the fish into the panko to coat on all sides, and pat to remove excess.

Check the temperature of the oil again. It should be around 325°F (165°C). Gently drop the fish into the heated oil and fry for about 2 minutes on each side or until nicely golden. Remove the fish to paper towels, using a slotted spoon.

Serve immediately with the chips, lemon wedges, shredded cabbage, and tonkatsu and wasabi tartar sauces.

HOMEMADE TONKATSU SAUCE

Makes about ⅔ cup (165 ml)

¼ cup ketchup

½ cup Kombu Dashi (page 15) or water

3 tablespoons soy sauce

3 tablespoons Worcestershire sauce

2 teaspoons dark brown sugar

½ teaspoon freshly ground black pepper

1 teaspoon potato starch dissolved in 1 tablespoon water

Most Japanese cooks use store-bought tonkatsu sauce to season deep-fried foods like tonkatsu and okonomiyaki. But you can also make your own.

———————

Combine all ingredients in a small pot and cook over low heat until the sauce thickens and reduces by one fourth. Taste and adjust seasonings. If you like the sauce sweeter, add more ketchup, sugar, or mirin. If you want more savory flavors to come out, add more soy sauce and Worcestershire sauce. It will keep in the fridge for up to a month.

WASABI TARTAR SAUCE

Makes about 1¼ cup (300 ml)

2 hard-boiled eggs, coarsely chopped

¾ cup (180 ml) mayonnaise

2 tablespoons crème fraîche or milk

1 shallot, minced

3 tablespoons minced dill pickle

1 teaspoon wasabi

1 teaspoon soy sauce

Combine ingredients and stir with a whisk. Taste and adjust salt, as needed.

SNAPPER EN PAPILLOTE WITH GINGER AND SAKE

Makes 4 servings

1 zucchini, sliced into ⅛ inch (3 mm) thick coins

Four 5-ounce (176 gram) filets of snapper, striped bass, halibut, cod, pollack, or other meaty fish

4 shiitake mushrooms, stems trimmed and sliced ¼ inch (6 mm) thick

4 sprigs fresh parsley

Sea salt, to taste (use about ¾ teaspoon to 1 teaspoon per pound of fish)

Freshly ground black pepper, to taste

4 scallions, cut into 2 inch (5 cm) lengths

1 ounce (28 grams) ginger, peeled and julienned needle thin

½ cup (120 ml) sake

4 tablespoons unsalted butter

4 lemon wedges

Cooking fish in a parchment pouch is a quick and easy way to prepare it—a French technique that my mother often used when she expected company, because she could assemble the fish-filled pouches an hour or two ahead of time and keep them in the fridge. When trapped moisture reaches the right temperature, it forms steam, which quickly cooks the ingredients through. The beauty of this wafu version is in the way the fish steams not only in its own juices but also in sake. The sake acts as a tenderizer and removes any fishy odor, the ginger gives it spice, and the herbs and lemon add a lovely scent when the pouch is cut open by each guest.

Preheat the oven to 400°F (204°C). Cut four large squares of parchment paper, about 13 x 15 inches (33 x 38 cm). On the center of each piece of parchment place one quarter of the zucchini coins to form a flat base. On top of the zucchini, place one filet of fish, one sliced mushroom, and a sprig of parsley. Season each generously with salt and pepper, and evenly distribute the scallions, ginger, sake, and butter on top.

To fold the parchment parcel, hold the cut edges of the parchment together. Carefully fold the edge of the parchment over and around the fish and press down on the edges to seal the packet. Fold the corner of each side of the packet to the center, then tuck the sides under the fish.

Place the parcels on a sheet pan and place on the center rack of the oven. Cook for 10 to 12 minutes. Open one parcel to check if the fish is cooked. It should be just firm to the touch and opaque through the center. Refold. (That parcel will be yours!) The parchment parcel should be slightly puffed and browned when it comes out of the oven. To serve, place one parchment parcel on each dinner plate. You may choose to cut open the parcels yourself or serve them still sealed and allow your guests to cut them open. Serve with lemon wedges.

CEDAR PLANK SALMON WITH SHIO KOJI MARINADE

Makes 3–4 servings

Special Equipment

One 5 x 11 inch (12 x 28 cm) cedar plank

For the Recipe

1 pound (454 grams) salmon filet, skin on

3 tablespoons (45 grams) Shio Koji (page 38), pureed, or regular shio koji

1 tablespoon olive oil

Freshly ground black pepper, to taste

Minced chives, for garnish

1 lemon, cut into wedges

Cedar plank cooking was invented by Native Americans in the Northwest. They would tie fish to cedar planks and place them around open fires and use the residual heat from the fires to cook the fish. The cedar infuses the salmon with a gentle smoky flavor and acts as a serving plate. There is no tradition of using planks to cook fish in Japan that I am aware of, but this dish works wonderfully well, with the shio koji marinade tenderizing and seasoning the salmon with a miso-like flavor. The fish can be prepped up to two days in advance, and I always keep a jar of homemade shio koji in my fridge to rub on vegetables, other fish, and chicken (see Shio Koji Marinated Roast Chicken, page 209).

―――――――

Marinate the salmon in the shio koji. Rub the salmon filet with enough shio koji to coat evenly. I use an amount equivalent to 10 percent of the weight of the salmon filet. Adjust the amount of shio koji according to the metric weight of your salmon. Let the salmon marinate in the fridge for at least 8 hours and up to 16 hours.

To prepare the cedar plank, soak it in hot water for 1 to 4 hours.

When ready to cook the salmon, remove it from the fridge and use a paper towel to wipe away any excess shio koji. The salmon should look almost like it was patted dry, with little to no obvious residue from the shio koji rub. Bring the salmon to room temperature, about 15 to 20 minutes.

In the meantime, remove the plank from the soaking water and pat it dry with a dish towel. Place the plank on a baking sheet. Lay the salmon on top of the plank. Brush with olive oil and season with ground black pepper.

If cooking in the oven, preheat the oven to 450°F (230°C). Place the baking sheet with the cedar plank and the salmon on the center rack. If cooking the salmon on a grill, set the salmon on top. Cook the salmon until almost opaque in the center, about 15 to 20 minutes. Finish by turning the oven up to a broil to brown the top of the fish for the last 1 to 2 minutes of cooking (if using the oven) or covering with a lid for about 10 to 15 minutes (if grilling). An instant-read thermometer will read 120°F (48°C) at the center of the filet when the fish is done.

Serve with a sprinkling of fresh chives and the lemon wedges.

SEAFOOD TAKIKOMI GOHAN (AKA PAELLA JAPONESA)

Makes 6 servings

12 littleneck clams

1 cup (240 ml) sake

3½ cups (875 ml) dashi (preferably Kombu and Bonito Dashi, page 20, or Chicken Dashi, page 25)

4 tablespoons extra-virgin olive oil, divided

1 yellow onion, chopped

3 garlic cloves, minced

3 large Roma tomatoes, diced

1 red bell pepper, trimmed, seeded, and sliced into strips, ¼ x 2 inch (6 mm x 5 cm)

1 teaspoon sweet paprika

¼ teaspoon saffron threads

1½ tablespoons usukuchi shoyu (light-colored soy sauce)

1 teaspoon sea salt, divided

½ teaspoon freshly ground pepper, divided

2 cups (400 grams) medium-grain rice (I like Koda Farms), or short-grain rice (Bomba, Calasparra, or Arborio)

12 medium shrimp, cleaned, skin and tail on

½ pound (227 grams) calamari, cleaned tubes cut crosswise in ¼ inch (6 mm) pieces, and tentacles

12 green beans, ends trim and cut crosswise in halves

2 lemons, cut into wedges, to serve

Flaky sea salt, to serve

1 sprig fresh Italian parsley, leaves only, chopped, for garnish

I learned how to make paella while living in Valencia during the summer of my freshman year of college. I rented a room from a widow who lived above an auto shop. As I walked down the narrow street to catch the bus to school, the mechanics would greet me with piropos—flattering words. The widow would stick her head out of the kitchen window and yell at them to leave the Japanese girl alone! I was a bit of a rarity in Valencia back then (this was the early 1970s). One day, the widow showed me how to make paella—the classic Spanish rice dish. The kitchen was small and dark, but I felt like the cooking brought life back into her house.

When I went back to Los Angeles, I tried to recreate the paella for my family. I found many of the ingredients, but we didn't have a paella pan or saffron threads, or Spanish rice, and my parents preferred seafood over rabbit, so I wafu-ed my former landlady's recipe. I used a cast-iron skillet instead of a paella pan. I skipped the saffron. I used Japanese rice (medium grain, from Koda Farms). I made a fragrant shrimp dashi for the stock, using the shells of peeled shrimp, and seasoned the paella with soy sauce and sake. It turned out delicious. I served the quasi-Spanish rice dish with parsley and lemon wedges. If I have saffron and cook it in a paella pan, I say this dish is a wafu paella, and when I don't, it's kaisen takikomi gohan, Japanese rice with seafood. What they have in common is the crispy caramelized bottom, which is called socarrat in Spanish and okoge in Japanese—and in both cases, it's what people want to eat the most.

Add the clams and the sake to a medium pan, close the lid, and bring to a simmer over medium heat. When the clams begin to open, after about 5 minutes, transfer them to a bowl, reserving the clam juice. Discard any clams that remain shut. Pour the clam juice through a fine mesh strainer to remove any residual sand. You can cook the clams earlier in the day and keep them in the refrigerator. Combine the clam juice with the dashi to make about 3½ cups of broth.

Heat 3 tablespoons of the olive oil in a large heavy-bottomed skillet (such as a 12 inch/30 cm skillet) or paella pan set over medium heat. Add the onions and garlic and cook until the onions are translucent, stirring ⟩

often. Add the tomatoes, bell peppers, paprika, saffron, soy sauce,
½ teaspoon of salt, and ¼ teaspoon of black pepper. Taste and add more
salt, as needed. Lower the heat and cook for 8 minutes. Add the rice to the
pan and stir until the rice is coated with oil.

Pour 3¼ cups of the dashi and clam juice mixture into the skillet, setting
¼ cup of the dashi aside. Distribute the rice into an even layer and
bring the dashi to a rapid boil. Simmer over the lowest heat possible for
15 minutes. Do not stir the rice mixture, so you can get that crispy crust
that forms on the bottom.

In a separate cast-iron skillet, heat the remaining 2 tablespoons of oil and
sear the shrimp on both sides, lightly browning the shell. Season with
½ teaspoon salt and ¼ teaspoon pepper. Remove from heat. The shrimp
will finish cooking when added to the paella.

Nestle the shrimp, calamari, and green beans into the rice mixture, close
the lid of the skillet or cover it with aluminum foil, and cook over low heat
for 8 to 10 minutes or until the shrimp and squid are cooked through.
Taste the rice. If the paella looks dry, or the rice is not cooked, add the
remaining dashi to the pan. The rice should be semidry. Put the lid or foil
back on top. Raise the heat to medium for 1 minute to crisp the bottom of
the rice in the skillet, being careful not to burn it. Turn off heat and allow
the rice to rest for another 10 minutes.

Serve with lemon wedges and flaky sea salt on the side. Garnish with
parsley.

Variation Sonoko Curry Powder (page 153) adds a fragrant spice to
the rice.

MEAT

Growing up in Kamakura, I didn't eat a
lot of meat; the city is by the sea, and the price
of meat was prohibitively high. Passing the
family butcher shop on my way to school, I
couldn't help but admire the display of huge
pieces of beef and pork in the glass case and
envy the butcher's sons for being able to have
all the tonkatsu and steak their stomachs
desired. On the occasions we did have meat,
it was special. Once a year, on New Year's Eve,
my grandmother would treat us to sukiyaki—a
classic wafu beef stew cooked in a hot pot with
loads of sugar. (She regarded beef and sugar as
part of the treat; see my less-sweet version on
page 169.) For Children's Day, May 5, she would
make us a juicy yofu (Western-style) meatloaf in
a cast-iron skillet and served with fluffy potatoes
(my recipe for this meal is on page 217). She
loved beef so much that her birthdays were
always celebrated with a Chaliapin steak at the
Imperial Hotel—a tender beef steak marinated
with grated onions named for the Russian opera
singer Feodor Chaliapin, who requested the dish
to alleviate his toothache. It is still on the menu
at the hotel today.

My family started eating more meat when
we moved to Los Angeles in the early 1970s.
We were culture shocked when our neighbor
showed us their freezer full of meat. He told
us that he bought meat in bulk, "half a cow"
that fed his family for a whole year! My mother
was thrilled that our house came with a big
fridge, an oven, and a barbecue grill. While
rice dishes like Salmon Chirashi Sushi with
Avocado, Grapefruit, and Herbs (page 191) or
Seafood Takikomi Gohan (aka Paella Japonesa,
page 203) were our wafu centerpieces when
we had company, we also adopted American
holiday dishes that featured meat—honey-baked
ham for Easter, barbecue for Memorial Day
weekend, turkey for Thanksgiving, roast beef
for Christmas. My mother would always invite
me to take part in styling these meats. Once,
I dressed a turkey in a vest and a bowtie made
of pie dough. I brushed it with egg yolk. I got
a lot of compliments from the dinner guests.
I know cooks who shoo away their kids when
they are cooking, but not my mother. She
always invited us to participate every step of
the way.

These days, my weeknight meals in Los
Angeles are mostly centered around vegetables.
I eat pasture-raised meat in moderation,
alongside vegetables: a wafu hot pot (Pork and
Cabbage Hot Pot, page 221), also called mille-
feuille, its name inspired by the old-school

French pastry; a whole chicken marinated in shio koji (page 209) to honor my meat-loving mother and grandmother. A feast of Carne Asada Japonesa with Two Sauces (page 224) with handmade corn tortillas is perfect for when I want to invite people over for a barbecue. Any time I have a piece of grilled steak or chicken, I always top it with yakumi (see Yakumi and Furikake, page 3), such as grated daikon radish, wasabi, ginger, and herbs, not only to brighten the meat dish but also to aid in digestion. All of my meat dishes team up well with grains, noodles, and vegetables, so browse through the book to look for a nice pairing.

SHIO KOJI MARINATED ROAST CHICKEN

Makes 4–6 servings

One 4 pound (1.8 kilograms) chicken

½ cup (120 grams) Shio Koji (page 38) or store-bought shio koji

¼–½ stick (27–57 grams) unsalted butter, softened, or more if you wish

2 garlic cloves, peeled and left whole

2 sprigs fresh rosemary

8 sprigs fresh thyme

1 pound (454 grams) fingerling potatoes, unpeeled and halved lengthwise

4 carrots, peeled and cut into bite-sized pieces

2 stalks celery, cut into 2 inch (5 cm) pieces

2 shallots, peeled, halved lengthwise

2 tablespoons extra-virgin olive oil

Sea salt, to taste

Freshly ground black pepper, to taste

Lemon wedges, to serve (optional)

Roast chicken is the quintessential home-cooked comfort food, and this one gets a Japanese touch from shio koji—fermented salt koji—the all-purpose seasoning made of salt and rice that has been inoculated with koji mold. (The mold, *Aspergillus oryzae*, is also used in Japan to make soy sauce, sake, rice vinegar, and miso.) Shio koji is like miso's cousin, and it's my kakushiaji—my secret seasoning. When used as a brine for roasting chicken, shio koji adds an umami punch to the meat. It also tenderizes, salts, sweetens, helps retain juiciness, and gives the skin a golden glow. You may wonder if shio koji works better than a dry brine or a wet brine: in fact it brings the best of both worlds. It's a wet brine without being too liquidy; it behaves more like a paste. Once you get comfortable making this recipe, you can try shio koji on other meats like turkey, duck, and pork shoulder. It is wonderful with fish, like my Cedar Plank Salmon with Shio Koji Marinade (page 201). If the skin is getting too dark in some places during roasting, cover the area with a cabbage or lettuce leaf (a trick I inherited from my mother).

A couple of days before you want to roast the chicken, remove it from the package and give it a rinse. Remove the giblets and pat the chicken dry with a paper towel or clean kitchen cloth.

Tuck the wing bones back and rub the entire chicken with the shio koji. Refrigerate, uncovered, for 12 to 24 hours in the refrigerator to dry out.

Remove the chicken from the fridge and wipe off the shio koji with a paper towel. Put the chicken back in the fridge, uncovered, for 2 hours to dry out the skin. Remove the chicken from the fridge 30 minutes before cooking.

Preheat the oven to 400°F (204°C) an hour before roasting.

Place the chicken on a rimmed baking pan. To butter the chicken, gently loosen the skin, starting at the neck and working under the breast. Scoop some softened butter with your fingers and then rub it under the loosened skin, being careful not to tear it. You will use about ¼–½ stick or more of butter, depending on how large your chicken is and how generous you want to be. Rub butter around the outside of the chicken as well. Tie the legs with a string. ›

Put the garlic cloves and the herbs in the cavity of the chicken.

Rub the cut potatoes, carrots, celery, and shallots with olive oil and toss with some salt and pepper. Arrange the vegetables around the chicken.

Bake the chicken for 20 minutes at 400°F (204°C) on the middle rack. Lower the temperature to 350°F (176°C) and continue cooking for 40 minutes or until a thermometer reads 165°F (73°C) at the thickest part of the breast. Check the internal temperature of the meat every 10 minutes, after 40 minutes of cooking. Remember to baste the chicken periodically with the juices, and, if the skin is getting too dark, put some cabbage or lettuce leaves on top so it doesn't dry out.

Remove the string and serve the chicken with lemon wedges, if you like. ⟩

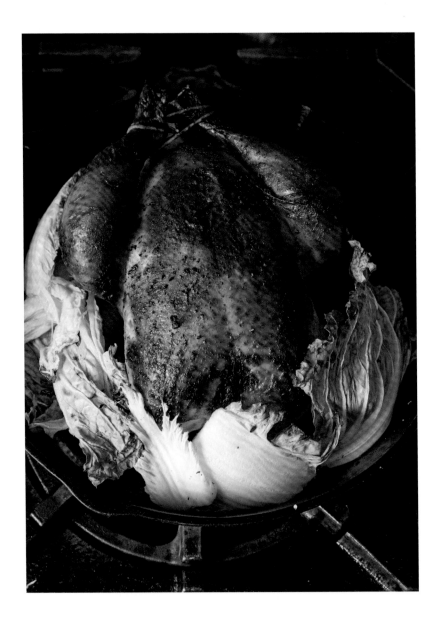

Balsamic Shio Koji Chicken on Rice

4 chicken thighs
(1½ pounds/680 grams),
skin on, deboned

¼ cup (60 grams) Shio Koji
(page 38)

1 tablespoon olive oil

¼ cup (60 ml) balsamic vinegar

1 batch Basic White Rice
(page 163), to serve

4 scallions, trimmed and grilled,
to serve

1 cucumber, Japanese
or Persian, sliced, to serve

Basting balsamic vinegar onto shio koji chicken gives it a layer of sweetness with notes of molasses and cherry.

Pat dry the chicken thighs with a clean paper towel. Turn the thighs skin down on a cutting board. Make ½ inch (12 mm) slits on the meaty side of each thigh, about 2 inches (5 cm) apart. Rub the shio koji all over the chicken thighs. Let the thighs marinate in the fridge for at least 1 day and up to 3 days. To cook the chicken, preheat the oven to broil and set the rack in the middle of the oven. Line a baking tray with foil.

Wipe off the shio koji marinade with a paper towel. Spread the thighs out on a baking sheet, skin side down, brush with olive oil, then baste with balsamic vinegar. Broil until the chicken browns lightly, about 3 to 4 minutes. Repeat the basting and browning two more times at 3- to 4-minute intervals. Allow 10 minutes cooking time on the meat side before you flip the chicken.

Turn the chicken over so it is skin side up. Cook until the skin is lightly browned. Baste with balsamic vinegar and broil until the skin is crispy and brown and the meat is cooked through, about 3 to 4 minutes, and the internal temperature registers 165°F (73°C) on the thermometer. Do not flip again, or the skin will lose its crispiness. Remove from the oven and let the chicken rest for 5 minutes, then slice it crosswise into 1 inch (2.5 cm) thick pieces. Serve with rice, grilled scallions, and sliced cucumbers, if you like.

Noodle Soup with Balsamic Shio Koji Chicken

You can also serve the chicken with cooked soba, ramen, udon, or somen noodles. Prepare 4 servings of cooked noodles. Set aside. Heat 1 quart (1 liter) of Kombu and Bonito Dashi (page 20) or your favorite dashi over medium heat. Season the dashi with ⅓ cup (80 ml) Basic Shoyu Tare (page 32). Taste and make adjustments. Bring the soup to a boil and keep it on a simmer over low heat while you prepare the toppings. Slice the scallions thinly. Slice the chicken into ¼ inch (6 mm) thick slices. Divide the noodles between four bowls. Pour the hot soup on top of the noodles. Divide the chicken into four servings and add to the bowls. Garnish with chives, shichimi pepper, and crumbled nori seaweed. Eat immediately, while the noodle soup is piping hot.

CHASHU PORK

Makes 6–8 servings

2 pounds (907 grams) pork belly, skin on, tied (see Kitchen Notes)

1 teaspoon sea salt

½ teaspoon freshly ground black pepper

2 tablespoons neutral oil (such as grapeseed or light sesame oil)

3 cups (720 ml) Bonito, Kombu, and Dried Shiitake Mushroom Dashi (page 22) or dashi of your choice

1 cup (240 ml) sake

3 green onions, green and white parts, cut into 2 inch (6 cm) pieces

1 ounce (28 grams) ginger, unpeeled and sliced into ¼ inch (6 mm) thick pieces

3 garlic cloves, sliced

2 dried red chilies, seeded

¾ cup (180 ml) Basic Shoyu Tare (page 32)

3 tablespoons Okinawa Black Sugar (Kokuto) Syrup (page 293) or molasses

Mustard, mayonnaise, wasabi, and/or Yuzu Kosho (page 10), to serve

Chashu, also called yakibuta or nibuta, is wafu chuka, or Chinese in origin. A braised pork dish that's been adopted by the Japanese as practically their own, it's that fatty round slice of meat that is used as a ramen topping. It's also a nice weeknight dish enjoyed in Chashu Pork (page 215), Egg, Corn, and Miso-Butter Ramen (page 261), and in Chilled Spicy Ramen Salad with Egg, Chashu Pork, Tomatoes, and Cucumbers (page 251), along with steamed rice mixed into fried rice, and served with vegetables. Chashu is preferably made with fatty cuts of pork, like pork belly and pork shoulder. Look for a slab that has a fairly even distribution of meat to fat and an even thickness. I usually work with a pork belly between one and three pounds in weight depending on how many people I plan to feed. The larger the slab, the longer it will take to cook the meat. It's easier to slice the fatty chashu if you let it rest in the fridge overnight and reheat it—although my students like to eat chashu right out of the pot in big chunks.

———————

Puncture the skin of the pork in several places with a sharp knife, being sure not to cut into the meat. Turn the pork over and score the meat lightly, no more than ¼ inch (6 mm) deep in 1 inch (2.5 cm) intervals. Season with salt and freshly ground pepper.

On a cutting board, lay the pork belly down and roll it up lengthwise into a tight roll, with skin facing out.

Using kitchen twine, tightly tie the pork belly at ¾ inch (2 cm) intervals.

Heat the oil in a large heavy-bottomed skillet over medium-high heat and sear the pork belly until browned on all sides, about 15 minutes. (I periodically rotate the pork belly with tongs to check how the meat is browning to avoid burning the skin.) When the meat is uniformly browned, remove from the heat and discard the fat in the pan.

Transfer the seared pork belly to a large Dutch oven (about 3 quart/ 2.8 liter capacity) and add enough water to cover the meat about ¾ of the way, then add the dashi, sake, green onions, ginger, garlic, red chilies, shoyu tare, and syrup. Bring to a boil over medium heat. Lower the heat and simmer the pork for 3 to 4 hours, turning it every 15 minutes, until the sauce has reduced by half and the meat is cooked. The internal temperature should be around 160°F (70°C). Remove from the heat and let the meat come to room temperature in the sauce. You can slice and ⟩

Chashu Pork (cont.)

serve the chashu at this stage, but it is better to let it rest in the fridge overnight to make the slicing easier. Cut it while it is cold and then heat the cut meat in hot broth or pan-fry it.

Serve chashu with mustard, mayonnaise, wasabi, and/or yuzu kosho. It will keep in the fridge for 3 to 4 days.

KITCHEN NOTES

You can use skin-on or skinless pork belly. The skin-on pork belly will render more fat than the skinless pork belly.

There are other ways to cook the meat. If you have a pressure cooker, the meat will cook much faster (about 30 minutes) and yield very good results. Alternatively, you can stick the meat along with the sauces and condiments in the preheated oven and roast it slowly at low temperature (350°F/180°C) for 2 to 3 hours, then turn up the oven (400°F/200°C) for 30 minutes to crisp the crackling. The internal temperature should be around 160°F (70°C). Remove from the heat and let the meat come to room temperature in the sauce.

Use the cooked sauce to season your ramen broth, if you like.

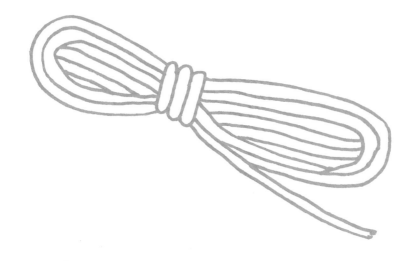

HATSUKO'S MEATLOAF WITH FLUFFY POTATOES

Makes 4 servings

For the Meatloaf

1 yellow onion, minced

1 carrot, peeled and cut into ¼ inch (6mm) dice

1 stalk celery, cut into ¼ inch (6 mm) dice

1 garlic clove, minced

3 ounces (90 grams) panko breadcrumbs

⅓ cup (80 grams) sour cream

2 tablespoons buttermilk or milk

1 pound (454 grams) ground pork

1 pound (454 grams) ground beef

1 egg

½ teaspoon freshly ground black pepper

½ teaspoon sea salt

1 teaspoon paprika

2 tablespoons chopped fresh Italian parsley, to serve

For the Fluffy Potatoes

3 russet potatoes, peeled and cut into large 2 inch (5 cm) chunks

Sea salt, to taste

3 tablespoons butter

Freshly ground black pepper, to taste

1 teaspoon aonori powder (optional) ›

Since beef was expensive in Japan when I was growing up, it was a real treat when my grandmother, Hatsuko Ishikawa, invited us over for a meatloaf with amakara (salty and sweet) sauce, made with soy sauce, honey, and vinegar. She made hers in a round cast-iron skillet and always served it with potatoes, which were tossed in the pan (with the lid closed) to make them fluffy. This recipe is enhanced with a miso-infused shiitake mushroom sauce, my own wafu version of meatloaf.

Preheat the oven to 350°F (176°C). *[handwritten: needs hotter oven or longer cooking time]*

To make the meatloaf, sauté the onions, carrots, and celery in a large frying pan until the onions are translucent, about 5 minutes. Add the garlic and set aside to cool.

In a large bowl, soak the panko in sour cream and buttermilk. Add the pork, beef, egg, pepper, salt, paprika, and parsley to the bowl with the soaking panko. Add the cooled vegetables and mix until just combined, being careful not to overmix. Shape into a round loaf in a cast-iron pan. *[handwritten: make flatter]* Set the rack in the middle of the oven and bake for 50 minutes or until the internal temperature is 160°F (70°C) and the meatloaf is cooked through.

While the meatloaf is baking, prepare the fluffy potatoes. Place the potatoes in a large saucepan with a handle and cover with 1 inch (2.5 cm) of water. Add a pinch of salt and bring to a boil over medium heat. Lower the heat and simmer for 10 minutes or until the potatoes are cooked through. Reserve 1 teaspoon of the starchy water the potatoes cooked in, then drain the potatoes and return them to the pan.

Add the butter to the potatoes while hot and use a spoon to make sure the potatoes are evenly coated. Now, close the lid. Holding the lid with one hand and the handle of the pan with the other, shake the potatoes in the pot until they are fluffy. This will take about two or three light shakes. Open the lid and transfer the fluffy potatoes to a bowl or platter. Sprinkle with salt and pepper, and with aonori powder, if you like. ›

For the Amakara Sauce

1 tablespoon unsalted butter

1 tablespoon Red Miso (page 40) or store-bought red miso

2 tablespoons honey

¼ cup (60 ml) sake

1 tablespoon rice vinegar

1 tablespoon soy sauce

6 shiitake mushrooms, cut into ⅛ inch (3 mm) thick pieces

1 teaspoon water reserved from cooking the potatoes

To make the sauce, in a medium saucepan melt the butter over low heat. Add the miso, honey, sake, rice vinegar, and soy sauce and cook for 2 minutes. Add the sliced shiitake mushrooms and continue cooking for 2 minutes. Add the reserved water from the potatoes to thicken the sauce and cook for 1 minute.

Brush the sauce on the meatloaf and bake for another 10 minutes.

Let the meatloaf rest for 15 minutes covered with aluminum foil before serving. Garnish with parsley and serve with the potatoes. It will keep in the fridge for 4 to 5 days.

PORK AND CABBAGE HOT POT

Makes 3–4 servings

For the Hot Pot

½ small napa cabbage
(2.2 pounds/1 kilogram),
about 8–10 leaves

1 pound (454 grams)
pork belly, sliced thinly

4 ounces (113 grams)
shiitake mushrooms,
stems removed (optional)

4 ounces (113 grams) shimeji
mushrooms, trimmed
and separated by hand into
4 bundles (optional)

2 ounces (55 grams) ginger,
peeled and grated,
reserving the juice

5 cups Kombu and Bonito Dashi
(page 20) or dashi of
your choice

¼ cup (60 ml) sake

1 tablespoon soy sauce,
plus more to taste

½ teaspoon sea salt,
plus more to taste

To Serve

Classic Ponzu Sauce (page 36) or
Quick Ponzu Sauce (page 36)
and/or Goma Dare
(page 223)

1 lemon, cut into 8 wedges

3 scallions, sliced crosswise,
⅛ inch (3 mm) thick

Shichimi pepper, for garnish

Some people refer to this hot pot as mille-feuille, which means a "thousand leaves" in French, but it is not French in origin. Since hot pots originated in Mongolia and China several hundred years ago, before coming to Japan, this recipe is classic wafu but with a modern name. If you can, use quality pork, such as Berkshire pork belly, which is prized for its succulent texture, marbling, and richness of flavor. Mushrooms are a nice addition but optional. Serve the hot pot with ponzu or goma dare sauce on the side. When all the pork and vegetables are eaten, season the remaining broth with shoyu tare and add some cooked udon or ramen noodles. Top with yakumi for a final slurp, if you like. We call this ritual of finishing up the broth "shime."

Lay a cabbage leaf horizontally on a clean cutting board. Put a slice or two of pork belly on top and cover it with another leaf, as if you were making a sandwich. Then cut each stuffed cabbage into three or four pieces about 2–2½ inches (5–6 cm) long. Repeat with the remaining cabbage and pork belly.

In a 2 quart (2 liter) Dutch oven or donabe clay pot, pack the cut pieces into concentric circles, starting from the outer rim and working your way to the center of the pot. Use the thick part of the leaves for the outside and the softer leaves for the inside of the circle. Pack the ingredients as tightly as possible, because the cabbage will shrink while cooking. If using the mushrooms, put them in the middle of the pot.

Combine the grated ginger and its juice, dashi, sake, soy sauce, and salt in a bowl. Stir and add the mixture to the pot. Start cooking over medium-high heat. Remove any foam on the surface with a skimmer. When it comes to a boil, lower the heat to a simmer and cook uncovered until the cabbage is tender and the pork is cooked, about 8 to 10 minutes. (The cooking can also be done at the table on a portable burner or stovetop. If using a portable burner, make sure to have good ventilation or air circulation.) Serve the hot pot immediately. Give everyone soup bowls so they can help themselves and pass around the ponzu sauce and/or goma dare, lemon wedges, sliced scallions, and shichimi pepper. ›

Variation Serve with udon or ramen noodles: Once the pork and vegetables have been eaten, use the remaining rich dashi to make noodle soup. Replenish with more dashi to make about 6 cups. Season the dashi with ¼–⅓ cup of Basic Shoyu Tare (page 32). Taste and adjust seasoning as necessary. Add 2 to 3 servings of udon or ramen noodles and simmer the soup until the noodles are heated through. You can also add a couple of beaten eggs into the mix after the noodles have been added and cook for another minute for richer flavor. Divide into bowls and serve with yakumi such as scallions, shichimi pepper, and Surigoma (Ground Toasted Sesame Seeds) (page 6). This soup is best eaten on the same day.

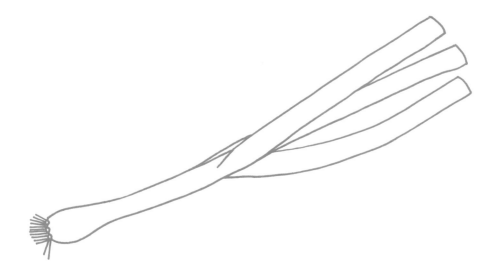

GOMA DARE

Sesame Sauce

¼ cup (60 ml) soy sauce

¼ cup (60 ml) mirin

¾ cup (180 ml) soy milk

3 tablespoons tahini or nerigoma (Japanese-style tahini)

1 garlic clove, grated

½ teaspoon of chili oil (optional)

Makes 1½ cups (350 ml)

This is a thick and creamy sauce made with equal amounts of soy sauce and mirin, soy milk, and a few tablespoons of tahini or nerigoma, Japanese ground-sesame sauce (page 6). If you like a spicy version, add chili oil. Try it on vegetables or as a dipping sauce for soba and udon noodles and in other hot pots.

In a medium saucepan, combine the soy sauce, mirin, and soy milk over medium-low heat, stirring constantly with a whisk until the mixture comes to a boil. Remove from heat and add the tahini or nerigoma, garlic, and chili oil (if using) and mix well. Bring to room temperature. Serve the goma dare alongside noodles, blanched vegetables, grilled vegetables, or poached chicken. It will keep, tightly covered, in the fridge for up to 2 weeks.

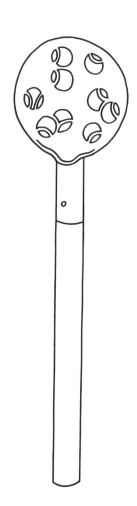

CARNE ASADA JAPONESA WITH TWO SAUCES

Makes 4 servings

For the Guacamole

3 large ripe avocados, pitted and peeled

1 garlic clove, minced (optional)

¼ white onion, minced

1 jalapeño pepper, seeded and minced

1 scallion, chopped

Juice of 1 or 2 limes, as needed

½ teaspoon sea salt, or more to taste

3 tablespoons chopped fresh cilantro leaves

For the Frijoles de la Olla

1 pound (454 grams) dry pinto beans

2 inch (5 cm) square strip kombu

½ teaspoon sea salt, or more to taste

Cotija cheese, for serving

For the Tomato Salsa

2 pounds (908 grams) Roma or heirloom tomatoes

2 garlic cloves, peeled and left whole

4–5 chile de árbol peppers

2–3 green onions, minced

½ bunch fresh cilantro, chopped

½ teaspoon sea salt, or more to taste

I lived in Mexico City during my formative years; the smell of masa tortillas, roasting chilies, onions, tomatoes, tomatillos, and meat on the griddle are embedded in my genes. Even after my parents settled back in Tokyo, my mother, who also adored Mexican food, would ask me to bring back corn tortillas and queso Cotija in my suitcase so she could make carne asada at home. My Mexican and Puerto Rican kitchen assistant Ruben and I once prepared a wafu carne asada lunch, using marinades infused with a simple teriyaki sauce to honor my mother, and also a spicy ponzu sauce made with guajillo and ancho chilies. Even the frijoles de la olla (stewed pinto beans) got an umami kick from a piece of kombu in the cooking water. It was a nice backyard wafu Mexican barbecue in Los Angeles that made me feel perfectly at home.

To make the guacamole, mash the avocado in a mortar with a pestle or use a fork to mash them in a bowl. Add the garlic (if using), onions, jalapeño peppers, scallions, lime juice, and salt. Taste and make adjustments. Stir in the cilantro. Keep refrigerated until ready to use.

To make the frijoles de la olla, first soak the beans overnight. The following day, discard the soaking liquid and rinse the beans with fresh water. Transfer the soaked beans to a pot and fill with water to cover. Add the kombu and simmer over low-medium heat. Remove the kombu after about 30 minutes, and continue cooking the beans for another 20 minutes, until the beans are cooked and smashable. Season with salt. Serve the beans in their liquid in a bowl and top with crumbled Cotija cheese. It will keep in the fridge for 3 to 4 days.

To make the tomato salsa, roast the whole tomatoes and garlic on a comal or in a skillet set over high heat to produce a nice char on the skin. When done, blitz the charred tomatoes, garlic, and chile de árbol peppers in a blender or food processor to reach a chunky, not soupy, consistency. Pour the mixture into a bowl and stir in the chopped green onions and cilantro. Add salt to taste.

For the Chili Ponzu Sauce

2 dried guajillo chilies

2 dried ancho chilies

1 cup (240 ml) Classic Ponzu Sauce (page 36) or Quick Ponzu Sauce (page 36)

For the Teriyaki Sauce

¾ cup (180 grams) Teriyaki Sauce (page 33)

1 ounce (28 grams) ginger, peeled, grated, and squeezed for its juice

For the Carne

2 pounds (908 grams) skirt steak

For Serving

Corn tortillas

Fresh cilantro, chopped

1 bunch red radishes, trimmed and quartered

1 white or yellow onion, chopped

Limes, quartered

Prepare two sauces for the carne asada.

For the chili ponzu sauce, place the guajillo and ancho chilies in a saucepan and fill with water midway. Simmer on medium heat until the chilies are soft, about 20 minutes. Remove them from the water and remove the stems. Place the stemless rehydrated chilies in a blender. Add the ponzu sauce and blend all the ingredients together until you achieve a smooth paste.

For the teriyaki sauce, combine the teriyaki tare and ginger in a small bowl.

Divide the steak into two baking dishes. Pour the chili ponzu sauce over one dish and the teriyaki marinade over the other. Let sit in the fridge for 4 hours to overnight until ready to grill.

Remove the marinated steak from the fridge and bring to room temperature, approximately 30 minutes. Preheat the grill on high—make sure the grill is hot so the meat doesn't stick. Place the meat on the grill and cook for about 4 to 5 minutes on each side to achieve a medium doneness. Alternatively, cook the meat in a skillet over medium-high heat, about 4 to 5 minutes on each side to achieve a medium doneness. Remove the meat from the grill or skillet and let sit for about 5 minutes. Cut the steak into strips or bite-sized pieces and serve on warm tortillas, topped with the guacamole, beans, and salsa, and the fresh cilantro, radish, onions, and a squeeze of lime. Enjoy!

GRILLED LAMB CHOPS WITH LEMONGRASS, GINGER, AND CHILI

Makes 6 servings

2 stalks fresh lemongrass

2 shallots, minced

1 ounce (28 grams) ginger, peeled and minced

3 tablespoons Teriyaki Sauce (page 33)

2 garlic cloves, minced

1 Thai or serrano chili pepper, seeded and finely chopped

¼ teaspoon cumin powder

½ teaspoon freshly ground black pepper

2 tablespoons extra-virgin olive oil

6 lamb chops, ¾ inch (2 cm) thick

2 limes, cut into wedges

During the summers in Kamakura, the part of Japan I grew up in, my grandmother would bring out a round cast-iron griddle to cook Genghis Khan Mongolian barbecue and invite the neighbors. Lamb is the typical protein in a Mongolian barbecue, but since the local butcher didn't carry it, my grandmother would opt for pork, beef, or chicken. The smoke from the griddle hurt my eyes, but I wanted to stay close to the action. During the party someone would retell the legend of Kublai Khan's attempts to conquer the Japanese archipelago in the twelfth century with 4,400 ships and 140,000 soldiers, which were thwarted when typhoons known as kamikaze ("divine wind") destroyed their fleet. I loved hearing these stories and reenacting them in my mind. Today, Genghis Khan barbecue is a regional specialty in Hokkaido, where lamb has been raised since the late nineteenth century. This recipe is my modern wafu interpretation. The lamb chops are marinated in a teriyaki sauce infused with the grassy citrus flavor of lemongrass from my garden.

To make the marinade, trim the bottom third from each lemongrass stalk. Peel and discard the outer layers of each stalk to reveal the tender white inner hearts. Thinly slice and then mince each stalk.

In a large bowl, combine the minced lemongrass, shallots, ginger, teriyaki sauce, garlic, chili pepper, cumin, black pepper, and oil.

In a bowl, cover the lamb chops in the marinade and refrigerate for 1 hour to overnight.

When you are ready to grill, bring the chops to room temperature. Scrape off the excess marinade with a knife. Heat a grill pan over high heat, add the chops to the pan, and sear for about 2 minutes, until browned. Flip the chops over and cook for another 3 minutes for medium rare; an instant-read thermometer inserted into the thickest part should register 134°F (57°C). Transfer to a platter and let rest for 5 to 10 minutes. Serve on a platter with the lime wedges.

Variation Serve with grilled vegetables such as zucchini, thinly sliced kabocha squash wedges, and onions, cooked on the same griddle after the lamb is done. The fat from the lamb will infuse the vegetables with umami. Season with salt and pepper.

NOODLES AND DUMPLINGS

Many "authentically" Japanese foods are, in fact, foreign dishes that have been wafu-ed over the centuries. Among the most prominent of these are noodles and dumplings, which first came to Japan from China.

These dishes, made with flour and water, are collectively called menrui in Japanese. They evolved from karakudamono, an eighth-century savory pastry made with ground rice, wheat, soybeans, and adzuki beans and seasoned with salt, miso, and vinegar, which eventually developed into the form of wheat noodles like somen and udon. Soba, which is made from buckwheat, originally came to Japan from China in the form of groats, porridge, and dumplings, and remained in that form for a long time, because of buckwheat's gluten-free nature—it was difficult to form into noodles when it didn't contain a binding agent like wheat gluten. But with the advent of the stone mill and noodle-making techniques from China and Korea in the seventeenth century, soba eventually turned into exquisite noodles.

Centuries later, after World War II, other noodles and dumplings like gyoza (fried dumplings), suigyoza (soup dumplings), and spaghetti found their way into the Japanese diet.

Chinese noodle and dumpling dishes like ramen, soup dumplings, gyoza, and shumai were brought over by Chinese settlers in Yokohama in the early twentieth century. I grew up in the busy district of Shibuya, Tokyo, in the 1960s, where there were countless ramen and chuck ryoriya—wafu-style Chinese restaurants—one of which was Hayashi, a very popular ramen shop. This tiny noodle shop was owned by the family of my Chinese Japanese schoolmate Hachan. There was always a line outside the shop that often continued across the street. I would go there with my friends and sit at the bar to watch Hachan's father make us his famous ramen. I acquired a taste for good ramen early on in my life. Hayashi uses a wafu blend of chicken and pork bones with kombu, dried shrimp, and bonito flakes in their soups. These days Hachan is often at the shop greeting customers.

Other places I frequented as a teenager growing up in Shibuya were kissaten (coffee shops) and shokudos (family-style restaurants), which created their own takes on foreign ingredients and dishes and offered enticing wafu spaghetti on their menus. These dishes were reimagined to suit Japanese palates, adding a dash of soy sauce to enhance the umami, or using miso as a secret seasoning or incorporating Japanese herbs like shiso, mitsuba, and myoga or pickles like umeboshi. One of my favorite places from this time is an old neighborhood hangout in Shibuya named Kabe-no-Ana (which translates to "hole in the wall"), which is famous for their original wafu spaghettis. I used to go there so often with my girlfriends that we know their menu by heart. Masumi's favorite is kinoko nasu (mushroom-eggplant spaghetti cooked with soy-butter sauce, garnished with nori); Peichun's is Neapolitan (ketchup spaghetti with sausage, onions, mushrooms, and shredded cabbage); Yumiko's is mentaiko (spicy pickled pollack roe spaghetti coated in butter, garlic, and olive oil); and mine is

ika natto (squid, fermented soybeans, and shiso spaghetti), a viscous delight.

I didn't often eat gyoza, the most popular Japanese pan-fried dumplings, until I was an adult. It was something you ordered at a Chinese restaurant, and not what my mother or grandmother made at home. (What my mother was serious about was making lasagna from scratch and her shrimp dumpling hot pot.) When I finally tasted gyoza, it became my favorite dumpling, and I eventually learned how to make it at home. If you come to my house, you will almost always get gyoza for starters, and my friends often request them.

This chapter is filled with an assortment of wafu-ed noodles and dumplings, from soba to spaghetti to gyoza to suigyoza, that draw inspiration from Japan and beyond.

ALMOST LIKE MOTHER'S LASAGNA

Makes 6–8 servings

Special Equipment

Metric digital scale

Food processor

Rolling pin

Pasta machine

Parchment paper

9 x 13 inch (23 x 33 cm)
deep casserole dish

For the Fresh Noodles
(makes 16 sheets of
fresh noodles), or substitute
1 pound (454 grams)
dried lasagna noodles
(not the no-boil variety)

17.5 ounces (350 grams) flour
or all-purpose flour,
plus more for dusting

3 medium eggs plus 1 egg yolk
(178 grams)
(roughly 50–52 grams each
by weight once cracked)

For the Béchamel Sauce

4 cups (1 liter) whole milk,
plus more if reheating

½ yellow onion

3 cloves

5 tablespoons (73 grams)
unsalted butter, plus more
for greasing the baking dish

¼ cup (30 grams)
all-purpose flour

Pinch freshly grated nutmeg

1 teaspoon sea salt

½ teaspoon freshly
ground pepper ⟩

Lasagna was my mother's teiban—her go-to dish—and made with a great generosity of spirit. Hers was a tall lasagna, five to seven layers, with a crispy brown top that we kids fought over. What made it wafu was that she added miso into the meat sauce as a kakushiaji—a hidden ingredient—to boost its flavor, and served the lasagna with rice on the side. When my mother became ill, my father, who had never set foot in the kitchen until then, started cooking, and he taught himself how to make her lasagna from scratch. He wanted to please my mother, and I think he did. I didn't have a chance to ask her for the recipe before she passed away, so I decided to make a version in her memory. I called my friend Francesco Allegro, who runs the pasta department at Rossoblu in Los Angeles, for guidance (he advised me to use lots of eggs and to make it tall, like my mother's). I added a little miso to the Bolognese sauce. Miso serves as the kakushiaji that deepens the umami. I also use mirin in the Bolognese sauce—another kakushiaji that tames the acidity of the tomato sauce. The effect is subtle but definite. If you don't have time to make fresh pasta, use dry lasagna noodles instead. Use a metric digital scale to weigh the pasta ingredients.

———————

To make the lasagna noodles, combine the flour and eggs in a bowl or a food processor fitted with the metal blade. Knead the dough for 5 minutes. Once thoroughly combined and bouncy to the touch, cover with a clean dish towel and allow the dough to rest for 45 minutes to 1 hour.

Set up your pasta machine and evenly dust a baking sheet with flour. After the dough has rested, cut it into four equal pieces. Cover the dough pieces with the dish towel so they don't dry out. Working one piece at a time, use your fingers or a rolling pin to flatten out each piece of dough until it's just thin and narrow enough to fit into the pasta machine at its widest setting, typically about 4½ x 8 inches (11 x 20 cm). Repeat 3 more times.

Begin rolling out the pasta, and run the flattened piece through each setting twice, getting thinner and thinner until the sheet is about ⅛ inch (3 mm) thick. The sheet should be about 5 x 32 inches (12 x 81 cm). Repeat with the remaining pieces of dough. After the 4 pieces of dough are ⟩

For the Bolognese Sauce

1 batch Miso Bolognese Sauce (see Pasta with Miso Bolognese Sauce, page 236)

For Assembly

1 cup (90 grams) grated Parmesan cheese

1 cup (236 grams) fresh mozarella cheese, shredded

rolled out, cut each into 4 noodles, about 5 x 8 inches (12 x 23 cm), for a total of 16 noodles. Place the pasta on your lined baking sheet, dusting each layer with additional flour to prevent sticking. Cover with a dish towel to prevent drying until you are ready to assemble the lasagna.

To make the béchamel sauce, heat the milk and the onion studded with cloves in a medium saucepan and cook over low heat for 15 minutes. Remove the onion. In a large saucepan, melt the butter over medium heat, add the flour, and whisk to combine. Continue whisking over medium heat until the mixture forms a loose white paste, about 2 minutes. Gradually add in the milk, stirring vigorously and allowing the mixture to thicken and warm between each addition. Once all the milk has been added, season with the nutmeg, salt, and pepper. Continue stirring, paying special attention to the bottom of the pot to prevent scorching. Heat until the mixture is steaming hot and thickened enough to coat the back of a spoon, about 20 minutes. Turn off the heat and set aside. Ideally, you should make the béchamel sauce as close to assembling the lasagna as possible. You can store it in the fridge for up to 3 days, but it will thicken a bit. To loosen it up, you can reheat over medium-low heat, add ½ cup of milk, and stir.

Heat the Bolognese sauce in a saucepan over medium heat for 5 to 10 minutes.

Preheat the oven to 400°F (204°C).

To assemble the lasagna, set aside ¼ cup of Parmesan cheese and the mozzarella cheese for the top layer.

Fill a large pot with water and salt and bring to a boil. Blanch the pasta in batches for 30 seconds and then transfer it to a large bowl of iced water to stop the cooking process. Drain and transfer the pasta to a sheet tray. Drizzle with a little olive oil to prevent the pasta from sticking together.

Butter the bottom of your casserole dish.

Ladle a thin layer of Bolognese sauce to cover the base of your casserole.

Put two sheets of cooked pasta on top of the sauce, cover in a thin layer of Bolognese, then a thin layer of béchamel, and sprinkle it with 1 to 2 tablespoons of the Parmesan cheese. Repeat the assembly until you have at least 5 to 7 layers, finishing with béchamel. You may have a little leftover pasta. Cover tightly with foil and place the dish in the middle rack of the oven and bake for about 30 minutes, until bubbly and piping hot in the center. Remove the foil, top with an even layer of the reserved Parmesan and mozzarella, increase the oven temperature to 425°F (218°C), and bake until the cheese on top is golden brown and crispy on the edges, about 5 to 7 minutes. Remove from the oven, and allow to cool and set for 15 minutes before slicing and serving.

To store the lasagna, tightly wrap and freeze for up to 3 months. Thaw in refrigerator and bake as instructed in the recipe. If the lasagna is cold, it may need an extra 20 minutes of cooking time.

PASTA WITH MISO BOLOGNESE SAUCE

Makes 4–6 servings

1 tablespoon olive oil

2 ounces (56 grams) pancetta, diced

1 small yellow onion, minced

2 garlic cloves, finely minced

1 medium carrot, peeled and finely chopped

1 medium stalk celery, finely chopped

2 tablespoons unsalted butter, divided

¾ pound (454 grams) ground beef chuck

¼ pound (127 grams) ground pork

1 cup (240 ml) milk

Pinch ground nutmeg

1 cup (240 ml) sake or white wine

One 28 ounce can (793 grams) plum tomatoes, coarsely chopped, with their juice

1 bay leaf

2 sprigs fresh thyme

3 leaves fresh sage

2 tablespoons miso

1 tablespoon mirin, or more to taste

Sea salt, to taste

Freshly ground black pepper, to taste

1 cup (240 ml) Kombu Dashi (page 15), Quick Chintan Dashi (page 26), or more if needed

1½ pounds (680 grams) pasta (tagliatelle, spaghetti, or rigatoni) or udon noodles

¼ cup (22 grams) freshly grated Parmesan cheese, plus more to taste, for garnish

The classic tagliatelle with Bolognese sauce gets a wafu kakushiaji ("secret umami enhancer")—sake, miso, mirin, and kombu dashi. For an even deeper layer of umami, make this sauce with chicken dashi or chintan dashi. What's not to love? Serve this sauce over traditional pasta or udon noodles, or use it to make a wafu-ed lasagna.

———————

Add the oil to a large pot set over medium heat. Add the pancetta and cook until lightly brown, about 3 minutes. Add the onions and stir and cook until they become soft and translucent, about 4 minutes. Then add the garlic, carrots, and celery, stir to combine, and continue cooking for about 4 minutes, until the vegetables are soft. Cooking over low heat helps bring out the aromas and amami—the sweetness.

Add 1 tablespoon of the butter to the pot and raise the heat to medium. Add the meat and cook until the pink is gone and the water from the meat has evaporated. Add the milk and continue stirring until it has evaporated. Add the nutmeg and stir to combine.

Add the sake or wine to the pot, scrape up any bits sticking to the bottom, and continue cooking over low heat until the alcohol has evaporated.

Add the tomatoes, bay leaf, thyme, sage, miso, and mirin. Stir to combine, and continue cooking, uncovered, over low heat for 1½ hours. Taste. Add salt and pepper as needed. The sauce will thicken as it cooks, so replenish with ½–1 cup of dashi if needed and continue cooking for another half hour.

To serve, bring a large pot of water to a boil over medium-high heat. Cook the pasta according to the package instructions, then drain, reserving some of the cooking liquid. In the meantime, reheat the meat sauce over medium-high heat. Add a little pasta water to emulsify the sauce. Add the cooked pasta and turn off heat. Add the remaining butter and toss several times to combine. Garnish with grated Parmesan.

SOBA NOODLES WITH ASPARAGUS AND SHISO PESTO

Makes 4 servings

For the Pesto

¼ cup (40 grams) toasted pine nuts

40 fresh shiso leaves, stems trimmed, 4 set aside for garnish

3 garlic cloves, peeled and left whole

½ teaspoon sea salt, or more to taste

Freshly ground black pepper

½ cup (44 grams) grated Parmesan cheese

½ cup (120 ml) extra-virgin olive oil, or more depending on your desired consistency

For the Assembly

Pinch sea salt

1 bunch asparagus, cut crosswise at a diagonal into 1 inch (2.5 cm) slices

1 batch Nihachi-Style Homemade Soba Noodles (page 241) or store-bought soba noodles

Grated Parmesan cheese, to serve (optional)

You can wafu any pasta dish by simply swapping the noodles. Soba and udon both work well with pesto sauce. I use homemade soba here, but you can also use store-bought. I make my pesto sauce with green shiso, which is like a cousin of basil but mintier. If you cannot find shiso leaves, use basil or arugula leaves.

———————

To make the pesto, combine the pine nuts, shiso, garlic, salt, pepper, Parmesan cheese, and olive oil. Process using an immersion blender on medium or low speed until your pesto starts to form. Scrape down the sides. Blend again until everything is combined. You can make the pesto a day in advance and keep it in the refrigerator.

Bring a large pot of water to a boil over medium-high heat. Add a pinch of salt. Cook the asparagus for 2 minutes or until al dente. Remove from the pot with a ladle and shock in ice-cold water. Then drain and set aside in a small bowl.

In the same pot, bring the water to boil again over high heat. Cook the soba noodles, two servings at a time, following the manufacturer's instructions. Once they are cooked, rinse vigorously in running water to remove any starch and then drain in a colander. Tap the bottom and sides of the colander to remove any excess water.

To serve, drizzle the pesto evenly over the noodles and gently toss to combine, taking care not to break the strands. Add the asparagus and more grated Parmesan cheese, if you like.

Variations

Serve these noodles cold with Goma Dare (Sesame Sauce) (page 223) or Basic Dipping Sauce (Tsuyu or Tsukejiru) (page 35).

These noodles are also delicious with pan-seared duck breast. The pairing works very well. I serve about 4 ounces (113 grams) per person. Score the boneless duck breast with a criss-cross pattern on the skin, being careful not to cut all the way through the skin. Salt and pepper it on both sides, then let it rest on the cutting board for 15 minutes. To pan-fry, place the duck skin-side down in a cold frying pan and slowly heat the pan over ›

Soba Noodles with Asparagus and Shiso Pesto (cont.)

medium heat. Fry the breast, letting the fat melt, and crisp the skin to a golden brown, about 5 to 10 minutes, depending on the size of the duck breast. Three quarters of the cooking is done on the skin side. Pour out the excess rendered fat throughout the cooking. Flip and sear the meat side for 1 to 2 minutes, until the thermometer registers 135°F (57°C) for medium-rare. Let rest for 10 minutes before slicing. Serve with soba noodles.

NIHACHI-STYLE HOMEMADE SOBA NOODLES

Makes 4 servings

Special Equipment
Metric digital scale
Rolling pin
Ruler (optional)

For the Noodles
¾ cup (90 grams)
all-purpose flour

3 cups (360 grams)
buckwheat flour
(see Resources, page 313)

¾ cup + 3 tablespoons
(225 ml) water, divided

1 cup (130 grams)
tapioca starch

Nihachi soba is one of the most popular styles of soba, with great flavor and good chew. According to one legend, a Korean monk who took up residency at the Todaiji temple in Nara during the Edo period (1603–1868) showed people how to use wheat flour as a binding agent to stabilize the finicky gluten-free soba noodles. Nihachi 2:8-style soba is believed to be named after its ratio of 20 percent wheat flour to 80 percent buckwheat flour. If you care to make soba noodles by hand, try nihachi. When making soba, maintain a beginner's spirit. It takes practice to get your noodles to look nice. I am still at it. It's my soba yoga. You can use soba noodles for all sorts of wafu dishes. Serve cold with dipping sauces like Goma Dare (Sesame Sauce) (page 223) or Basic Dipping Sauce (Tsuyu or Tsukejiru) (page 35), or make a soba salad. Or serve hot with Miso Bolognese Sauce (page 236). Use the metric system on your digital scale to measure the ingredients.

To make the noodles, in a large bowl, sift together the all-purpose and buckwheat flours. Set aside.

Set aside 3 tablespoons of the water and pour the rest into the flour. Using your fingertips, quickly toss together the flour and water until well combined. If any flour sticks to your fingers, scrape it off and add it back to the dough. Continue working the dough until it forms a crumbly mass.

Using the palms of your hands, knead the dough in a circular motion—Wax on! Wax off!—until the crumbly mass turns into little balls. Gather the small balls and shape them into one large ball. If the dough feels dry, add another tablespoon of water. Continue kneading until the dough becomes smooth and shiny with no visible cracks. The dough should feel semidry, not sticky. Press the ball into a disc about 1 inch (2.5 cm) thick. This process will take about 5 minutes. If your dough still feels dry, you can add a tablespoon or two of water and knead until the dough feels smooth and firm but not dry.

Lightly dust a cutting board with a tablespoon of tapioca starch. Using a rolling pin, roll the disc approximately 8 inches (45 cm) square and ⅛ inch (3mm) thick. You want the dough to have an even thickness. ›

Generously dust the upper half of the dough with tapioca starch and then fold the lower half on top of it. Dust the folded dough and fold again, perpendicular to the rectangle you just folded. You should have a stack of dough that is four layers deep. Beginning from the short, folded side, slice the dough into thin noodles that are even in size, about ⅛ inch (3mm) thick, or wider if you prefer thicker noodles like fettuccine, about ½ inch (13 mm). If you have trouble cutting the noodles straight and even in size, use a ruler to guide you. Gently transfer the noodles to a baking sheet, shaking off the dusting starch by tapping the noodles on both ends.

Don't bundle the noodles like you would with pasta or they will break. The noodles are best cooked and eaten on the same day, but they will keep for up to 3 days if you wrap them in plastic wrap and keep refrigerated.

To cook the noodles, bring a large pot of unsalted water to a rolling boil over high heat. Drop the noodles into the boiling water, two servings at a time—not more, to prevent the noodles from sticking together. Cook for 90 seconds for thin (⅛ inch/3 mm) noodles, and a minute or two longer for thicker noodles. Scoop the noodles with a spider or large sieve (not tongs!) and transfer them to a strainer. Give the noodles a vigorous rinse under cold running water to remove any surface starch, then shock in a bowl of ice-cold water. Drain thoroughly by tapping the bottom of the colander. Do not toss the noodles, or they will break. Serve immediately in a basket or plate with the dipping sauce, grated daikon radish, chopped scallions, and wasabi.

STORAGE Fresh uncooked soba noodles keep in the fridge for 2 or 3 days, but for the best flavor, eat them right away.

MENTAIKO SPAGHETTI

Makes 3–4 servings

14 ounces (400 grams) spaghetti

1 large garlic clove, halved

3½ ounces (100 grams) mentaiko (cured Alaskan pollack) (about 4 pieces)

2 tablespoons extra-virgin olive oil

2 tablespoons unsalted butter, softened

1 teaspoon soy sauce

1 teaspoon lemon juice

1 teaspoon lemon zest

8 fresh shiso leaves, thinly sliced, for garnish

½ sheet dried nori seaweed, cut into thin strips, for garnish (keep in a ziplock bag until ready to use)

Lemon wedges, to serve

Mentaiko pasta was invented by the chef of Kabe-no-Ana (Hole in the Wall), a restaurant in my old neighborhood of Shibuya in Tokyo that has been in existence since the 1950s. I used to hang out there with my girlfriends. It's an affordable, unpretentious place that serves an amazing array of wafu pastas. I like mentaiko spaghetti because the only cooking you do is the pasta. You just toss the hot pasta in the bowl of roe, butter, and olive oil, and that's it.

———————

Cook the pasta to al dente following package instructions. Drain, reserving some of the cooking liquid.

While the pasta is cooking, rub a large bowl with the garlic halves. Use the garlic for another dish.

Puncture the skin of the mentaiko and scrape out the roe into a large bowl. Discard the skin. Save 1 tablespoon of the roe in a small bowl for garnish, if you like.

Add the olive oil, butter, soy sauce, lemon juice, and lemon zest, and whisk to combine.

Add the cooked pasta to the mentaiko mixture and toss to combine. If the pasta looks dry, add a couple tablespoons of the pasta water and continue tossing until the broth emulsifies.

Distribute the mentaiko pasta between four plates. Garnish with shiso and nori. Serve immediately with lemon wedges, if you like.

UDON AL YUZU KOSHO

Makes 4 servings

2 egg yolks

⅔ cup (160 ml) heavy cream

Zest and juice from ½ lemon

1½ teaspoons Yuzu Kosho (page 32) or store-bought yuzu kosho

¼ cup (60 ml) Kombu and Bonito Dashi (page 20) or Kombu Dashi (page 15)

1 pound (454 grams) udon noodles or linguine

4 tablespoons (56 grams) unsalted butter

Sea salt, to taste

1 teaspoon freshly ground black pepper

½ cup (45 grams) freshly grated Parmesan cheese

1 sheet dried nori seaweed, to serve

4 fresh shiso leaves, sliced into thin strips (chiffonade), to serve

4 tablespoons large-flake bonito shavings, to serve

This is a riff on Italian Pasta al Limone—a cheesy and luscious noodle dish, livened up with lemon zest and juice. The udon noodles give a wafu bite, and the yuzu kosho, a spicy and fragrant Japanese condiment made with yuzu, chili peppers, and salt, adds an unexpected brightness. The udon is garnished with nori, bonito flakes, and shiso leaves. I like to eat this cold during the summer.

———

Bring a large pot of water to a boil over medium-high heat.

While waiting for the water to boil, make the sauce. In a medium bowl, combine the egg yolks, heavy cream, lemon zest, 1 tablespoon lemon juice, yuzu kosho, and dashi. Stir to combine thoroughly. Taste. Adjust with additional yuzu kosho for a saltier tang or with additional lemon juice for more brightness. Set aside.

Cook the udon in the pot of boiling water until al dente, following the manufacturer's directions. Scoop the cooked pasta out of the pot and place straight into a large serving bowl with about one ladleful of the cooking broth. Immediately add the butter to the hot pasta and stir until the butter is fully melted and each noodle is glossy and coated.

Give the egg mixture one more stir and gently pour it over the hot buttered noodles. Toss until all the noodles are evenly coated. Taste again and adjust with salt, pepper, and freshly grated Parmesan, as desired. Serve immediately, inviting eaters to top their bowls with torn nori, threads of fresh shiso, and shaved bonito flakes.

SHRIMP DUMPLING HOT POT WITH DAIKON NOODLES

Makes 4 servings

For the Dumplings

12 ounces (340 grams) shrimp, peeled, deveined, and coarsely chopped

2 scallions, minced

1 tablespoon minced ginger

1 tablespoon sake

½ teaspoon sea salt

¼ teaspoon freshly ground black pepper

2 teaspoons potato starch or cornstarch

2 tablespoons Chicken Dashi (page 25), Quick Chintan Dashi (page 26), or store-bought chicken broth

1 tablespoon toasted sesame oil

30 Handmade Dumpling Wrappers (page 259) or store-bought dumpling wrappers

For the Soup

6 cups (1.4 liters) Chicken Dashi (page 25), Quick Chintan Dashi (page 26), dashi of your choice, or store-bought low-sodium broth

1 pound (454 grams) daikon radish, julienned into noodle-like strips, about 8 inches (20 cm) long

3–4 tablespoons red or white miso, or more to taste

Sea salt, to taste

Freshly ground black pepper, to taste

1 scallion, sliced into thin rounds, for garnish

Lemon peel, to serve

Shichimi pepper, to serve

This is one of my favorite dumpling hot pots. It features shrimp dumplings and noodles made of daikon radish. The soup is Chinese in origin, with a wafu infusion of miso. The long, spaghetti-like strands of daikon can be achieved with a mandoline or by hand.

———————

In a medium bowl, combine the chopped shrimp, scallions, ginger, sake, salt, pepper, starch, dashi, and sesame oil. Using your hands, mix until the ingredients are well combined and smooth. You can make the filling earlier in the day and keep it refrigerated.

Lay 10 dumpling wrappers on a clean and dry cutting board. Put 1 heaping teaspoon of shrimp filling on each wrapper.

Prepare a small bowl of water to dip your finger. Lightly wet the edge of half of the wrapper with water and fold in half to create a half-moon. Press firmly around the edges to seal and keep the filling intact while cooking. Put the finished dumpling on a plate and repeat with the remaining wrappers and filling.

Bring a large pot of water to a boil over medium-high heat. Add the dumplings and cook for 2 to 3 minutes. They are cooked when they float to the surface. Remove the dumplings from the water and drain and set aside.

While the dumplings are cooking, prepare the soup. Heat the dashi in a pot set over medium-low heat and bring to a boil. Lower the heat and add the daikon noodles. Cook for 4 minutes, or until fork tender. Lower the heat to a simmer, season the dashi with miso, and stir. Add salt and pepper to taste. Add the cooked dumplings to the heated soup and let it simmer for an additional 1 to 2 minutes.

Distribute the daikon noodles and the dumplings into 4 bowls. Top with the hot miso soup and garnish with scallions. Serve with lemon peel and shichimi pepper.

CHILLED SPICY RAMEN SALAD WITH EGG, CHASHU PORK, TOMATOES, AND CUCUMBERS

Makes 4 servings

8 ounces (226 grams) Chashu Pork (page 215) or cooked ham or chicken, shredded or sliced thinly

1 large tomato, cut into bite-sized wedges, or 12 cherry tomatoes, halved

2 Persian cucumbers (or any cucumbers of your choice), enough to make 2 cups julienned pieces

1 avocado, pitted, peeled, and sliced into ¼ inch (6 mm) wedges

4 eggs, beaten

1 teaspoon cane sugar (optional)

Pinch sea salt

4 teaspoons vegetable oil, divided

4 servings Handmade Ramen Noodles (page 267) or store-bought ramen noodles

For the Spicy Vinegar Dressing (If you wish to make a mild vinegar dressing, omit the toban-djan)

1½ cups (400 ml) Chicken Dashi (page 25), Quick Chintan Dashi (page 26), Kombu and Bonito Dashi (page 20), or store-bought low-sodium broth

½ cup (120 ml) rice vinegar

½ cup (120 ml) soy sauce

2 tablespoons cane sugar, or more to taste

2 tablespoons toasted sesame oil, or more to taste ⟩

When the temperature starts getting up into the eighties, the only thing my family wants to eat is hiyashi chuka, a cold vegetable ramen noodle salad that cools you off the moment you take the first bite. It's Chinese in origin ("chuka" means "Chinese style"), but the seasonings and toppings are different in its Japanese form. This classic wafu version consists of a medley of sliced cucumbers, tomatoes, egg ribbons, and ham and is served with a soy-vinegar dressing or goma dare, a sesame dressing. I like the addition of avocado and chashu pork, along with a spicy sauce made with toban-djan, a Chinese broad bean chili paste. Once you learn how to make egg ribbons, you will be sprinkling them onto all your salads and pastas. You can, however, substitute the egg ribbons here with a soft-boiled egg. Hiyashi chuka is always accompanied with amazu (pickled ginger), which offers a nice acidity and spice to this colorful noodle. For protein, chicken, shrimp, crab, and pork all work well, or even leftover grilled meat from last night's dinner.

Put the chashu pork and all the prepared tomatoes, cucumbers, and avocado on a quarter-sheet tray and keep in the fridge until time to assemble the dish.

To make the egg ribbons, lightly whisk the eggs, sugar (if using), and salt in a small bowl. In a well-seasoned 9 inch (22 cm) cast-iron or nonstick skillet, heat 1 teaspoon of the oil over medium-high heat.

Add a quarter of the beaten egg mixture and quickly spread it over the entire pan to make a thin crepe. Cook for about 1 minute. Turn off the heat and cover the pan with a lid for 1 minute. When the egg is cooked, carefully flip the crepe onto a cutting board and let cool. Repeat with the rest of the oil and the egg mixture. When all the crepes have cooled, cut them each in half down the widest part and stack them. Trim the round edges to make a rectangular shape. Slice the stack into ⅛ x 2 inch (3 mm x 5 cm) ribbons. Place on the tray with the meat and vegetables and keep refrigerated until you're ready to assemble the dish. ⟩

1 ounce (28 grams) ginger, peeled and grated

1–2 teaspoons toban-djan (fermented broad bean chili paste)

For the Garnishes

1 cup nori seaweed ribbons (½ dried nori sheet cut into thin ribbons, ⅛ x 2 inches/ 3 mm x 5 cm) (keep in a ziplock bag until ready to use)

1 cup (254 grams) julienned Young Ginger Pickle (page 149) or store-bought pickled ginger

2 tablespoons toasted white sesame seeds

Goma Dare (Sesame Sauce) (page 223) (optional)

To make the spicy vinegar dressing, combine the dashi, vinegar, soy sauce, sugar, toasted sesame oil, ginger, and toban-djan in a bowl and mix well. Set aside.

Bring a pot of water to a rapid boil over high heat. Add the ramen noodles and cook until tender but still toothsome, about 1 minute (if using store-bought noodles, follow the package instructions). Shock the noodles in ice-cold water and drain.

As soon as the noodles are drained, assemble the hiyashi chuka by placing the chilled noodles on a plate and topping with avocado, cucumbers, tomatoes, egg ribbons, and chashu pork. Garnish with nori, pickled ginger, and toasted white sesame seeds. Serve the vinegar sauce at the table (and the goma dare, if you wish) and let diners season their own plate.

PORK, NAPA CABBAGE, AND GARLIC CHIVE GYOZA

Makes about 50 gyoza

For the Gyoza

50 dumpling wrappers, store-bought or homemade (page 259)

1 batch Pork and Napa Cabbage Gyoza Filling (page 256)

2 tablespoons toasted sesame oil, plus an additional 1 teaspoon for extra-crispy gyoza

To Serve

2 tablespoons La-yu (Spicy Chili Oil) (page 258) or store-bought

¼ cup (60 ml) soy sauce

⅓ cup (80 ml) kurozu (black vinegar) or rice vinegar, or lemon wedges

During the Second World War, a squad of Japanese soldiers from Utsunomiya in Tochigi Prefecture was sent to Manchuria in northern China, where they acquired a taste for Chinese dumplings. When they returned to Japan, they tried to recreate them at home, and the rest is history. Today, Utsunomiya City is known as a mecca for gyoza, with more than two hundred gyoza shops. There is even a statue of Venus enrobed in a gyoza wrapper there. Gyoza are thinner than their Chinese ancestor and often served as a side dish, as a prelude to ramen or one of many dishes on the menu at an izakaya—a drinking establishment that serves a variety of small dishes.

At home, I often serve gyoza as an appetizer, but most people don't stop at five dumplings. They easily gobble up ten, or even more, so I always make about fifty dumplings at a time. I like to pair pork with a variety of greens like garlic chives, napa cabbage, scallions, chard, and kale, as well as herbs like basil and cilantro. No matter what ends up going into the mix, I keep the ratio of meat to vegetables at about one to one. Filling the dumpling wrappers makes for a wonderful family activity, though you may wind up with some odd and funny shapes. You can make dumpling wrappers from scratch, but I often use commercial wrappers because they are quite reliable.

Fill a small bowl with water and put it next to the cutting board where you will make the gyoza. The water will be used to wet and seal the gyoza wrappers. Place your bowl of filling alongside your cutting board with a spoon for doling out.

Line a baking sheet with parchment paper and set it next to the cutting board. Spread out as many wrappers on your cutting board as will fit without overlapping. Put 1 heaping teaspoon of filling on each wrapper.

To wrap a gyoza, dip your fingertip into the water and use it to dampen the whole edge of the wrapper. Lift the front and back edges and pinch them together in the center; the water will form a seal between the two edges. You can opt not to pleat the dumpling, but pleating makes for a tighter seal and adds visual appeal. Pleat with ¼ inch (6 mm) folds along the front or back edge, folding the pleats so the folds point toward the center. >

Fold two or three pleats on the right. Do the same with the left, with the pleats pointing toward the center. Press firmly on each pleat to completely seal the wrapper. Put the sealed uncooked gyoza on the baking sheet, flattening the bottoms so they stand upright. Repeat with the remaining wrappers.

To cook the gyoza, heat 2 tablespoons of sesame oil in a 10 inch (25 cm) nonstick skillet over medium-high heat. You will get the best results when the pan is heated evenly. Place half of the gyoza into the pan, forming three rows with all the dumplings facing in the same direction and standing in the pan, not lying down. Fry the gyoza for 3 to 4 minutes, until the bottoms are evenly browned. Pour about ¾ cup (180 ml) water into the pan, enough to cover the bottom third of the gyoza. Be ready to cover the pan immediately with a lid because the water will splash and make a mess on your stovetop. Lower the heat and simmer with the lid on until almost all the liquid is gone, 4 to 5 minutes.

Remove the lid and increase the heat to medium-high. Cook until the bottom of the gyoza become dry and crispy, 1 to 2 minutes. For an even crispier finish, add another ½ teaspoon sesame oil to the pan and swirl it around, lifting the gyoza up with a spatula so the oil can spread evenly underneath them. Continue to cook for about 1 minute, until the bottoms of the gyoza are crisp. Remove the pan from the heat and loosen the gyoza with a spatula. Transfer to a serving plate, with the gyoza either bottom side up or bottom side down. This is a matter of preference: The Japanese serve bottom side up. The Chinese serve bottom side down. While your diners are eating the first batch, cook the remaining batch in the same way.

Serve immediately with la-yu, soy sauce, and/or kurozu or lemon wedges for dipping. >

Pork and Napa Cabbage Gyoza Filling

Makes enough for roughly 50 dumplings

2 scallions, sliced into ¼ inch (6 mm) pieces crosswise

¾ pound (340 grams) napa cabbage, minced

¼ pound (115 grams) garlic chives or scallions, minced

2 teaspoons sea salt, divided

1 pound (454 grams) ground pork (preferably pork shoulder)

1 ounce (28 grams) ginger, peeled and minced

2 garlic cloves, minced

1 tablespoon soy sauce

2 teaspoons potato starch or cornstarch

½ teaspoon cane sugar

1 teaspoon toasted sesame oil

Freshly ground black pepper, to taste

2 tablespoons water or Chicken Dashi (page 25)

In a large bowl, combine the scallions, cabbage, and garlic chives, add 1 teaspoon of the salt, and massage for a couple of minutes. Let stand for a couple of minutes and massage again until excess water comes out. Squeeze the cabbage mixture to remove any remaining excess water.

In a large bowl, combine the pork with the remaining salt, the ginger, garlic, soy sauce, potato starch, sugar, sesame oil, pepper, and water or dashi, mixing vigorously with your fingertips until combined and creamy in texture. Add the cabbage and chive mixture. Cover and refrigerate for at least 30 minutes or up to overnight.

La-yu

Spicy Chili Oil

Makes about ¾ cup (180 ml)

1 tablespoon toasted white sesame seeds

1 tablespoon toban-djan (broad bean chili sauce)

1 teaspoon gochugaru (Korean chili powder), or more to taste

½ teaspoon Sichuan peppercorns, toasted and coarsely ground

¼ cup (60 ml) toasted sesame oil

¼ cup (60 ml) neutral oil (rice bran oil, avocado oil)

1 dried chili pepper (togarashi, Guntur, Kashimir, or Mexican) seeded

1 clove garlic, minced

1 ounce (28 grams) peeled and minced ginger

Scallion, green parts only, cut into 2 inch (5 cm) pieces

1 tablespoon sakura ebi (tiny dried shrimp), minced (optional)

1 teaspoon soy sauce (optional)

½ teaspoon sugar (optional)

La-yu is not only an essential companion to gyozas but adds spice to noodles and cooked vegetables as well. I leave it on the table for everyone to drizzle freely on their foods. While there are many commercial chili oils available online or at Japanese grocery stores, homemade tastes so much better. You can enhance the umami with sakura ebi (tiny dried-shrimp variety) that have been dried in their shells; add minced ginger and garlic for spice, sesame seeds for crunch. This la-yu is more than an oil. Its solids can be eaten with a spoon.

Combine the sesame seeds, toban-djan, gochugaru, and Sichuan peppercorns in a small bowl.

Heat the sesame oil and neutral oil in a small skillet over medium-high heat. Add the chili pepper, garlic, ginger, scallions, and shrimp, if using, and cook for 2 minutes over low heat, or until everything is lightly toasted but not browned. Strain the solids and set them aside. Return the oil to the skillet. Bring the heat up to medium and cook the oil until it begins to smoke a little.

Pour half of the hot oil over the spice mixture and stir for about 30 seconds to combine well. Add the remaining half and mix well. Add the solids and mix. Let cool to room temperature.

Season with soy sauce and sugar, if using.

Transfer the la-yu to a glass or metal container with a tight-fitting lid. It will keep for up to 1 month in the refrigerator.

Handmade Dumpling Wrappers

Makes about 50 wrappers (approx. 3½ inches/9 cm in diameter)

Special Equipment

3 inch (7.6 cm) cookie cutter or drinking glass with equivalent rim size

Stand mixer with dough hook

Pasta machine (optional)

Ingredients

1 cup (240 ml) water, plus more as needed

½ teaspoon sea salt

1½ cups (187 grams) all-purpose flour

1½ cups (187 grams) bread flour

2 teaspoons light sesame oil or vegetable oil

1 cup (125 grams) potato starch or tapioca starch, for dusting

Bring the 1 cup water to a boil in a small pot set over medium heat and leave it at a rolling boil for 1 minute. Remove from the heat and dissolve the salt in the hot water.

Sift the flours together in a medium bowl. Add ¾ cup of the hot salted water to the flour mixture, stirring with your hands. Continue adding the remaining hot salted water, one tablespoon at a time, until the dough is shaggy, using up to 1 full cup of water. Add the oil and mix to form a round dough. If the dough feels dry, add another tablespoon of water. Let the dough rest for 15 minutes.

Place the dough in the bowl of the stand mixer fitted with the dough hook. Work the dough at medium speed for 8 to 10 minutes, until it is smooth and no longer sticky.

Alternatively, you can apply the traditional method: Stomp on the dough if you would like to try a feet-on, machine-free method. Put the dough in a 1 gallon ziplock bag and double-bag it with a large 2 gallon ziplock bag. Put a towel or sheet on the floor and place the bag of dough on top. With clean, shoeless feet, stomp the dough about 100 times, pausing after every 25 stomps to turn the dough 90 degrees and fold into three like an envelope. The dough will become smoother and shinier as it's worked.

Cut the dough in quarters and form 4 logs. Wrap the logs in plastic wrap and let them rest for 30 minutes on the kitchen counter.

Unwrap the logs and slice each crosswise into approximately 15 pieces. Flatten each disc with a rolling pin so that it is paper thin, about 3 inches (7.6 cm) in diameter, then use the cookie cutter or glass to make round wrappers. Use the rolling pin to flatten the wrappers again, so they are about 3½ inches (9 cm) in diameter, leaving the center a tad thicker than the edge.

Sprinkle each wrapper with starch and put it on a clean baking sheet. Cover all the dough with a clean dish towel while you are working to prevent it from drying out. Once the wrappers are done, wrap them in plastic wrap and store in the refrigerator. Use or freeze within 1 day for best results. Rolled-out dumpling wrappers can be stored in the fridge for 3 or 4 days or in the freezer for a month.

CHASHU PORK, EGG, CORN, AND MISO-BUTTER RAMEN

Makes 4 servings

2 ears fresh corn
or 1 cup frozen corn

8 cups (1.9 liters)
Bonito, Kombu, and Dried
Shiitake Mushroom Dashi
(page 22), Pork Bone Dashi
(page 24), Quick Chintan
Dashi (page 26), or any
dashi you prefer

2 teaspoons sea salt,
or more to taste

2 teaspoons Koumiyu
(page 264), divided

1 batch Chashu Pork (page 215)

1 batch Seven-Minute
Eggs (page 265)

1 batch Memma (page 263)

1 batch Handmade
Ramen Noodles (page 267)
or 4 servings store-bought
fresh ramen noodles

4 teaspoons Miso-Honey
Butter (page 50)

For the Garnishes

1 sheet dried nori seaweed,
cut into 4 pieces (stored in
a ziplock bag to keep crisp)

1 ounce (28 grams) ginger,
peeled and grated

2 scallions,
sliced thinly crosswise

½ cup (70 grams) Surigoma
(page 6)

Shichimi pepper, to taste

Freshly ground black pepper,
to taste

Yuzu Kosho (page 32) or store-
bought yuzu kosho (optional)

It wouldn't dawn on any of my schoolmates, including my friend Hachan, who is the co-owner of the famous ramen shop Hayashi, in Shibuya, to make ramen from scratch at home when there are so many good ramen shops (more than five thousand in Tokyo alone, and twenty thousand across Japan) and so much good, packaged ramen available in Japan. But I like a challenge. This is a classic wafu ramen—with a yofu, Western twist. It's got butter.

The ramen can be served year round, but fresh, in-season corn will make this experience extra special. I chose baby corn for this recipe, but any fresh corn will do. Memma are braised bamboo shoots, a standard crunchy accompaniment to ramen, but you can swap for other vegetables like grilled, roasted, or pan-fried eggplant, zucchini, or summer squash. Cherry tomatoes and leafy greens also make colorful and nutritious additions. And if you want a totally vegan ramen, fry up some tofu to throw in (see Crispy Tofu with Dipping Sauce, page 125).

The time-consuming part is making the ramen soup—which, like any good broth, takes time—and the noodles. The good news is that you can make the latter in advance and keep them on standby. Or you can make a quick pork and chicken dashi using ground meat. I season the ramen with shio, or sea salt, but you can use miso or soy sauce if you prefer. The amount of seasoning to use is a matter of personal preference. With salt, start with ½ teaspoon per serving (about 2 cups/480 ml of ramen soup). With miso and soy sauce or tare, start with 2 teaspoons per serving. Taste and make adjustments.

Do as I do when I teach ramen workshops, and have each person prepare their own, including cooking the noodles. Just make sure that the soup—the seasoned dashi for ramen is called soup—is boiling hot. Lukewarm ramen soup does not make the cut. See below for how I prepare for a ramen party.

Place the corn in a medium pot filled with cold water. Bring to a boil and cook for 1 to 2 minutes, until the corn is just tender. Drain and let cool. If you are using baby corn, use whole. Otherwise, roughly shave the kernels of the cobs into a bowl. Set aside.

Place 9 cups (2.2 liters) of the dashi in a 3 quart (3 liter) pot and bring to a boil over medium-high heat. Lower the heat to a simmer. ❯

Season the soup by adding salt, one teaspoon at a time, to the pot. Stir and taste until the desired flavor is reached. The rest of the salting will be done with a teaspoon of miso-honey butter on top of each serving, so allow for the extra flavor.

Bring the seasoned soup to a second boil and then lower the heat to keep it at a simmer while you work on cooking the noodles, which only takes a minute. If the soup starts to evaporate and gets too salty while you are working on the noodles, add more plain dashi or water. Stir and taste again.

Put ½ teaspoon of koumiyu in each of the four bowls.

Slice the chashu pork into ⅛–¼ inch (3–6 mm) thick pieces and reheat it in the hot soup for a minute. Set the slices on a plate along with the eggs, memma, and garnishes.

To cook the noodles, bring a stock pot of unsalted water to a rolling boil over high heat. Add 2 servings of the noodles at a time and cook for about 1 minute. Take one noodle out of the water and taste. The cooked noodles should be chewy and springy. When the noodles are ready, scoop them out with a strainer. Drain the noodles and divide them among the first two bowls. Repeat, cooking the remaining noodles.

While the noodles are cooking, bring the soup back to a rolling boil. Pour the boiling soup over the noodles in the bowls. Top with pork, egg, memma, corn, garnishes, and a dab of miso-honey butter. Serve immediately with chopsticks and spoons.

Variations

Add fried tofu (see Crispy Tofu with Dipping Sauce, page 125) and grilled, roasted, or pan-fried vegetables like kabocha squash, eggplant, bean sprouts, cherry tomatoes, green beans, okra, and mushrooms. For a vegan ramen, use Kombu Dashi (page 15) or Vegetable Dashi (page 18) as a soup base.

For a spicy ramen: Add 1 teaspoon or more of toban-djan (fermented broad bean chili paste) or any of your favorite chili sauces to the soup.

If you prefer a more savory flavor: Omit the honey from the Miso-Honey Butter.

MEMMA

Braised Bamboo Shoots

Makes 6–8 servings

8 ounces (230 grams) canned bamboo shoots

1 tablespoon toasted sesame oil

1 cup (240 ml) dashi of your choice

¼ cup (60 ml) Basic Shoyu Tare (page 32)

1 tablespoon mirin

1 teaspoon chili oil

Memma is a classic accompaniment to ramen noodles. You can also enjoy memma as a side dish with rice.

Slice the bamboo shoots into ½ inch (12 mm) batons, about ¼ inch (6 mm) thick.

Heat the oil in a medium skillet set over medium heat, add the bamboo shoots, and cook for 2 minutes. Add the dashi, shoyu tare, and mirin, and cook until the liquid is mostly absorbed by the bamboo, about 15 minutes. Drizzle with chili oil. Cool and store in the fridge for up to 1 week.

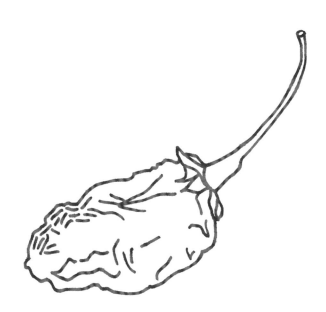

KOUMIYU

Fragrant Chili Oil

Makes about ¾ cup (180 ml)

1 small leek,
green and white parts divided

1 cup (240 ml) neutral oil
(avocado oil, rice bran oil)

2 garlic cloves, minced

1 tablespoon ginger,
peeled and minced

2 dried chili peppers
(such as togarashi or
Mexican) (optional)

Drizzle this oil over your favorite noodles and pasta dishes, as well as grilled foods. Add a couple of dried anchovies if you want a more oceanic flavor. For a more complex spicy flavor, try La-yu (Spicy Chili Oil) (page 258).

———————

Cut the leek sections lengthwise, then thinly slice into even pieces, about 2 inch (5 cm) long. Dry with a paper towel.

In a medium skillet, heat the oil over medium-low heat. Add the leeks, garlic, ginger, and chilies and cook for 15 to 20 minutes or until the leeks, garlic, and ginger are just golden. Strain through a fine mesh strainer lined with a paper towel. Let cool and then transfer to a container with a tight-fitting lid. Store in the fridge and use within 2 weeks.

SEVEN-MINUTE EGGS

This is a versatile soft-boiled egg that can be served with noodles, salads, and vegetables.

———————

Bring 4 eggs to room temperature. Bring a medium saucepan of water to a boil, filled deep enough to cover the eggs once you add them. Once boiling, reduce to a steady simmer and gently lower the eggs into the pot using a slotted spoon. Start a timer for 7 minutes. To ensure that the yolks set in the center, gently swirl the water every 1 to 2 minutes as the eggs cook. After 7 minutes, drain the pot, and immediately place the eggs in an ice bath to stop the cooking. Leave to cool for about 2 minutes. Peel the eggs. They will keep in the fridge for 3 to 4 days.

Variation

You can marinate the peeled seven-minute egg for 1 to 2 days in Basic Dipping Sauce (page 35).

HANDMADE RAMEN NOODLES

Makes 4–6 servings

2½ cups (300 grams) bread flour

⅓ cup (50 grams) heritage-grain flour (such as Sonora, Pasayten, or Rouge de Bordeaux)

1 cup (115 grams) cake flour or all-purpose flour, plus more for dusting

2 teaspoons (10 grams) Baked Baking Soda (below)

1½ teaspoons (7 grams) sea salt

1 cup (240 ml) water

2 cups (250 grams) potato starch or tapioca starch, for dusting

Special Equipment

Stand mixer with dough hook

Pasta machine

These noodles are made with a blend of bread flour, cake flour, and whole-wheat heritage-grain flour for good flavor. What makes them springy, yellow, and slightly nutty smelling is the addition of baked baking soda to the dough mixture. It is similar to kansui, an alkaline solution (potassium carbonate and sodium bicarbonate) that regulates the acidity and the pigments of the dough. You can find kansui in Chinese grocery stores, but I find baked baking soda more suitable for home cooks.

———————

Place the flours in a medium bowl and whisk them together.

In a small bowl, whisk together the baked baking soda, salt, and water until the baking soda and salt are dissolved.

Add the baking soda mixture to the blended flour in three equal additions, mixing with a wooden spoon after each addition. Once the dough resembles a shaggy ball, transfer it to a plastic bag and let it stand at room temperature for 30 minutes. The dough will look a bit dry, but it will relax with time and take on moisture.

To knead the dough, place it in the bowl of the stand mixer fitted with the dough hook. Mix at the lowest speed for 5 minutes or until the dough is smooth. If the dough still feels dry and crumbly, add 1 or 2 tablespoons of water.

Turn the dough onto a floured surface and shape into a disc by tucking the edges under with your hands. Cover the dough with a dish towel and allow to rest in a bowl for a minimum of 3 hours or up to overnight in the refrigerator.

To make the noodles, set up the pasta machine and a cutting board. Cut the dough into four pieces. Flatten each one with your hands and spread it wide enough so that it's slightly narrower than the pasta machine's width. Dust the dough evenly and generously with potato or tapioca starch on both sides to prevent it from sticking to the machine. Begin rolling the pasta through the pasta machine, twice per setting, starting with the widest setting and lowering the dial until the width is at ⅛ inch (3 mm). The dough may feel dry and break apart in the beginning, but don't be ▸

tempted to add water. Simply fold it and start again. Cut each sheet of rolled dough into pieces 8 to 12 inches (20 to 30 cm) long using a knife.

Dust the dough again with a generous amount of starch and run it through the spaghetti setting. Gently set the noodles on a baking sheet, sprinkling them with more starch so they don't stick together.

Store the noodles in the fridge for 4 or 5 days or in the freezer for a month.

Baked Baking Soda

½ cup (136 grams) baking soda

This is the ingredient that gives ramen its bright yellow color and springiness. Note that when baked, the baking soda will look exactly the same.

Preheat the oven to 250°F (120°C). Line a baking sheet with parchment paper.

Spread the baking soda on the prepared baking sheet in an even layer. Bake for 1 hour. Let cool, then transfer the baked baking soda to a jar with a tight-fitting lid. It will keep for a year.

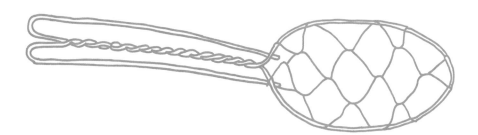

How to Prepare for a Ramen Party

3 days (stored in fridge) to 1 month (stored in the freezer) in advance
- Make 8–12 cups of dashi: Chicken Dashi (page 25); Pork Bone Dashi (page 24); Bonito, Kombu, and Dried Shiitake Mushroom Dashi (page 22), or Vegetable Dashi (page 18); or Quick Chintan Dashi (Quick Pork and Chicken Broth) (page 26)

2 days (stored in the fridge) in advance
- Make the Koumiyu (Fragrant Chili Oil) (page 264)
- Prep the ramen dough and let it rest overnight (page 267) or buy some noodles
- Make the Chashu Pork (page 215)
- Make the Memma (Braised Bamboo Shoots) (page 263)

1 day (stored in the fridge) in advance
- Make the Seven-Minute Eggs (page 265)
- Make the Miso-Honey Butter (page 50)
- Cut the ramen dough into noodles, if making your own
- Prepare whatever garnishes you like (see Yakumi and Furikake, page 3)

On the day of the party
- Season the broth
- Slice and heat the chashu pork
- Slice the eggs and serve on a plate
- Serve the yakumi in small bowls
- Add the koumiyu to the ramen bowls
- Cook the noodles and distribute into the ramen bowls
- Pour the hot soup over the ramen
- Arrange the toppings, miso-honey butter, and yakumi
- Slurp!

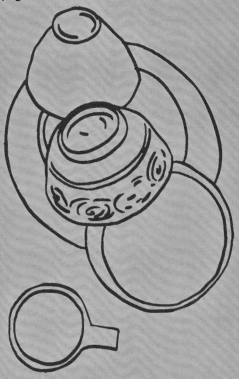

SWEETS AND BAKED GOODS

I was raised in a family that loves putting their hands in flour. Growing up, we made wagashi (traditional Japanese sweets), yogashi (Western baked goods), and pan (bread, derived from the Portuguese word "pão"), and later in life I learned how to make pizza, too. I remember how excited my sister Fuyuko and I got as kids when we saw the conical mound of white flour (like Mount Fuji!) on our grandmother's blue scale. You would find us standing right next to her in the kitchen ready to help.

Wagashi are generally sweets made from mochi, steamed and pounded mochigome (a sweet rice), and beans (such as adzuki and lima beans), that are boiled, mashed, and sweetened to form anko, sweet bean paste. Seasonal fruits and nuts are also sometimes added. Wagashi have gone through a process of cultural infusion over a period of centuries. Anko, for example, is believed to have arrived from China as early as the fifth century as a medicinal food and was later used as a meat substitute filling in steamed buns. Then came Chinese confections and sugar, along with the ritual of drinking tea, in the seventh century. Until that point, most Japanese sweets were made of fruits, nuts, vegetables,

mushrooms, and seaweed. In the sixteenth century, the Portuguese traders and missionaries brought yogashi like pão de ló (sponge cake) and confeito, a type of sugar candy. They also introduced biscuits, a type of pan that had a long shelf life to last during the sea voyage. Those cakes and sweets were wafu-ed over time and became something distinctly Japanese. Bread was also brought in by English and German bakers who came to Japan in the late nineteenth century to bake for European settlers in Yokohama. Legend has it that milk bread may have been invented by the British baker Robert Clarke, who opened the Yokohama Bakery in Japan back in 1862.

Bread became more accessible to Japanese people in the years following the Second World War, as a result of the American government sending surplus wheat flour and powdered milk to Japan. Japanese children like me were regularly fed koppe pan—a big, oblong wheat bun—at school. These days, Japanese people consume more bread than rice, and you will find some fine bakeries in Japan, as well as some of the best pizzerias.

Over the past century, Japanese people have

also developed a serious taste for Western sweets and now produce some of the most refined European-influenced pastries in the world. My sister Fuyuko apprenticed herself for seven years to the craft of French pastry making, working for the late master chef Gaston Lenôtre in Paris, and later with Wittamer in Brussels. She became a full-fledged pastry chef in Tokyo, and recently moved to Los Angeles, where she opened a cottage pastry shop. Together, we have done workshops and have worked as vendors at the Hollywood Farmers Market.

Sweets and baked goods in the U.S. have seen their own infusion of wafu ingredients like matcha, miso, mochi, and sesame seeds, and the arrival of products like milk bread. But wagashi haven't fully taken hold. There are a few artisanal wagashi shops, like Fugetsudo in the Little Tokyo neighborhood near me in Los Angeles. Founded in 1903 by the Kito family, it specializes in traditional mochi and yofu-style mochi made with chocolate, coffee, and peanut butter. Most Americans have yet to discover anko. Some of my friends turn their noses up at it because the key ingredient is sweetened beans. But I ask you to give this incredible dessert a chance. Anko is the soul of wagashi and other sweets in East Asia. It has incredibly complex flavors—nutty, creamy, sweet, umami. The quality of the beans, the amount of sugar used, the length of time the beans spend simmering in sugar water, and the "ude"—the skill of the wagashi artisan—all determine the flavor of anko.

If you plan a trip to Japan, I urge you to visit an artisanal wagashi shop; the difference between their versions and those made for shelf stability, rather than flavor, is like night and day. These experts make wagashi in small batches. They are seasonal and express the artistic touch of the wagashi maker. You must show up at the shop and get in line. When your turn comes to buy, choose the wagashi that speaks to you. The shop attendant will put it in a box, wrap it nicely, and tie it with a string for you to take home and enjoy with tea. Most wagashi must be eaten within a day. It's the evanescent quality of these sweets that makes them even more precious, like falling cherry blossoms in springtime.

The recipes in this chapter combine Western and wagashi sweets. Yes, there is Anko (Adzuki Bean Paste) (page 301), if you want to give it a try, though you can also buy it. You'll also find my Miso Apple Pie (page 281), a wafu take on the classic American dessert, as well as milk bread and wafu pizzas, in these pages.

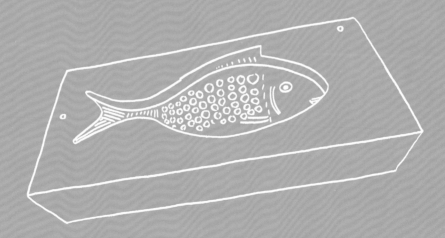

MOCHI FRUIT COCKTAIL WITH SHISO MINT SYRUP

Makes 4–6 servings

1 cup (240 ml), fresh plum juice (see Kitchen Note) or store-bought cold-press fruit juice (berry, apple, pineapple)

1 cup (240 ml) water

1 tablespoon (5 grams) agar powder

6 stone fruits (one or more varieties, such as plums, peaches, and nectarines), pits removed, diced into ½ inch (1.25 cm) pieces

Fresh mint leaves, for garnish

For the Mochi Balls

¼ cup (35 grams) shiratamako (sweet rice flour)

2 tablespoons water, or more, as needed

For the Shiso Syrup

½ cup (120 ml) water

½ cup (100 grams) cane sugar

10 fresh shiso leaves

Pinch sea salt

Fruit cocktail was my mother's favorite way to end a meal—hers was mostly out of a can, preferably Del Monte, the brand she discovered when she came to America. She mixed the canned fruit with fresh apples, oranges, and bananas and served the fruit cocktail in a large punch bowl she bought secondhand at the Rose Bowl Flea Market in Pasadena. If there were bruised leftovers floating and fermenting in the opaque liquid, it was my mother who took a spoon to finish them off. She then drank the syrup like a martini. I had a kind of love-hate relationship with her fruit cocktail, but now that my mother has passed away, love is what remains.

Here is my wafu version of a summer fruit cocktail made with a variety of fresh sliced stone fruit, agar jelly, and mochi balls made from glutinous rice flour called shiratamako. I love the various textures—crispy, soft, gooey. I choose a few plums in season—heirloom varieties from the farmers market like Armenian, Santa Rosa, greengage, damson, and mirabelle. You can serve the fruit cocktail with a dollop of Anko (Adzuki Bean Paste) (page 301), sweetened black soybeans (see recipe in Yogurt with Sweet Black Soybeans, Fruit, and Toasted Coconut Flakes, page 59), or ice cream—or all three!—with the shiso syrup on the side.

Heat the fruit juice in a small saucepan over low heat until lukewarm. Set aside.

Add the water to a small saucepan, then slowly add the agar powder, stirring until it dissolves. Turn the heat on medium-low and continue to stir until the agar mixture comes to a boil. Turn off the heat and let cool for 2 to 3 minutes. Add the lukewarm fruit juice and stir. Transfer the agar mixture to a heat-resistant container, about 6 x 6 inches (15 x 15 cm). It will set in approximately 20 minutes at room temperature. When set, cut it into ½ inch (1.5 cm) squares and refrigerate. You can make the agar and store in the fridge the day before you plan to serve it.

To make the mochi dumplings, mix the flour and water in a small bowl to form a paste, about the consistency of a soft playdough. Make little balls, about ¾ inch (2 cm) in diameter. Bring a small pot of water to a boil over medium heat and drop the balls into the boiling water. After they rise › to the surface, allow them to cook for another minute. Scoop them out of the water and shock them in cold water. Drain. The mochi will harden with time, so make this fruit salad just before serving.

To make the shiso syrup, combine the water and sugar in a medium saucepan and bring to a boil. Boil just until sugar is fully dissolved. Turn off the heat and add the shiso leaves and a pinch of salt. Stir to combine and let the syrup come to room temperature. The shiso leaves can be left to steep in the syrup for up to 4 hours. Remove and discard the leaves before serving. Store in the fridge for up to 2 weeks.

Serve the chilled mochi and jelly squares with sliced stone fruit wedges and shiso syrup, garnished with mint leaves.

Variation

You can also serve this fruit cocktail with Kokuto Syrup (page 293).

KITCHEN NOTES To make fresh plum juice, combine 1 pound (454 grams) ripe plums, 5 ounces (150 grams) cane sugar, and 1¼ cups (300 ml) water in a medium saucepan and bring to a boil over medium heat. Lower heat and simmer for 15 minutes. Taste and adjust with more sugar, as needed. Strain the juice through a fine mesh strainer. It will make 1½ cups of plum juice, and you can enjoy the pulp with yogurt. The juice keeps for 3 days in the fridge or in the freezer for 3 months.

Some fruit juices may need a little more agar powder to achieve a jelly-like consistency that can be cut easily with a knife, but use 5 grams for every cup of fruit juice as a starting point and make adjustments, as needed.

ORANGE AGAR WEDGES

Makes 4–6 servings

4 pounds (1.8 kg) oranges (such as cara cara and Valencia)

2–3 tablespoons (24–36 grams) cane sugar, plus more as needed

1 tablespoon (5 grams) agar powder

⅔ cup (160 ml) water

Fresh mint leaves, for garnish (optional)

In Japan, instead of the gelatin often found in American desserts, we use a seaweed-based gelling agent called kanten, or agar, which originated in ancient China and came to Japan more than twelve hundred years ago. The texture of agar desserts is slightly less jiggly than those made with gelatin, but it is just as effective for making sliceable desserts. In this recipe, I wafu orange gelatin wedges using agar, which works delightfully well with fruit juices. Compared to gelatin (which cannot be substituted here), agar sets more quickly at room temperature. This wafu dessert has great eye appeal. The key is to cut out the fruit without tearing the orange skin. Use a small, sharp knife.

———————

Leave 2 oranges whole, and cut the others in half at the equator. Working carefully, scrape out the fruit with a spoon, a small knife, and your hands without tearing the skin. You will use the hollowed-out orange peel halves to hold the jelly. If the shell doesn't sit straight, trim the bottom with a knife, being careful not to make a hole. Set the hollow orange shells on a cookie sheet.

Blend the scooped-out fruit to make 1¼ cups (300 ml) of juice. Strain the juice through a fine mesh strainer to remove any pulp. Taste and add 1–2 tablespoons sugar, if desired. Set aside.

In a small dry bowl, combine the agar powder and 1 tablespoon of sugar and mix well.

Add the water to a medium saucepan, then slowly add the agar mixture, stirring until the mixture dissolves. Turn heat on medium-low and continue to stir until the water comes to a boil. Turn off the heat. Let cool for 2 to 3 minutes. Add the orange juice and stir.

Cut the two whole oranges into segments. Using a knife, cut the white membrane that separates each segment of the fruit. Cut the segments in thirds. Divide the pieces of orange between the hollowed-out orange shells. Then pour the warm orange juice mixture into each shell.

Allow the jelly to set at room temperature, then transfer to the fridge to finish setting. After it's chilled, about 3 hours. Slice each one into wedges, as you would a whole orange.

Serve immediately, with mint, if you like.

DORAYAKI

Makes 8 dorayaki

¾ teaspoon baking soda

2 tablespoons water

3 eggs

¾ cup (150 grams) cane sugar

2 teaspoons honey

2 teaspoons mirin

¼ teaspoon sea salt

1½ cups (180 grams) all-purpose flour

Vegetable oil, for the pan

1 batch Anko (page 301) or 300 grams store-bought anko

½ cup (120 ml) heavy cream, whipped (optional)

Dorayaki are nothing like the stacks topped with butter and drizzled with maple syrup, perhaps with a side of eggs and bacon, that Westerners associate with pancakes. In Japan, they appear as a teatime snack, with anko—sweet adzuki bean paste, which tastes a little like sweet potato—sandwiched between them. The pancakes taste like castella, a honey cake based on the Portuguese and Spanish pastries that were introduced to Japan during the sixteenth century. Centuries later, Japanese people now regard dorayaki as a classic wagashi (Japanese) confection, and not too many shops in Japan make dorayaki as good as those at Usagiya in Tokyo. Whenever I am back there, it's an essential stop. This recipe is my homey version. Use anko, as below, or replace it with your favorite jam (my kitchen assistant Kali and my sister Fuyuko love their dorayaki filled with whipped cream and currant jam).

———

Combine the baking soda with the water and stir. Let stand for a few minutes until fully dissolved.

Meanwhile, in a medium bowl, combine the eggs, sugar, honey, mirin, and salt. Beat with a whisk or hand mixer until fully combined but not whipped. Add the baking soda mixture and whisk again to combine. Add the flour and fold it in until just combined, being careful not to overmix. Cover with a dish towel and let rest for 30 minutes to 1 hour. Don't worry if there are still a few lumps in the batter after whisking; the resting time will help to dissipate them. The batter can be used after a half-hour rest, but it's best if you wait 1 hour.

Set a large nonstick frying pan over medium-low heat and brush with just enough oil to coat, wiping out any excess with a paper towel. Ladle enough batter into the pan to make a pancake about 3 inches (8 cm) in diameter, about 2 tablespoons. Cook until both sides are deep golden brown, about 3 to 4 minutes per side. Repeat with the remaining batter. You should now have 16 pancakes.

Serve hot or at room temperature. Top eight of the pancakes with a spoonful each of bean paste and whipped cream, if using, and top with the remaining pancakes to make sandwiches, then serve. Eat the dorayaki within a day of making them.

MISO APPLE PIE

Makes one 9 inch pie

For the Pie Crust

16 tablespoons (228 grams)
cold unsalted butter

1 ⅜ cups (170 grams)
all-purpose flour

1¼ cups (170 grams)
Sonora flour or all-purpose flour,
plus more for dusting

½ teaspoon sea salt

½ cup (120 ml) ice-cold water

1 egg, beaten

1 tablespoon cane sugar

For the Filling

1 batch Miso-Stewed Apples
(page 285)

My mother believed that apples taste best when baked in pies. When we were kids, she always baked in the middle of the night, when everyone was asleep. Cool temperatures and peace of mind were high on her list of optimum conditions. But such peace was often disrupted when the smell of baking interrupted the sleep of her five children. We would come down to the kitchen in our pajamas and eat the sliced apples floating in salted water, as my mother hurried to peel more.

My sister Fuyuko, who is a pastry chef, and I have tried for years to replicate our mother's slab apple pie recipe. Mother passed away a few years ago, but Fuyuko and I eventually came up with a pie she would be proud of. Fuyuko taught me the basics, and I tweaked the apple filling, adding miso to give it a wafu element. Just for fun, I entered it into the KCRW annual pie contest, and it won second place in the apple pie category. My hidden ingredient did wonders!

———————————

To make the dough, put a piece of parchment paper on a flat surface. Using a box grater, coarsely grate the cold butter onto the parchment. Chill the grated butter in the freezer until it hardens, about 10 minutes.

In a large bowl, blend the flours and salt using a pastry cutter. Add the chilled grated butter and start blending the dry ingredients and the butter until the mixture resembles a coarse meal, with a few large pea-size lumps of butter remaining.

Make a well in the middle of the dough, and sprinkle in the water. Mix the water into the dry ingredients until the dough is crumbly and hydrated just enough to come together in a shaggy mound. Try not to overmix; bits of butter should still be visible in the dough.

Divide the dough into two even portions, about 9 ounces (255 grams) each. Place each on a piece of plastic wrap and roughly roll out into 7 x 7 inch (18 x 18 cm) squares about ½ inch (1.25 cm) thick. Wrap the dough and place it in the refrigerator for 30 minutes.

After the dough is chilled, place one portion on a piece of parchment paper. Lightly dust the surface of the dough with flour and place a second sheet of parchment paper on top. Roll out the dough into a square about 10 x 10 inches and ⅛ inch thick (25 x 25 cm x 3 mm). If the dough sticks to the paper, remove the top layer, dust the dough again with flour, put the paper back on top, and continue rolling. Remove the top layer of ➤

parchment and prick the surface of the dough with a dough docker or a fork. Re-cover the dough with parchment and put it in the fridge to chill for 30 minutes. Repeat with the remaining dough. Keep both pieces refrigerated until ready to make the pie.

Pull out one piece of dough from the refrigerator and remove the parchment covering. Place it on a baking sheet lined with parchment paper and spread the cooked and chilled apples on top, leaving a ½ inch (1.25 cm) space on the sides. Brush the beaten egg along the sides. Reserve the rest of the beaten egg and put the half-assembled pie back into the refrigerator.

Pull out the second piece of pie dough from the refrigerator and remove the parchment paper. Cut slits in the dough, each about 9 inches (23 cm) long, across *almost* the entire length of the slab of dough, leaving about a ½ inch (1.25 cm) border uncut on all sides. The goal is to create a top crust of ½ inch (1.25 cm) thick strips, all attached to each other by the intact border.

Once the top crust has been cut, retrieve the bottom crust with the pie filling from the fridge. Use your rolling pin to gently roll up the top crust. Line up the top and bottom pieces of dough, and gently unroll over the pie filling. Once completed, seal the edges together by gently folding them up and over and crimping. Cover again with a sheet of parchment and allow the whole thing to chill in the refrigerator again for at least 1 hour before baking.

When you're ready to bake, preheat the oven to 400°F (204°C). Remove the chilled pie from the fridge and brush the surface with the remaining beaten egg and sprinkle the top with sugar. Bake the pie on the middle rack of the oven until crisp and evenly golden brown, about 1 hour, rotating halfway through to ensure even baking. Remove from the sheet tray and transfer to a cooling rack.

KITCHEN NOTES

For the pie crust, and for all baking, I strongly recommend that you measure by weight and not volume. It is best practice to follow the gram measurements here.

If the unbaked sheets of dough become soft and difficult to handle, refrigerate them for about 10 minutes and try again.

STORAGE You can store the formed pie dough (disc or square) in the freezer for up to 3 months. Wrap it tightly in aluminum foil or store it in a freezer bag. Thaw the pie dough in the refrigerator overnight. ▷

MISO-STEWED APPLES

Makes about 6 cups (1 kg)

5 large apples (approximately 7 oz/200 grams each) whole, skin on, preferably honeycrisp, Fuji, or pink lady

Approximately ½ cup (96 grams) cane sugar (use the equivalent of 15 percent of the weight of the peeled and sliced apples; adjust as needed)

1 tablespoon lemon juice

1 tablespoon Red Miso (page 40) or store-bought red miso, plus more to taste

To make the apple filling, wash and peel the apples. Cut them into quarters and remove the cores with a knife. Cut the quarters into four slices, about ½ inch (1.25 cm) thick. Measure the weight of the apple slices on a digital scale. Put them in a medium bowl and add enough sugar to equal 15 percent of the weight of the apples. (For example, if the chopped apples weigh 1,000 grams, you would add 150 grams of sugar.) Add the lemon juice. Mix to combine and let the apples macerate until the sugar dissolves and the apples are juicy, about 1 hour.

Transfer the macerated apples to a medium stainless-steel saucepan. Cover with a lid and cook over low heat until the apples are soft and translucent, about 30 minutes, stirring with a wooden spoon from time to time, being careful not to overcook or burn them. You want the apple slices to retain their shape. Add the miso and gently combine. Taste and add more as needed. The miso flavor will be more pronounced when the apples cool down. Remove from the heat. Cool the apples completely before using.

Rose and Leaf Decorations

Do as my sister and I did when baking with my mother and use any leftover dough to make decorative rose petals and leaves. To make roses, roll out the dough and cut out five circles 1 inch (2.5 cm) in diameter. Using your hands, form each circle into a petal shape. For the center of the flower, cut out a strip of dough, roll it, and pinch the bottom slightly. Put one petal around the bud and then the next one, overlapping them slightly until all the petals are attached. Open up the rose petals to make it look like it is in full bloom. To make the leaves, use a small paring knife to carve out the shape of leaves from the pie dough. Score the dough to make it look like a leaf. Refrigerate and rest for 30 minutes before baking.

Preheat the oven at 360°F (182°C). When ready to bake, place the roses and leaves directly on a sheet tray covered with parchment paper. Brush with a beaten egg. Sprinkle sugar on the leaves but not on the roses, to avoid burning the petals. Bake for about 20 minutes for the leaves and 35 minutes for the roses, or until the roses are golden brown. Arrange the roses and leaves on top of the baked pie.

SESAME BUTTER COOKIES

½ cup (100 grams) cane sugar

11 tablespoons (155 grams) unsalted butter

3 tablespoons (45 grams) tahini or nerigoma (Japanese-style tahini)

1 teaspoon vanilla extract

¾ teaspoon rose water

1½ cups (185 grams) ll-purpose flour

1¼ teaspoon Sonoko Curry Powder (page 153) or store-bought Japanese curry powder

½ teaspoon turmeric

¼ teaspoon ground cardamom

½ teaspoon ground cinnamon

¼ cup white sesame seeds

¼ cup black sesame seeds

1 tablespoon flaky sea salt, for garnish

Makes 24 cookies

This recipe was inspired by mantecadito, a Puerto Rican thumbprint cookie. My kitchen assistant Daniela and I wafu it with Japanese curry powder, resulting in fragrant shortbread with a subtle spicy flavor. It is not too sweet, so you can also enjoy it with cheese.

Preheat the oven to 350°F (176°C). Line two cookie sheets with parchment paper.

Using a stand or handheld mixer, cream the sugar, butter, tahini or nerigoma, vanilla, and rose water together in a medium bowl.

Combine the flour, curry powder, turmeric, cardamom, and cinnamon in a medium bowl. Add dry ingredients to the cream and sugar mixture and mix at medium speed to combine, until it forms a smooth dough.

Pour the white and black sesame seeds onto a plate, allowing them to mix together. Scoop out the cookie dough, one leveled tablespoon at a time, and roll into balls. Roll each ball in the sesame seeds, covering it on all sides, and set it on one of the lined cookie sheets, 2–3 inches (5–7.6 cm) apart, 12 cookies on each sheet. Sprinkle flaky sea salt on the cookies. Refrigerate until firm, about 10 minutes.

Remove the cookie sheets from the fridge. While the balls are still firm and cold, use the bottom of a glass to flatten each one to 2 inches (5 cm) in diameter. Bake in the oven for 10 minutes on the middle rack, then rotate the sheets and bake for another 7 to 8 minutes, until the edges are slightly brown. Remove from the oven to cool, about 10 minutes. The cookies will be puffy and soft. After 10 minutes, carefully transfer the cookies to a wire rack to cool completely.

Store in an airtight container for up to 1 week.

KITCHEN NOTE For all baking, I strongly recommend that you measure by weight and not volume. It is best practice to follow the gram measurements here.

SPICED MOLASSES COOKIES

Makes 36 cookies

¾ cup (174 grams)
unsalted butter, melted

1 cup (200 grams) cane sugar

¼ cup, approximately
(84 ml) molasses

1 egg

2 cups (240 grams)
all-purpose flour

2 teaspoons baking soda

½ teaspoon salt

3½ teaspoons Sonoko Curry
Powder (page 153) or
store-bought Japanese
curry powder

1 teaspoon ground cinnamon

⅛ teaspoon ground cloves

For the Coating

1 cup brown sugar

1 teaspoon Sonoko Curry Powder
(page 153) or store-bought
Japanese curry powder

This is a riff on ginger molasses cookies—an old-time holiday favorite. Similar to the Sesame Butter Cookies recipe (page 286), I use Japanese curry powder to make a Western cookie with a wafu twist. They are crispy, chewy, subtly spicy, and addictive. These cookies also work well when used as a base for New York–style cheesecake instead of the usual ginger snaps. I also freeze these cookies and use them to sandwich ice cream and serve it with fruit and Okinawa Black Sugar (Kokuto) Syrup (page 293). My students love this dessert.

Line two cookie sheets with parchment paper.

To make the cookie dough, in a large bowl combine the butter, sugar, molasses, and egg with a wooden spoon until well mixed. In a medium bowl, combine the flour, baking soda, salt, curry powder, and spices. Add the dry ingredients to the butter mixture and stir just until well combined. Cover the dough with plastic wrap and chill it in the refrigerator until it becomes firm, about 1 hour. (At this point, the unbaked cookie dough can be formed into logs, wrapped tightly in plastic wrap or aluminum foil, and refrigerated or frozen for later use.) When you are ready to bake, preheat the oven to 350°F (176°C). Scoop out the dough with a tablespoon and roll into 1 inch (2.5 cm) balls.

To make the coating, place the brown sugar and curry powder in a small bowl and combine with a fork. Roll each ball of dough in the sugar mixture until lightly coated. Place the dough balls on a parchment paper–lined baking sheet about 2 inches apart and gently flatten each into a disc using the bottom of a glass or jar.

Bake for 10 minutes on the middle rack of the oven, rotating the cookie sheet halfway through to ensure even baking. The cookies should be puffy and slightly soft in the center; they will firm up and deflate as they cool. Cool for 5 minutes and then remove from the cookie sheet and let them continue to cool on a rack.

KITCHEN NOTES

If baking dough from frozen, add an extra minute to the total baking time.

For all baking, I strongly recommend that you measure by weight and not volume. It is best practice to follow the gram measurements here.

CHUNKY CHOCOLATE MISO BANANA BREAD

Makes 1 loaf

4 medium bananas, overripe and brown all over

1¾ cups (210 grams) all-purpose flour

1 teaspoon ground cinnamon

¼ teaspoon ground nutmeg

1 teaspoon baking powder

½ teaspoon baking soda

3 tablespoons (42 grams) butter, softened

¾ cup (165 grams) brown sugar

2 tablespoons (30 grams) Red Miso (page 40) or store-bought red miso

3 tablespoons (30 grams) sour cream or buttermilk

2 eggs, beaten

1 teaspoon vanilla extract

½ cup (85 grams) chocolate chunks, preferably dark chocolate

⅔ cup (80 grams) chopped walnuts

3 tablespoons Okinawa Black Sugar (Kokuto) Syrup (page 293) or molasses (optional)

2 tablespoons toasted black sesame seeds

After I found myself with too many jars of homemade red miso in the fridge (leftover samples from the farmers market where I am a vendor), I started using more miso in my cooking, wherever salt was called for. Miso in my salad dressing, stews, compound butter, carrot cake, and, of course, my soups. I had some overripe bananas, so my kitchen assistant Ruben made some banana bread and inoculated it with miso for fun. It came out so good that we brought a few loaves to the farmers market, sliced them up, and hoped they would sell. People didn't want the slices—they bought the whole loaves, and we sold out instantly. Most miso banana bread recipes call for white miso, which is milder and sweeter than red miso. I prefer using red because it is caramelly, with subtle notes of Parmesan cheese. When adding red miso, begin with less than what the recipe calls for because every miso is slightly different. Baste the top of the decorative banana with some molasses-y kokuto syrup, if you like, for a nice shiny finish.

———————

Preheat the oven to 350°F (176°C). Butter a 10 x 5 inch (25 x 13 cm) tin loaf pan and dust with flour to prevent the batter from sticking to the pan.

Peel the bananas. Slice one banana in half lengthwise and put it aside. This will be used for decoration. Mash the remaining bananas in a bowl with a fork until they are chunky.

In a medium bowl, whisk together the flour, cinnamon, nutmeg, baking powder, and baking soda.

Put the butter, sugar, and miso in the bowl of a stand mixer fitted with a whisk attachment, or use a hand mixer, and mix until fluffy, about 5 minutes. Slowly add the buttermilk, then the beaten eggs, a little at a time, followed by the vanilla extract, and mix until well incorporated. Add the mashed bananas, dry ingredients, chocolate chunks, and walnuts and mix until just blended. Avoid overmixing. Transfer the dough to the prepared pan.

Arrange the halved banana on top of the batter, cut side up. Brush the top of the banana with the kokuto syrup, if using. Sprinkle the sesame seeds on top and around the banana. Bake for 60 to 65 minutes or until a toothpick or chopstick inserted into the center comes out clean. Allow ▸

Chunky Chocolate Miso Banana Bread (cont.)

the bread to cool on a rack for 30 minutes before taking it out of the pan. The banana bread will keep in the fridge for 2 to 3 days, or in the freezer for 1 month.

KITCHEN NOTE Be sure to use overripe bananas. Buy yellow bananas a week in advance of the baking and allow them to ripen in a brown bag.

OKINAWA BLACK SUGAR (KOKUTO) SYRUP

Makes ⅔ cup (80 ml)

1 cup (136 grams) Okinawa black sugar (also known as kokuto) or dark brown sugar

1 cup (240 ml) water

This is an all-purpose syrup that I use like maple syrup or molasses. If you can't find Okinawa black sugar, you can use dark brown sugar.

Add the sugar and water to a medium saucepan and cook over low heat for 30 minutes or until it thickens into a syrup. Store for 2 months in the fridge.

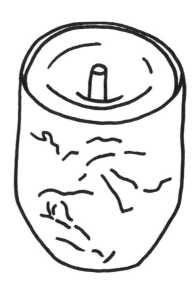

AMAZAKE ICE CREAM WITH CHERRY SYRUP

Makes 4–6 servings

Special Equipment

Electric rice cooker

For the Ice Cream

7 ounces (200 grams) freeze-dried rice koji

¾ cup (150 grams) glutinous sweet rice

3 cups (720 ml) warm water (150°/65°C), divided

1 whole cinnamon stick

1 teaspoon vanilla extract

1 teaspoon freshly squeezed ginger juice

½ teaspoon sea salt

2 tablespoons heavy cream

1 teaspoon honey

For the Cherry Syrup

1 cup fresh or frozen cherries, pitted

2 tablespoons water

¼ cup (50 grams) cane sugar

½ teaspoon vanilla extract

1 teaspoon lemon juice

For Garnish

12 cherries, whole with stems

Mint leaves, to serve (optional)

Amazake is a fermented rice drink with many cousins—sake, soy sauce, miso, mirin, and shio koji (to which it bears the most similarity). When rice is inoculated with rice koji, the two ingredients produce a creamy, naturally sweet, delicate, floral probiotic beverage. Although the name "amazake" sounds a bit like "sake," there is no alcohol involved, so even children can enjoy it. Here, amazake is turned into an ice cream infused with cinnamon and ginger. You will need an electric rice cooker for this recipe. Basic rice cookers are inexpensive—just get one that can keep your cooked rice at "keep warm" temperature to create an optimum environment for fermenting it.

———————

To make the ice cream, place the rice koji in a small bowl and bring to room temperature for at least an hour.

Rinse the rice until the water runs clear. Put the rinsed rice in a rice cooker along with 1½ cups (360 ml) of warm water and leave to soak in the cooking water for 1 hour. After soaking, set to "cook" and allow the rice to cook to completion. It will be on the soft side.

When the rice is finished cooking, allow the rice cooker to switch to the "keep warm" setting and stay there. Add another 1½ cups (360 ml) of warm water. You want to use the additional water to bring the temperature of the rice down to 150°F (65°C). Once the temperature is adequately reduced, add the rice koji and the cinnamon stick to the cooker pot and stir to combine.

With the rice cooker open, drape a kitchen towel over the rice, then lower the lid; the towel will keep it slightly ajar. If your lid is spring-loaded, you may need to gently weigh it down in order to keep it closed enough. Average rice cookers are set to maintain a temperature of 150°F (65°C) when on the "keep warm" setting. We want to maintain a temperature just below that in order for optimal fermentation. Leave the porridge covered with the kitchen towel and slightly ajar to ferment for 8 to 10 hours.

After 8 to 10 hours, your porridge should be very evenly hydrated and flavored by the cinnamon stick. Turn off the rice cooker, open the lid, and allow the mixture to cool slightly. Remove the cinnamon stick, then › stir in the vanilla extract, ginger juice, and salt. Use an immersion blender to reach the consistency of your liking—still slightly coarse, or fully pureed (I like mine very smooth and creamy). Add the cream and honey and stir. Taste and adjust to your liking with a pinch more salt or a drop more vanilla or ginger juice, cream, or honey. Keep in mind that freezing will mute the flavors slightly. Transfer the blended mixture to a freezer-safe container, and store in the freezer until fully firmed up for an ice cream (about 2 to 4 hours) or stir every 30 to 45 minutes for a semi-freddo texture.

To make the cherry syrup, add all the ingredients to a small saucepan and bring to a simmer over medium heat. Stir until the sugar is fully dissolved. Maintain a low simmer and gently mash the cherries with the back of a wooden spoon as they cook. Allow the mixture to simmer for another 8 to 10 minutes, until all the fruit is very soft and broken down. Remove from the heat and allow to cool slightly. Pour through a fine mesh strainer to remove the solids. Store in a tight-lidded container in the fridge. The syrup can be served chilled out of the fridge or still warm.

To serve, scoop generous balls of the ice cream into cups, drizzle with the cherry syrup, and top with a pair of whole, stem-on frozen cherries and a mint leaf.

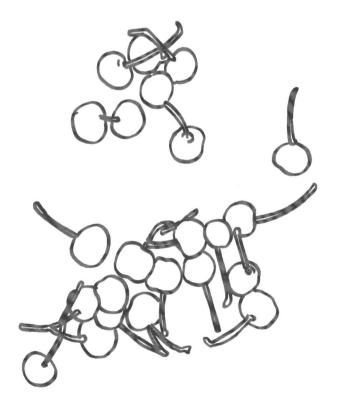

PUMPKIN AND ANKO PIE

For the Pie Crust

8 tablespoons (113 grams) cold unsalted butter

⅔ cup (85 grams) all-purpose flour, plus more for dusting

⅔ cup (85 grams) Sonora flour (or other whole-grain flour)

½ teaspoon salt

¼ cup (60 ml) ice-cold water

For the Filling

15 ounces (425 grams) canned pumpkin puree

½ cup (110 grams) light brown sugar

¼ teaspoon Kosher salt

1½ tablespoons Okinawa Black Sugar (Kokuto) Syrup (page 293) or molasses

1½ teaspoons ground cinnamon

1½ teaspoons ground ginger

⅛ teaspoon ground nutmeg

⅛ teaspoon ground cloves

2 eggs

½ cup (120 ml) heavy cream

⅓ cup (80 ml) milk

1 batch Anko (page 301) or store-bought anko (see headnote)

1 cup (240 ml) whipped cream, for serving (optional)

Makes 6 servings

There is a kabocha squash and adzuki bean dish called itokoni, literally "simmered cousins." It's an odd name, but it makes perfect sense: both ingredients are highly nutritious and have a relatively long shelf life. But to wafu a quintessential American pie with these ingredients? How audacious! You can make my recipe for anko or use store-bought, as most Japanese cooks do. Anko comes in two different varieties: Koshian is a finely pureed, smooth paste; and tsubuan is a coarse paste with some beans left whole. I prefer tsubuan, because it has a better texture. My kitchen assistant Tracy and I also added some Okinawa Black Sugar (Kokuto) Syrup to the pie. It gives a molasses-y flavor to the filling; if you can't find kokuto, just use molasses.

———————

Preheat your oven to 350°F (176°C).

Make your pie crust first. Coarsely grate the cold butter with a box grater onto parchment. Chill the grated butter in the freezer until it hardens, about 10 minutes.

In a large bowl, whisk the flours and salt. Add the butter and mix with your hands until the mixture resembles a coarse meal, with a few large pea-size lumps of butter remaining.

Make a well in the middle of the dough and sprinkle in the water. Mix the water into the dry ingredients until the dough is crumbly and hydrated enough to come together in a shaggy mound. Try not to overmix the dough.

Place the dough on a piece of plastic wrap and roll out into a 7 x 7 inch (18 x 18 cm) circle that is ½ inch (2.5 cm) thick. Wrap the dough and place it in the refrigerator for 2 hours (it will keep for up to 3 days there or 1 month in the freezer).

After the dough is chilled, place it on a surface lightly dusted with flour and put a piece of parchment paper over the top. Roll the dough into a 10 x 10 inch (25 x 25 cm) circle that is ⅛ inch (3 mm) thick. Place the dough into a 10 inch (25 cm) pie pan. Shape the crust, prick with a fork or a dough docker, then place a piece of aluminum foil on top and add weights or beans to keep the crust from rising. ›

Pumpkin and Anko Pie (cont.)

Bake for 1 hour in the middle rack. Remove the weights and foil and set aside to cool.

To make the pumpkin filling, combine the pumpkin puree, brown sugar, salt, the kokuto syrup or molasses, cinnamon, ginger, nutmeg, cloves, eggs, cream, and milk and with a mixer or by hand mix until smooth.

Fill the bottom of the pie shell with the adzuki bean paste. Next, add the pumpkin filling to come just below the rim of the pan. Bake in the middle rack for 45 minutes to 1 hour.

Let cool. Serve plain or with whipped cream.

KITCHEN NOTE For the pie crust, and for all baking, I strongly recommend that you measure by weight and not volume. It is best practice to follow the gram measurements here.

ANKO

Adzuki Bean Paste

Makes 2 cups (900 grams)

1½ cups (300 grams) adzuki beans

1½ cups (300 grams) cane sugar

2 pinches sea salt or kosher salt, or more to taste

Anko is a sweet paste made of adzuki beans. It is used as a filling for bean cakes and bread and comes in a variety of textures and flavors similar to chestnut and sweet potato, depending on the variety of beans, sweetener, and how much they are processed (used whole or mashed). Here, I will show you the classic tsubuan version, which is coarsely mashed, so you can still see and taste the beans. Most Japanese cooks use store-bought anko. It's reliable, but it is often on the sweeter side. I recommend you start with store-bought anko so you get an idea of the different textures and flavors. Then make your own, which is ultimately the tastiest, from scratch.

Wash the adzuki beans under water. Transfer to a medium pot and fill with hot water (not boiling) to cover. Let stand for 1 hour. Discard the water. Resoak the beans overnight in hot (not boiling) water. Cover with a lid.

When you are ready to make the anko, drain the beans and, in the same pot, add enough water to cover, about 4 cups. Bring to a boil over medium heat. Drain the beans and return to the pot with 4 more cups of water and bring to a boil over medium heat again. Reduce the heat to a simmer and cook the beans for 1 hour, until they are soft, removing any surface foam. To test readiness, remove a bean with a spoon, let cool for a few seconds, then squish it with your fingers. If it squishes easily, it is ready.

Add ⅓ of the sugar to the pot and continue cooking the beans over medium-low heat for 5 minutes. Add another ⅓ of the sugar and cook for another 5 minutes before adding the remaining sugar. Stir well with a paddle. Add a pinch of salt. Take a teaspoon of beans from the pot, wait for them to cool down, and then taste. If you'd like more salt, add another pinch, and stir again.

Remove the beans from the heat and drain, reserving the liquid. Return the bean liquid to the pot and simmer over medium heat for 10 minutes or until the liquid becomes syrupy. Add the beans to the syrup and simmer for 10 minutes longer, ›

Anko (cont.)

mixing frequently with a spatula, until the liquid is mostly absorbed. The beans should be semi-crushed and have a shiny and smooth but slightly lumpy texture. To test the smoothness, scoop up a ladleful and then drop it back into the pot. If it slides off too fast, it has too much liquid; it needs more time cooking. If the lump leaves a tail, it's perfect. The anko will continue to thicken as it cools down. Remove from the heat and spread the beans on a cookie sheet and allow to cool. Then transfer the anko to a container with a tight-fitting lid. You can keep it in the refrigerator for 1 week or in the freezer for 1 month.

WAKAME MILK BREAD WITH FURIKAKE

Makes 2 loaves

Special Equipment

Stand mixer with dough attachment

Two 8½ by 4½ inch (22 x 11 cm) metal loaf pans

For the Roux

½ cup (120 ml) water

¼ cup plus 2 tablespoons (90 ml) whole milk

¼ cup (34 grams) bread flour

For the Dough

2 tablespoons (28 grams) salted butter, melted, divided

3 large eggs

1 cup (240 ml) whole milk, at room temperature

5⅓ cups (639 grams) bread flour, plus more for dusting

½ cup, approximately (60 grams) rye flour or Sonora flour

¼ cup plus 2 tablespoons (80 grams) cane sugar

¼ cup (27 grams) nonfat or low-fat powdered milk

1½ tablespoons instant yeast

1¾ teaspoons table salt

8 tablespoons (113 grams) salted butter, cut into 8 pieces, softened

½ cup dried wakame seaweed, rehydrated and cut into ½ inch pieces, excess water squeezed out (about 1 cup hydrated) ›

Pan, or bread, was introduced to Japan by Portuguese traders in the sixteenth century. Most Japanese people didn't eat bread as part of their daily diet until after World War II, but my maternal grandmother grew up in a modern Japanese family who eagerly adapted the yofu—Western style—ways. She was one of the few people in Kamakura who owned an oven, and she had a routine of baking bread on Mondays. She made toast with butter and homemade jam for breakfast and egg or ham "sando-witchy" (we didn't call sandwiches "sandos" like they do today) for lunch. She would invite me or one of my siblings, and years later my son, to help her knead the dough with our feet. She served an English-style breakfast, setting the small breakfast table with ironed tablecloths and cloth napkins and serving Darjeeling tea, brewed slowly in a teapot, in teacups with saucers. She lived to be 102, and I think of her every time I bake bread.

Milk bread is a soft and airy bread that has made a successful wafu crossover in the United States. The softness comes from the use of a roux called tangzhong, which is made with milk, flour, and water. This is the bread that my grandmother used to make. It has a milky-sweet flavor and soft texture that tears into feathery strands. This recipe, which I developed with my kitchen assistant Courtney, contains wakame seaweed for an oceanic flavor and furikake for a crispy crunch.

To make the roux, in a medium saucepan, combine the water, milk, and flour, then whisk until free of lumps. Set over medium heat and cook, whisking constantly, until the mixture thickens (a silicone spatula drawn through the mixture will leave a trail) and bubbles slowly, 2 to 4 minutes. Scrape into a medium bowl, press a sheet of plastic wrap directly against the surface, and cool to room temperature.

To make the dough, brush a large bowl with the melted butter, reserving the rest. Add two of the eggs to the cooled roux and whisk until well combined. Add the room-temperature milk and whisk until homogeneous and smooth. ›

For the Topping

2 tablespoons Grapefruit
Furikake (page 8)
or toasted sesame seeds

In the bowl of the stand mixer, whisk together the bread and rye flour, sugar, powdered milk, yeast, and salt. Attach the bowl and dough hook to the mixer and, with the machine running on low, slowly add the roux-egg mixture. With the mixer still running, add the softened butter one tablespoon at a time. Add the softened wakame seaweed pieces. Increase the speed to medium-low and knead until the dough is very strong and elastic, 10 to 12 minutes; it will stick to the sides of the bowl. Scrape the dough into the prepared bowl, then brush the surface with melted butter. Cover the bowl with plastic wrap and let rise in a warm spot until doubled in bulk, about 1½ hours. Meanwhile, coat the loaf pans with melted butter.

Lightly flour the counter. Gently punch down the dough, then turn it out onto the prepared counter. Using a chef's knife or bench scraper, divide the dough into four equal portions, each about 12½ ounces (355 grams). Shape each portion into a smooth ball. Using your hands, pat one ball into a 4 x 7 inch (10 x 18 cm) rectangle, then fold the dough into thirds like a business letter. Pinch the seam to seal. Turn the dough seam side down and place on one side of one of the prepared loaf pans so the seam is perpendicular to the length of the pan. Shape a second portion of dough, then place it in the pan alongside the first, positioning it the same way; there should be just a small amount of space between the two pieces of dough. Cover the pan with a clean kitchen towel. Repeat the process with the remaining portions of dough, then place under the towel alongside the first pan. Let rise until the dough domes 1–1½ inches (2.5–4 cm) over the rim of the pan, about 1 hour.

Meanwhile, heat the oven to 350°F (176°C) with a rack in the middle position. In a small bowl, whisk the remaining egg until well combined; set aside. When the dough is properly risen, gently brush the tops with the egg and sprinkle with the furikake. Bake until the loaves are well risen and golden brown, 30 to 35 minutes. Cool in the pans on a wire rack for 15 minutes. Gently invert the bread out of the pans, stand them upright on the rack, and cool for at least 1 hour before slicing.

SPICY CURRY TOMATO PIZZA

Makes one 16 inch (40 cm) pizza

Special Equipment

Pizza stone

Pizza peel or rimmed
baking sheet

For Assembly

½ batch Pizza Dough (page 309)

2 cups (240 grams) all-purpose
flour, plus more for dusting

½ cup (60 grams) semolina flour

Extra-virgin olive oil, for drizzling

For the Curry Tomato Sauce

2 teaspoons soy sauce

1 tablespoon plus 1 teaspoon
Sonoko Curry Powder (page 153)
or store-bought Japanese
curry powder

2 garlic cloves, pressed through
a garlic press or minced

One 28-ounce can whole peeled
tomatoes, crushed by hand

1 tablespoon olive oil

1½ teaspoons sea salt

1 teaspoon red pepper flakes
(optional)

For the Toppings

1–2 small Yukon Gold potatoes,
thinly sliced about ⅛ inch
(3 mm) thick

3 mushrooms of your choice,
thinly sliced about ¼ inch
(6 mm) thick

¼ red bell pepper, sliced
into ½ x 3 inch
(1.25 x 7.6 cm) batons

½ teaspoon Sonoko
Curry Powder (page 153),
or store-bought Japanese
curry powder, plus more
for sprinkling ⟩

I think of this as "wafu okonomi" pizza. "Okonomi" means "as you like it," and I use the name here because there are infinite possibilities as to what you put on it. My kitchen assistant Courtney and I make two versions, one with a mildly spiced Japanese curry tomato sauce, as you see here—a wonderful wafu twist on a classic pie—and another with a yuzu kosho béchamel sauce with herbs and vegetables from my garden. The pizza dough is inspired by Joe Beddia's *Pizza Camp* cookbook, and the tomato sauce gets wafu-ed with curry powder, soy sauce, and yuzu kosho.

To make the curry tomato sauce, combine the soy sauce, curry powder, garlic, tomatoes, olive oil, salt, and red pepper flakes, if using, and mix well. Let rest in the fridge for a few hours for the flavors to blend. It will keep, refrigerated, for 1 week.

Place the pizza stone on the lowest shelf of your oven and preheat the oven to 500°F (260°C) or to its highest temperature. Heat the stone for at least 1 hour before baking the pizza.

Remove the pizza dough from the fridge and let it stand at room temperature for 15 minutes.

Meanwhile, prepare the toppings. Toss the potatoes, mushrooms, and red bell peppers with the curry powder. Drizzle with olive oil. Set aside.

When you are ready to assemble and bake the pizza, place the all-purpose flour in a bowl. Lightly dust the countertop, then dunk the dough in the bowl with your hand before transferring it to the floured countertop. Press the dough firmly with your fingers to flatten the center and work your way out toward the edge to make the dough into a wider pie, about 7–9 inches (17–23 cm) wide. Be careful not to disturb the outermost lip, which will become your crust.

Carefully pick up the dough and stretch it, being careful not to tear it. You can place the dough over your floured fist and let gravity help with the stretching, until it is about 14–16 inches (35–40 cm). Alternatively, if you'd like two smaller pizzas, you can divide the dough in two. Put the stretched dough back on the dusted counter. Generously and evenly coat a pizza peel, or a rimmed baking sheet flipped upside down, with semolina flour. Gently transfer the dough to the peel or baking sheet.

Take about ¾ cup (180 ml) of the curry tomato sauce and spread it on the dough with a spoon or spatula. Arrange the potatoes, mushrooms, ⟩

Extra-virgin olive oil,
for drizzling

1 scallion, sliced thinly crosswise

1 cup grated mozzarella cheese

¼ cup fresh herbs (cilantro, parsley, fennel fronds, and any edible flowers), for garnish

red peppers, and scallions evenly over the pizza. Sprinkle over the grated mozzarella and then some of the herbs and some more curry powder. As Joe Beddia advises, do not take more than 5 minutes to do this part, to avoid the dough sticking to the pizza peel or baking sheet.

Use the pizza peel or baking sheet to slide the pizza dough so that it sits safely on the stone. Carefully pull the pizza peel or sheet out, shut the oven, and bake until the crust turns deep brown. This may take up to 10 minutes, depending on your stove. When the pizza is done, use the pizza peel or sheet to transfer the pizza out of the oven and onto a cutting board. Finally, sprinkle with more herbs and drizzle on some extra-virgin olive oil, if you like. Enjoy!

Yuzu Kosho White Sauce Pizza

Makes one 16 inch (40 cm) pizza

½ batch Pizza Dough (page 309)

For the Béchamel Sauce

3 tablespoons unsalted butter

3 tablespoons all-purpose flour

1½ cups (360 ml) milk

3½ teaspoons Yuzu Kosho (page 32) or store-bought yuzu kosho

Sea salt, to taste

Freshly ground black pepper, to taste

For the Toppings

1 cup grated Gouda cheese

2 to 3 leaves Swiss chard, kale, sorrel, or any hearty leafy green, whole or cut to fit the pizza

1 cup blanched asparagus, broccolini, or any pea variety, or enough to cover pizza evenly

1 cup fresh herbs (cilantro, parsley, fennel fronds, and/or any edible flowers), for garnish

Juice from ½ lemon or yuzu, for drizzling

This is an elegant pizza with a cream sauce that is seasoned with kosho—a citrusy chili paste that adds brightness and heat to the sauce.

To make the béchamel sauce, melt the butter in a small saucepan over medium-low heat. Add the flour and whisk into the butter until smooth, about 2 minutes. The sauce will remain white in color. Slowly whisk in the milk until thickened by the roux. This will take about 3 to 4 minutes. Remove from the heat. Stir in the yuzu kosho and add salt and pepper to taste.

Roll out the pizza and prepare your oven as directed above. To assemble the pizza, take about ¾ cup (180 ml) of the béchamel sauce and spread it over the dough, all the way to the edges. Cover the pizza with the grated Gouda cheese. Arrange the leafy greens and other vegetables and sprinkle over some herbs and flowers. Bake the pizza following the instructions above.

Remove the pizza from the oven and squeeze the fresh yuzu or lemon juice over the leafy greens.

PIZZA DOUGH

Makes two 1 pound (454 grams) balls of dough

1½ cups (360 ml) cool water

2 teaspoons cane sugar

½ teaspoon active dry yeast

1 tablespoon extra-virgin olive oil

2½ cups (300 grams) all-purpose or bread flour, plus more for dusting

1 cup, approximately (120 grams) Sonora flour or other whole-wheat heritage-grain flour

4 teaspoons sea salt

In a large bowl, whisk together the water, sugar, and yeast. Add the olive oil and whisk until combined. Add the flours and switch to mixing with your hands. Mix until everything is incorporated and there is no dry flour left in the bowl. Use a spatula or dough scraper to scrape down the sides of the bowl. It will look like a lumpy ball. Cover the bowl with plastic wrap or a dampened kitchen towel and let it rest on the counter for 30 minutes.

When the dough has finished resting, add the salt to the dough and fully incorporate it, using a dough scraper or wet hands. Shape the dough into a smooth round ball, place it in a bowl, cover the bowl with plastic wrap, and let rest in the fridge for 24 hours.

After the dough has rested, transfer onto a well-floured surface. Put some flour on your hands so the dough doesn't stick to you while kneading. Fold the dough onto itself over and over again by grabbing the sides of the dough and folding them to meet in the middle, rotating a quarter turn after each fold. When you have a smooth, round ball again, cut the dough in half. Weigh both sides to make sure they are even.

Repeat the folding and rotating process with half of the dough. Set the other half aside. Fold and rotate until the dough is extremely smooth and round. If your dough gets too sticky, dust it with more flour. Set aside and cover with a kitchen towel until it doubles in size. This will take about 3 or 4 hours. Repeat with the other half of the dough. Test the readiness of the dough by pressing into it with your finger. If the dough rises back slowly, it's ready. Now, it's time to make your pizza!

If you want to assemble the pizza later, return the dough to the fridge in a lidded container for another slow rise—but don't keep it in there for more than 24 hours, or it will turn sour and become hard to work with.

Tomorrow's Bento

A bento box is a portable lunch—a physical and creative expression of the cook. Japanese cooks are always thinking ahead about what to put in tomorrow's bento box. The only thing I would prepare on the day of is the rice; it just tastes best fresh. Here are my guidelines for making your own bento, using leftovers from recipes in this book, or anything else you might have in your fridge.

- Include seasonal and fresh foods
- Embrace leftovers from last night's dinner
- Keep everything at the same temperature to avoid spoilage
- Cut food into bite-sized pieces so you can eat it with chopsticks or a fork
- Avoid saucy or watery foods to prevent leakage
- Try to achieve a balance of flavor and nutrition
- Be creative

Here's a bento menu, to inspire you:

- Cedar Plank Salmon with Shio Koji Marinade (page 201)
- Kinpira Gobo (page 116)
- Broiled chicken (see Balsamic Shio Koji Chicken on Rice, page 212)
- Seven-Minute Eggs (page 265)
- Potato Salada (page 110)
- Onigiri (Miso-Honey Butter with Toasted Onigiri, page 49) with Umeboshi (Pickled Ume Plums) (page 147) and Furikake (see Yakumi and Furikake, page 3)
- Freshly cooked Basic White Rice (page 163) or Basic Brown Rice (page 164)
- Blanched baby corn
- Blanched snow peas
- Cherry tomatoes
- Sliced cucumbers

Resources

The following are a few reliable online resources to help in your search for all the ingredients in this cookbook. Be a regular supporter of your local farmers market and farm stands. Look for sustainably raised food whenever possible. Japanese condiments can be found in Japanese groceries, specialty grocery stores, and online.

Flour, Grains, and Pulses

Anson Mills / ansonmills.com
    Heirloom grains and flours, including sobakoh
    (soba-grade flour) and grits

Dry Storage / drystorageco.com/flour-shop
    Heirloom flours

Hayden Flour Mills / haydenflourmills.com
    Heirloom grains, noodles, crackers,
    and baking mixes

King Arthur Baking Company / kingarthurflour.com
    Flours and bakeware

Koda Farms / kodafarms.com
    Premium Japanese-style rice, chickpeas,
    and Mochiko flour

Laura Soybeans / laurasoybeans.com
    Non-GMO soybeans for making miso and natto

Masienda / masienda.com
    Masa harina, heirloom corn, single-origin
    ingredients, and cookware like tortilla presses,
    molcajetes, and more, all sourced from Mexico

Rancho Gordo / ranchogordo.com
    Heirloom beans

Sequatchie Cove Farm / sequatchiecovefarm.com
    Heirloom grains, organic vegetables, eggs, cheese,
    and pasture-raised beef, pork, and chicken.

Tehachapi Heritage Grain Project /
tehachapigrainproject.org
    Heirloom grains and flour

Tofu and Natto

Meiji Tofu / meijitofu.com
    Artisanal non-GMO tofu

New York Natto / nyrture.com
    Artisanal non-GMO natto

Dumpling Wrappers and Noodles

Nanka Seimen / nankaseimen.com

Umi Organics / umiorganic.com/our-noodles

Japanese Groceries

Mitsuwa Marketplace / mitsuwa.com

Nijiya Market / nijiya.com

Tokyo Central / tokyocentral.com

Tokyo Fish Market / tokyofish.net

Sunrise Market / sunrisemart.com

Uwajimaya / uwajimaya.com

Fresh Seafood

Kai Gourmet / kaigourmet.com

Primetime Seafood / primetimeseafoodinc.com

Riviera Seafood Club / rivieraseafoodclub.com

Yokose Seafood / instagram.com/yokose_seafood/.

Spices, Seeds, Nuts, and Oils

Diaspora Co / diasporaco.com
Growing a better spice trade and sourcing, milling, and blending the highest quality spices and masala

Mountain Rose Herbs / mountainroseherbs.com
High selection of quality spices, teas, and oils

Speciality Grocery Stores that Carry Japanese Condiments

Altadena Beverage / altadenabev.com

Andrade's Catch / andradescatchri.com

Cookbook / cookbookla.com

Farm Shop / farmshopca.com

Gjusta Grocer / gjustagrocer.com

The Japanese Pantry / thejapanesepantry.com

LA Home Farm / lahomefarm.com

Little Flower Bakery / littleflowercandyco.com

Little King / littleking.online

McCalls Meat & Fish Co. / mccallsmeatandfish.com

Milk Street / store.177milkstreet.com

Miracle Plum / miracleplum.com

Onggi / onggi.com

Wellspent Market / wellspentmarket.com

Wine and Eggs / wineandeggs.com

Zingerman's Deli / zingermans.com

Cookbooks

Now Serving / nowservingla.com

Omnivore / omnivorebooks.myshopify.com

Vroman's Bookstore / vromansbookstore.com

Miso, Freezed-Dried Koji, and Soy Sauce

Cold Mountain Miso / coldmountainmiso.com

Moromi Shoyu / moromishoyu.com

Shared Cultures / shared-cultures.com

South River Miso Company / southrivermiso.com

Seaweed

Daybreak Seaweed / daybreakseaweed.com

Japanese Dashi Products

Yagicho Honten / yagicho-honten.tokyo
Woman-owned, 280-year-old grocery shop, with premium-grade bonito flakes, kombu, dried shiitake mushrooms, and beans

Ceramics, Clothes, Houseware, Pottery, etc.

Colleen Hennessey Clayworks / colleenhennessey.net

Dosa / dosainc.com

Hitachiya / hitachiyausa.com

The Lazy Potters / thelazypotters.com

Mt. Washington Pottery / mtwashingtonpottery.com

Shoshi Watanabe / shoshiwatanabe.com

Toiro Kitchen & Supply / toirokitchen.com

Tortoise General Store / tortoisegeneralstore.com

Tsuchikara Pottery / mitsukosiegrist.com

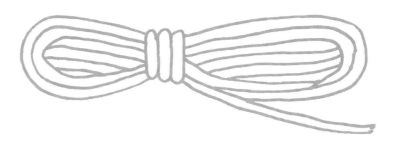

Acknowledgments

I want to thank everyone on the Knopf team for believing in me—Cassandra Pappas, Kelly Blair, Kevin Bourke, Lisa Montebello, Sara Eagle, Amy Hagedorn, and especially Tom Pold for his consummate patience and dogged work ethic; I will cherish our creative discussions. I also want to thank Tom for visiting my favorite hole-in-the-wall in Tokyo and trying the bastardized spaghetti. I believe I completely wafu-ed him.

I want to thank my agent, Danielle Svetcov, for guiding my path as an author. She helped me develop the idea for this book and find a wonderful home for it. She called me to help when I felt stuck creatively and even invited me to go for a long walk with her family when she came to Los Angeles. I owe her tons of grapefruit shrub.

Arigato to Rick Poon, who gave me the elegant images of my food and garden. I admire his patience, warmth, and diligence.

Thanks to Juliette Bellocq for helping me define and express my wafu ideas with her beautiful drawings and for her generous and kind spirit.

Thanks to Jennifer Brown for her sharp and creative editorial support. I probably wafu-ed her, too.

Arigato to Mamiko Nishiyama for providing me with her expertise in dashi and sake, and for being the best travel mate.

Thanks to Glenn Roberts for sending me live flours and for sharing his wisdom and love for good food. After more than a decade of listening to him talk passionately about the restoration of heritage grains and preservation of foodways, I am finally starting to understand why they matter so much.

Thanks to Erin Hogan and Lydia Esparza for your creative input on the book. I owe you tons of gyoza.

315

I want to thank my kitchen assistants past and present, especially for their recipe testing and tasting, creative input on this project, and sharing their laughter and tears. Special call-outs to Kali Bush Vineburg for keeping me organized and motivated; Tracy Tober for her kindness and helping me produce the best curry powder; Francesca Basilico for inspiring me to wafu Italian dishes; Ruben Acevedo for restoring the Mexican in me with his ideas for posole and carne asada; Katie DeVries for bringing so much vitality and order to my kitchen; Courtney Weiss for our fun doughy adventures; Capri Williams for making the most beautiful edible and native garden; and Fuyuko Kondo for teaching me how to make a flaky pie crust and for being such a caring sister. Gushing thanks also to Nancy Hsu, Kelly Friedman, Chantael Takeuchi, Joyce Kuhn, Daniela Swamp, Melissa Bishop, Cassie Davis, Jessica Li, Chloe Chappe, Ramon Nieto, and Hannah Tierney.

Arigato to all my friends for keeping my soul nourished and my mind open to new experiences.

I want to acknowledge and express my deepest appreciation for the entire community that has supported me during the writing of this book.

Last, but not least, warmest thanks to my family for your love and support—Katsuhisa Sakai, Sakae Sakai, Binah Yeung, Tyler and Emmalina Forbes, Barbara and Elena Cavallo, Hiroshi Kondo and family, Sachiko Kanda and family.

And to my students, who have taught me so much over the years.

Kali Bush-Vineberg, Rex and Claire Ito, Tracy Tober

Index

A Note on the Type

This book was set in Hoefler Text, a family of fonts designed by Jonathan Hoefler, who was born in 1970. First designed in 1991, Hoefler Text was intended as an advancement on existing desktop computer typography, including as it does an exponentially larger number of glyphs than previous fonts. In form, Hoefler Text looks to the old-style fonts of the seventeenth century, but it is wholly of its time, employing a precision and sophistication only available to the late twentieth century.

Composed by North Market Street Graphics,
Lancaster, Pennsylvania

Printed and bound by C&C Offset, China

Designed by Cassandra J. Pappas